# Research and Development in British Theatre

# Research and Development in British Theatre

*Edited by*
Tom Cantrell, Katherine Graham, Mark Love-Smith and
Karen Quigley

*methuen* | drama
LONDON • NEW YORK • OXFORD • NEW DELHI • SYDNEY

METHUEN DRAMA
Bloomsbury Publishing Plc, 50 Bedford Square, London, WC1B 3DP, UK
Bloomsbury Publishing Inc, 1385 Broadway, New York, NY 10018, USA
Bloomsbury Publishing Ireland, 29 Earlsfort Terrace, Dublin 2, D02 AY28, Ireland

BLOOMSBURY, METHUEN DRAMA and the Methuen Drama logo are trademarks of Bloomsbury Publishing Plc

First published in Great Britain 2025

Copyright © Edited by Tom Cantrell, Katherine Graham, Mark Love-Smith, Karen Quigley and Contributors, 2025

Tom Cantrell, Katherine Graham, Mark Love-Smith, Karen Quigley and Contributors have asserted their right under the Copyright, Designs and Patents Act, 1988, to be identified as Editors of this work.

For legal purposes the Acknowledgements on p. xiii constitute an extension of this copyright page.

Cover image © Johan Persson / ArenaPAL

All rights reserved. No part of this publication may be: i) reproduced or transmitted in any form, electronic or mechanical, including photocopying, recording or by means of any information storage or retrieval system without prior permission in writing from the publishers; or ii) used or reproduced in any way for the training, development or operation of artificial intelligence (AI) technologies, including generative AI technologies. The rights holders expressly reserve this publication from the text and data mining exception as per Article 4(3) of the Digital Single Market Directive (EU) 2019/790.

Bloomsbury Publishing Plc does not have any control over, or responsibility for, any third-party websites referred to or in this book. All internet addresses given in this book were correct at the time of going to press. The author and publisher regret any inconvenience caused if addresses have changed or sites have ceased to exist, but can accept no responsibility for any such changes.

A catalogue record for this book is available from the British Library.

A catalog record for this book is available from the Library of Congress.

ISBN: HB: 978-1-3503-0036-1
PB: 978-1-3503-0035-4
ePDF: 978-1-3503-0038-5
eBook: 978-1-3503-0037-8

Typeset by Deanta Global Publishing Services, Chennai, India
Printed and bound in Great Britain

For product safety related questions contact productsafety@bloomsbury.com

To find out more about our authors and books visit www.bloomsbury.com and sign up for our newsletters.

*To the students and colleagues who have inspired and encouraged this exploration, and to everyone who manages to set out without knowing where they will end up.*

# Contents

| | | |
|---|---|---|
| List of Contributors | | ix |
| Foreword *Jenny Sealey* | | xi |
| Acknowledgements | | xiii |
| Introduction | | 1 |
| 1 | Warped virtuosity and wobbly visuals: Skill-learning in R&D  *Karen Quigley* | 17 |
| 2 | Interview with Selina Thompson | 34 |
| | Questions and Prompts #1 | 41 |
| 3 | R&D in public: Scratch at Battersea Arts Centre  *Mark Love-Smith* | 42 |
| 4 | Interview with Gilly Roche | 60 |
| | Questions and Prompts #2 | 70 |
| 5 | R&D at the National Theatre Studio: *London Road*  *Tom Cantrell* | 71 |
| 6 | Interview with Lillian Henley | 91 |
| | Questions and Prompts #3 | 99 |
| 7 | Percolating and plummeting: Artist perspectives on R&D  *Deborah Pearson* | 100 |
| 8 | Interview with Rosemary Jenkinson | 117 |
| | Questions and Prompts #4 | 122 |
| 9 | Questions, materiality and negotiation: The role of the designer in R&D  *Katherine Graham* | 123 |
| 10 | Interview with Rosie Elnile | 139 |
| | Questions and Prompts #5 | 147 |
| 11 | Developing a dramaturgical praxis through repetitive R&D  *Rebecca Benzie, Harry Kingscott and Nora J. Williams* | 148 |
| 12 | Interview with Alex Kelly and Rachael Walton of Third Angel | 162 |
| | Questions and Prompts #6 | 169 |
| 13 | Movement direction as research and development  *Ayşe Tashkiran* | 170 |
| 14 | Interview with Georgina Lamb | 184 |
| | Questions and Prompts #7 | 190 |
| Afterword  *Duška Radosavljević* | | 191 |
| Index | | 197 |

# Contributors

Please note: Interviewee biographies are included as introductions to each interview.

**Rebecca Benzie**
Rebecca is Lecturer in Theatre at the University of York. Her research interests include feminist theatre practices, new playwriting and acts of commemoration. She is an experienced theatre practitioner and dramaturg, specializing in devised theatre and text adaptation. Her monograph, *Feminism, Dramaturgy, and the Contemporary British History Play*, was published in 2024 with Bloomsbury's Engage Series.

**Tom Cantrell**
Tom is Professor of Theatre and Head of the School of Arts and Creative Technologies at the University of York. He has published widely on acting processes, including *Acting in Documentary Theatre* (2013), *Acting in British Television* (2017) and *Exploring Television Acting* (2018), co-written with Christopher Hogg.

**Katherine Graham**
Katherine is Senior Lecturer in Theatre at the University of York where her research focuses on the agency of materials in performance. She has also worked extensively as a lighting designer for theatre and dance and has published work about light in *Theatre and Performance Design Journal*, *Studies in Theatre and Performance* and *Contemporary Theatre Review*. She is co-editor, with Kelli Zezulka and Scott Palmer, of *Contemporary Performance Lighting: Experience, Creativity, Meaning* (2023).

**Harry Kingscott**
Harry is the Young Artists Producer at Derby Theatre. He has worked extensively as a movement director and performer. His practise, having trained at the École de Théâtre Jacques Lecoq, centres around physical expression, choral movement, clown and mask work. As a freelancer, he regularly worked with young people of all ages and now runs the youth theatre and young artists programmes at Derby Theatre.

**Mark Love-Smith**
Mark is Senior Lecturer in Theatre at the University of York. He has research interests in devised and physical theatre, community theatre and the interplay of writing, directing and devising. His latest publication is the Routledge Performance Practitioners book on Frantic Assembly, co-written with Professor Mark Evans.

## Deborah Pearson
Deborah is Senior Lecturer of Dramaturgy at UAL's Screen School and Associate Research Fellow at Birkbeck. Her work spans playwrighting, directing, live art and visual art. She is founder and a co-director of UK-based curation collective Forest Fringe and the winner of several distinctions both for her practice and for Forest Fringe, including twice being named on the Stage 100 List.

## Karen Quigley
Karen is Senior Lecturer in Theatre at the University of York. Her first monograph, *Performing the Unstageable: Success, Imagination, Failure*, was published by Bloomsbury in 2020. She has also published research on a range of subjects including site-specific performance, solo spectatorship, embodied voice, British television comedy and theatre-fiction.

## Duška Radosavljević
Duška is a dramaturg, writer and researcher in contemporary theatre and performance practices, and currently Professorial Research Fellow at the Royal Central School of Speech and Drama. Publications include *Aural/Oral Dramaturgies: Theatre in the Digital Age* (2023), *Theatre Criticism: Changing Landscapes* (2016), *Theatre-Making: Interplay between Text and Performance in the 21st Century* (2013) and *The Contemporary Ensemble: Interviews with Theatre-Makers* (2013).

## Jenny Sealey
Jenny has been Artistic Director of Graeae Theatre Company, an internationally celebrated international leader and innovator in accessible world-class theatre, since 1997. Credits for Graeae include *Self-Raising* (2024), an opera; *The Paradis Files* (2022); and the musical, *Reasons to be Cheerful* (2010). She has directed many plays for young people and has adapted several novels for BBC Radio 4. Jenny co-directed the London 2012 Paralympics Opening Ceremony alongside Bradley Hemmings. In 2022, Jenny was made an OBE. She has been awarded the Liberty Human Rights Arts Award and is an honorary Doctor of Drama at the Royal Conservatoire of Scotland and Middlesex University and a Fellow of the Central School of Speech and Drama and Rose Bruford College.

## Ayşe Tashkiran
Ayşe is a movement director, teacher and researcher in the field of movement in theatre. She has created movement for a wide variety of companies. For the past twenty years she has also been at the helm of the MA MFA Movement: Directing and Teaching at Royal Central School of Speech and Drama. She is an associate artist at the RSC.

## Nora J. Williams
Nora is Associate Dean for Access and Participation at BIMM University. Her research interests include practice-as-research, dramaturgies, violence and intimacy, particularly in relation to classical and canonical plays. Her monograph, *Canonical Misogyny: Shakespeare and Dramaturgies of Sexual Violence*, is forthcoming in 2025.

# Foreword

Jenny Sealey

I owe my career as an actor and as director to research and development.

As we all know, there is no specific rule book, so you enter an R&D with your heart in your throat and your brain scrambled with fear. I have always worried about my own chaotic 'making it up as I go along' methodology, but this book, which is a glorious delving into the world of other people's R&D, has made me realize I am not alone. It demonstrates a beautiful vulnerability in everyone's approach as they detail how they have been brave enough not to know and to allow what will happen to happen.

I have many treasured memories. Exploring the stage directions as a storytelling/audio description device for *Bent* by Martin Sherman with a group of disabled men, diverse in ethnicity, disability and sexuality. It was a deeply sombre moment when we realized that the whole team, under Hitler's regime, would have been the first to go. This strengthened our belief that the stage directions held such dramatic emotional weight that we should vocalize them in the production – so we did. The space to talk, to remember the history of the Holocaust, discrimination and survival and also to reflect on where disabled people were in 2005 (when we did the play) allowed us to underpin the production with the politics of the past and the present. It was invaluable.

The R&D for *Reasons to be Cheerful* (2017), Graeae's first musical co-production with Theatre Royal Stratford East exploring the narrative around Ian Dury's songs, was set up to serve the writer. I got together a motley crew of specific actors who I knew were good at working with new writing along with one or two musicians. Little did I know most of them had great punk/rock voices and one of them could play two saxophones and the drums. He had kept that quiet. This gang went on to be the cast. They seamlessly slipped into the roles and through the week we pushed and challenged the form to give the writer a new playing field to take to the next draft. The right people were in the room, and I had a writer, Paul Sirett, who was open, generous and not remotely precious. At the end of the R&D, Paul asked to audition to be in the band. He had played the guitar all over the world with some major bands. How did I not know that?!

I carved out a mini R&D for myself to read this book on R&D. What a rich and varied book and how necessary it was and is to read, highlighting the urgent case to keep this on the agenda. When reading it, you can create your own pattern as this is not a linear book, but each chapter is full of diverse processes and discoveries.

You can admire the care Purni Morell took over the multiple R&D periods the National Theatre Studio had for *London Road* and her support of the writer and composer to ensure they did not get swallowed by the NT before the work was ready to move into a full piece. Try not to harbour envy of those that have the resources (a note to self), but learn from the wisdom of knowing when to jump from R&D into full rehearsals.

Gilly Roche's irreverence and undisciplined nature is liberating. Gilly's commitment to give students freedom to play and to fuck up is inspiring, and to be given resources to do this validates their experience as they become 'theatre makers'. It is a glorious rite of passage.

As a huge fan of David Jubb and all things Battersea Arts Centre, I loved the detailed analysis of what 'scratch' was, can be and is, and how it is firmly embedded within the theatre ecology. A scratch performance held by the support and generosity of an audience is sometimes the 'end product' and that can be either alright or not, but it requires the wisdom to know the difference.

R&D is when the stars align – or they don't – but either way a gem or a germ of something triggers what comes next. Selina Thompson talks about R&D being about skilling up, learning new technology, soul searching, excavating, binning ideas, having more ideas, having no ideas but trying something anyway. It is about creating a safe space in which to be unsafe and to announce that failure is truly permissible and actually invited.

My question is how do we judge failure? I am not sure I can answer it. Thompson also talks about marketing and who our work is for. An audience gives our work purpose, and this is worth remembering. Is failure when we become so immersed in our art that we forget who our audience is? As artists, we put our heart on the line, we expose our innermost feelings, we share the good, the bad and the ugly of ourselves and the world. We allow ourselves to be extremely vulnerable, but if an audience 'fails' to understand what it is we have shown them, have they failed us or have we failed them? Can the work of the theatre world ever be art for art's sake?

I have learnt about failure the hard way. When I haven't taken on feedback or acknowledged that something is not quite working in the way I have presented it. Or where I have ignored the fact that it is not connecting with an audience in the way I intended and have been hot-headed and thought 'well, I think it works'. I have been sorely bitten by press and audiences alike. BUT at the same time, we do not make work by committee and not everyone goes on the same journey when they see a piece of work. So, I don't really know the answer to 'how do we judge failure?'

Moving on, the book has some helpful questions and prompts – a reminder for those of us who have done it before and a starter pack for someone doing it for the first time.

At the time of writing, we are weeks away from a general election, and there is a hope that a new government may invest more in the arts. But that more will never be enough. So how do you, the reader of this book, continue the activism necessary to make the case for the vital nature of R&D? In simple terms, R&D lessens the 'risk' of something not working in rehearsals and the dreaded running out of time to rectify the issues, so it makes good economic sense. I think it must be more than just that though. It is an investment in the arts as a fundamental human right, and this is much harder to articulate to government bodies. Maybe we need an R&D on how to make the case for R&D. See you there.

# Acknowledgements

We are very grateful to the School of Arts and Creative Technologies at the University of York, where we met and began to work as collaborators. While we have been working on this book, we have been lifted up by our colleagues in a variety of ways. Special thanks to David Barnett for reading and commenting on some of the chapters and for his unflagging enthusiasm for the project, to Duncan Petrie and Áine Sheil for their ongoing support and to the whole Theatre team for contributing to this work via the teaching we do together.

Many thanks to Anna Brewer and Aanchal Vij at Bloomsbury for their sensitive and thoughtful stewardship of this book project. Anna's confidence in us and what we hoped the book might offer to the discipline spurred us on at vital moments, for which we are grateful.

The idea for this book started with plans for a symposium, due to take place at York in Spring 2020. From then to now, a lot of life has passed through the book team, and we thank our families and friends for their care and support while we have been working on this manuscript.

Finally, of course, we would like to thank our contributors and our interviewees. In particular, we thank all the students with whom we have shared R&D spaces as they have begun their own R&D journeys.

# Introduction

Our collaboration on this book emerges from our shared teaching of theatre research and development (henceforward, R&D). We co-designed and now co-teach a final-year module, the Independent Group Production Project, on the BA in Theatre: Writing, Directing and Performance at the University of York. On the module, students organize themselves into small groups to stage an extant play of their choosing as part of a theatre festival. The students can be assessed as actors, designers, directors or festival producers. As part of their work on the module, each group is given four weeks of R&D before they begin rehearsals for the play. The R&D period is not assessed, but rather we frame it as a period of experimentation and risk-taking that embraces failure as a crucial component. As supervisors, we are in the room with the students, collaborating with them as participants in the R&D, co-constructing the sessions with them. This period allows students to explore ways of working, to develop particular skills together and to think widely about the play they have chosen and how they might tell its story. Though the students do go on to stage assessed productions, we hold the R&D period apart from this outcome; from the start, we demarcate R&D as a separate space: an exploratory process that is valuable in its own right.

Sitting at the heart of this module, then, is our shared understanding of R&D as one of the most creatively fertile, collaborative and exciting periods in theatre-making. As theatre-makers and as researchers we have been struck by the richness and plurality of R&D practices across the theatre industry. Yet our students' questions, seeking research which they might use to guide them or to contextualize their own work, reveal the relative paucity of literature on the subject. This book responds to this need for scholarship. It aims to uncover, analyse, celebrate and question the rich range of practices under the term 'R&D'. Equally, we acknowledge that within this breadth of practice, R&D is not always utopian; there are political tensions around the term itself, and a complex funding landscape (explored later in this introduction) that raises additional questions about how the value of art(ists) is recognized. Embracing the pluralities, contradictions, tensions and possibilities of R&D, this book illuminates the depth and nuance of its many practices and manifestations.

## The dynamic, evolving practices of R&D

This book views R&D through its messy, various, asymmetrical forms. We position 'R&D' as a dynamic and evolving range of practices and the term itself as an umbrella: embracing a rich variety of approaches but yet worthy of delineation. The term

'R&D' is widely deployed by makers but not yet wholly defined by those who study theatre and performance processes. R&D *can* include devising but not necessarily: it might be used on an extant play (as evidenced by our teaching above). R&D *might* result in a production or output but might just as easily be an end in itself. R&D *could* be part of a formal rehearsal period but might stand alone, entirely untethered from anything that is later seen by an audience. This sense of R&D as a slippery and contingent practice is amplified across the volume, as contributors repeatedly point to idiosyncratic and shifting processes. R&D is discussed in these pages as, variously, 'coming together with other people to dream and hope about what the show could be' (Henley, p. 96); a space to explore 'the difference between the idea that you've got and the next thing it could become' (Morell p. 82); an 'open period when almost anything related to the initial inkling could be on the table' (Pearson p. 103); a process in which there may be 'lots of layers going on at the same time' (Walton p. 162); and a 'porous' space that resists linear thinking (Elnile p. 145). Our working definition of R&D in theatre-making, then, is that it is a period of time (often, but not always, delimited in advance) during which theatre-makers (often in a group but sometimes alone) explore a particular topic, scope a possible project or develop an element of their craft, without the need for a direct line between R&D and output or product.

While this is the first scholarly volume exclusively devoted to R&D as a specific theatre-making methodology, there exists a wealth of research in immediately adjacent and sometimes overlapping areas of practice. One such area is the body of literature exploring collaborative approaches to theatre-making, often positioned as a corrective to hierarchical structures of creative control and decision-making or the historic primacy of the director. Significant publications include the edited collections *Collaboration in Performance Practice: Premises, Workings and Failures*, edited by Colin and Sachsenmaier (2015), and Blain and Minor's *Artistic Research in Performance through Collaboration* (2020). These works provide useful insights into the wider context of collaborative practice, but their focus is wider than ours: they explore collaborative approaches through particular artists, companies and projects but don't make a distinction between R&D and other kinds of practice. Similarly, approaches to ensemble practice have been explored by Radosavljević (ed.) in *The Contemporary Ensemble: Interviews with Theatre-Makers* (2013) and by Cornford in *Theatre Studios: A Political History of Ensemble Theatre-Making* (2021). Ensemble approaches have also been shared in practical, 'how to' guides such as Burnett Bonczek and Storck's *Ensemble Theatre Making: A Practical Guide* (2013). These studies demonstrate the rich breadth of collaborative, collective approaches to theatre-making and feature interviews with a range of contemporary practitioners. On occasion, they engage with practices from particular R&D processes, such as Blain and Turner's account of a collaborative adaptation of Camus's *L'Etranger* by a group of theatre-makers, musicians, a lighting designer, animator and director:

> Over the course of the R&D process, collaborative strategies were tried out that aspired to create a shared consciousness between the collaborators, a shared consciousness that identified and then resolved the tensions and conflicts

that inevitably arose from a group of individuals coming together to develop a performance project. (in Blain and Minor 2020: 209)

Insights such as the capacity of R&D to create this 'shared consciousness' are useful to our study. Again, though, these studies subsume R&D into notions of ensemble across a range of processes within theatre, rather than focusing on how R&D as a modus operandi might unite and strengthen such ensemble approaches.

This study is also indebted to the wide body of research into devising practices. In their introduction to *Making a Performance: Devising Histories and Contemporary Practices*, Govan, Nicholson and Normington write:

> If devising is most accurately described in the plural – as *processes* of experimentation and sets of creative *strategies* – rather than a single methodology, it defies neat definition or categorisation. New practices have arisen from a combination of creative conversations and dissatisfaction with how current modes of practice address contemporary climates. (2007: 7, original emphases)

The plurality contained within the term 'devising' and the experimental focus of its practices mean that studies in this field are analogous to explorations of R&D in a number of ways. As we have noted, R&D is a methodology that is deployed on scripted as well as devised projects, but our study sits alongside such publications as Heddon and Milling's *Devising Performance* (who explore companies for whom 'devising' and 'collaborative creation' refer to 'a mode of work in which *no* script – neither written text nor performance score – exists prior to the work's creation by the company' (2005: 3)) and Oddey's *Devising Theatre: A Practical and Theoretical Handbook*, in which Oddey states that 'A devised theatrical performance originates with the group while making the performance, rather than starting from a play text that someone else has written to be interpreted' (1994: 1). Syssoyeva and Proudfit's edited collection, *Women, Collective Creation, and Devised Performance: The Rise of Women Theatre Artists in the Twentieth and Twenty-First Centuries*, closely engages with Heddon and Milling's work and proposes the term 'collective creation':

> There is a group. The group wants to make theatre. The group chooses – or, conversely, a leader within the group proposes – to make theatre using a process which places conscious emphasis on the *groupness* of that process, on some possible collaborative mode between members of the group, which is, typically, viewed as being in some manner more collaborative than members of the group have previously experienced. (2016: 6, original emphasis)

Given the focus on the ensemble across the chapters of this book, Syssoyeva and Proudfit's definition is highly relevant here. This sentiment of an R&D process being 'in some manner more collaborative' than other forms of theatre-making echoes across the case studies and analyses that comprise our study. Indeed, some, but not all, of the chapters will explore forms of devising, falling within the definitions that Oddey and Heddon and Milling propose.

Several of our contributors reflect on ways in which R&D and rehearsal processes can bleed into one another. Accordingly, this book will also engage with the plentiful scholarship on such processes. Key examples include Harvie and Lavender's (eds) *Making Contemporary Theatre: International Rehearsal Processes* (2010) and Simonsen's *The Art of Rehearsal: Conversations with Contemporary Theatre Makers* (2017). Though they don't name R&D specifically, Simonsen's interviewees frequently talk about phases of the kinds of generative research, exploration and development before rehearsals begin that we might recognize as such. Director, dramaturg and writer Rachel Chavkin, for example, notes of her work with The TEAM – 'a Brooklyn-based ensemble whose mission is to create new works about the experience of living in America today' (The TEAM 2024) – that

> the words rehearsal process are probably misnomers for The TEAM, because to me rehearsal implies working on and refining an agreed upon set of things that are going to happen [...]. Whereas with The TEAM we can't rehearse until we've made the thing, so actually for a TEAM process which might be anywhere from a year and a half to, typically closer to three to five years, even, most of that process is 'what the hell are we doing?' [. . .] The TEAM tends to start with an overall investigation. (Simonsen 2017: 61)

Chavkin's words again demonstrate the looseness of terminology when articulating the generation and development of new projects and how often rehearsals build on earlier ensemble work.

Marsden's *Inside the Rehearsal Room: Process, Collaboration and Decision-Making* (2021) similarly links R&D with the notion of a 'workshop period', and several of the theatre-makers and critics he cites identify the importance of exploratory phases of this kind and of carving out unpressured time for such work. The theatre critic Lyn Gardner notes this, pointing out that you

> discover very little when you are in a rush. Even the sharing culture of funded R&D weeks can be problematic when you know that on Friday afternoon venue bookers, producers and artistic directors – the people who are crucial to the future life of your show – will be in the room. (55)

While the focus of Marsden's book is on rehearsals, it is clear that the practitioners interviewed frequently view rehearsal as part of a wider ecosystem of preparatory processes for developing a project.

So, a potential contradiction: this study serves to celebrate the breadth and multiplicity of practice that constitutes R&D while also seeking to delineate R&D as distinct from the processes of devising, rehearsal, ensemble-building, collaborative theatre-making and new play development, despite the apparent overlaps between these. To address this contradiction we return to where we started: it is a widely used term in the industry, but searching library databases for 'R&D and theatre' produces no meaningful resources for the theatre researcher or student. Entering this lacuna, our study aims to draw out tacit understandings of R&D practices within multiple theatre-making identities (performers, ensembles, producers, designers and more), turning a critical lens to the role and value of R&D across theatre practice. However, we also have an ulterior motive. As we explore below, R&D is not just a term understood by theatre-makers; it is also the favoured term used in governmental funding plans to refer to investment in exploratory, experimental and speculative practices, particularly in relation to its industrial strategies. As we will demonstrate, the government clearly understands that financially supporting R&D in industry leads to a significant return on their investment. Yet this does not appear to be true of the arts. Our aim is that by making visible the rich practices of theatre R&D and the creative innovations that this work has yielded, we will strengthen the case for R&D within the arts to be a central tenet of governmental approaches to arts funding.

## Funding and support for R&D: The political context

Over the past few years there has been a gradual alignment between R&D and science and technology, with the arts disappearing from the government's R&D ambitions. For instance, the House of Commons Library has published an overview of 'Research and Development Funding Policy' (Rough, Hutton and Housley 2023) which charts the development of government policy on R&D in recent years (2017–23). Its authors state that 'Research and development (R&D) funding is defined as expenditure on research, *mostly in science and technology*, that results in new products, processes and understanding' (6, emphasis added). In its 2017 Industrial Strategy, the government announced a commitment to spend 2.4 per cent of gross domestic product (GDP) – around £48 billion – on R&D by 2027, a move which 'could increase public and private R&D investment by as much as £80bn over the next 10 years' (Department of Business, Energy and Industrial Strategy 2017: 66). Three years later, the government published its 'UK Research and Development Roadmap', in which it reiterated its commitment to 2.4 per cent of GDP by 2027 and outlined how it would fulfil its ambitions for R&D (Department for Science, Innovation and Technology and Department for Business, Energy and Industrial Strategy, 2020). While the focus of the roadmap was on science and technology, the arts were briefly mentioned, though only in connection with ideas of market value:

> We need to do more to make the most of our world-class research base and to increase the productivity of UK businesses all over the UK. We need to ensure our excellence in discovery research, design, engineering, data science, and creative arts translates into commercial applications – increasing the productivity of our existing industries and creating new growth opportunities for the UK. The UK has lower levels of R&D activity by businesses compared to our competitor nations, and that investment is focussed on large investors in a few sectors. (24)

However, since 2020, in the face of mounting financial challenges, these targets have been revised downwards. The 2017 Industrial Strategy and its associated fiscal commitments were replaced in March 2021 with a new plan: 'Build Back Better:

Our Plan for Growth' (HM Treasury 2021). The positioning and scope of R&D in this document was rather different, becoming explicitly linked to science. Indeed, the then prime minister Boris Johnson wrote in his introduction that 'We will make our country a science and technology superpower' (7). All reference to the arts had disappeared from this revised plan. This repositioning of R&D as a facet of science and technology was further emphasized in a strategy document, 'R&D People and Culture Strategy', published in July 2021 (Department of Business, Energy and Industrial Strategy 2021). The title shouldn't be assumed to reflect an engagement with the cultural industries; rather, the tone had further shifted away from the arts and culture. Culture, in this sense, referred to the government's focus on understanding, expanding and improving the workforce for R&D across a number of sectors and building inclusive workspaces. The introduction was written by Amanda Solloway MP, Minister for Science, Research and Innovation (Solloway's ministerial portfolio further demonstrating the alignment of R&D and science). In it, she wrote:

> When the government published its R&D Roadmap last year, we set out our bold and ambitious vision to make the UK a global science superpower, which is supported by our commitment to the fastest ever increase in public funding in R&D over the coming years. Since then, our appreciation of the vital importance of science and innovation has only grown. (4)

This focus on science has dominated the government's R&D agenda and spending commitments in recent years. Their 'Science and Technology Framework' (Department for Science, Innovation and Technology 2023) includes the strategic vision for R&D: that '[t]he UK's R&D investment matches the scale of the Science and Technology Superpower ambition, and the private sector takes a leading role in delivering this' (10). Their 2.4 per cent commitment has been dropped, but significant ongoing investment is still pledged in the documents, including being 'committed to invest £20bn in R&D in 2024/25' (ibid.).

## R&D investment in the arts

Where, then, does this leave investment in R&D within the arts? This question has exercised several researchers who have analysed the government's gradual erasing of the arts in their formulation of R&D policies, strategies and investment. Back in 2017, in response to the government's Green Paper 'Building Our Industrial Strategy' (a precursor to the Industrial Strategy announced later that year – see above), Hasan Bakhshi and Elizabeth Lomas called for a wider definition of R&D which would '[r]ecognise R&D as a legitimate practice in the arts, humanities and social sciences, not just science and technology' (Bakhshi and Lomas 2017: 2). Central to this call was the link between the definition of R&D and access to tax relief for R&D activities, a key incentive for companies to develop and support R&D practices in their organizations.

Bakhshi and Lomas noted that R&D practices in the arts, humanities and social sciences fall within the remit of the *Frascati Manual*, the internationally recognized guide used to statistically measure R&D and compare various public funding structures, subsidies and tax breaks, and which provides a definition for R&D which is widely employed. The definition reads:

> Research and experimental development (R&D) comprise creative and systematic work undertaken in order to increase the stock of knowledge – including knowledge of humankind, culture and society – and to devise new applications of available knowledge. (OECD 2015: 44)

For activities to qualify as R&D, the *Manual* states that they must fulfil five criteria. They must be 'novel, creative, uncertain, systematic and transferable and/or reproducible' (2015: 45). However, Bakhshi and Lomas note that

> [t]he Manual, whilst expanding in the later editions to acknowledge that R&D does occur across some arts, humanities and social sciences knowledge domains, still needs to rebalance its emphasis on science and technology and further widen the scope of its R&D definition. (Bakhshi and Lomas 2017: 3)

One of the effects of this emphasis on science and technology is that the UK government has tended to be reductive in its application of the *Frascati Manual's* definition of R&D. In its information for 'Research and Development (R&D) expenditure credit', HM Revenue and Customs states that 'Research and Development (R&D) tax reliefs support UK companies working on innovative projects in science and technology [...]. You cannot claim if the advance is in the arts, humanities, social sciences, including economics' (HMRC 2023). Bakhshi and Lomas note a contradiction in HMRC's use of definitions drawn from the *Frascati Manual* while requiring

> that the R&D relates to scientific or technological delivery despite the Manual's wider scope. The arts, humanities and social sciences whilst having the capacity to deliver R&D against the definition and being of great significance to the creative industries, are specifically excluded for HMRC's purposes. (2017: 3)

The government, by failing to offer this tax relief, actively disincentivizes R&D within the arts by employing a narrower definition of R&D than that which is laid out in the internationally recognized – and widely deployed – guide. Bakhshi, Breckon and Puttick are clear about the implications of this exclusion: 'the UK's application of the definition of R&D means that UK tax policy does not recognise the role that AHSS [Arts, Humanities and Social Sciences] R&D plays in delivering innovation, productivity and growth, and the role that tax relief can play in incentivising R&D which has its origins in the AHSS disciplines' (2021a: 6). Bird et al. (2020) have amassed data evidencing this situation. In their report, 'R&D in Creative Industries Survey – 2020', for the Department for Digital, Culture, Media and Sport, the research team found that 'enterprises in the creative industries do perform R&D but tend to spend relatively little on the activity and tend not to have a specific R&D budget' (10). Surveying R&D activities carried out by a wide range of creative industry firms, they note the discrepancy between the numbers of companies that carry out activities that would be captured by the *Frascati Manual*'s definition of R&D (more than 55 per cent of all firms surveyed) and the numbers whose activities are actually captured by the current tax relief definition (only 14 per cent). In music, performing and visual arts specifically, seventy-three companies were surveyed, and the numbers here show an even smaller proportion eligible for tax relief: 40 per cent of them conducted R&D activities on the *Frascati* definition but only 7 per cent by HMRC's definition (12). This discrepancy in the current funding policy has led Talem, Pugh and Fairburn to state in their 'Policy Recommendations' that a key action should be to '[l]obby for changes in the eligibility criteria for R&D tax credits to better fit the nature of creative sector R&D [. . .]. The Frascati Manual definition might be a good place to start' (2022: 23). The chapters and interviews that follow explore a rich range of R&D processes that clearly meet the manual's criteria – 'novel, creative, uncertain, systematic' – and that can frequently be understood as 'transferable and/ or reproducible' (OECD 2015: 45). We hope, therefore, that this study adds further weight to the arguments calling for R&D tax relief to be available in the theatre sector.

Several of the policy researchers cited above have noted the question of definitions as a recurring motif. In a finding that speaks to the aims of this collection, Bakhshi, Breckon and Puttick note that 'in several cases the businesses did not themselves describe their [arts, humanities and social sciences] work as R&D at all – but might label it "innovation", "experimentation" or "use of research evidence" instead' (2021b: 131). The fact that this work is not defined as R&D has an impact on how this work is accounted for and how visible it is:

> An implication is that these businesses do not include investment in AHSS R&D in their R&D budgets. And businesses whose R&D activities are dominated by AHSS may not have an R&D budget at all. In this context, it is striking that in a Department for Digital, Culture, Media and Sport (DCMS) survey of R&D in the creative industries, only 8 per cent of respondents said they had a formal budget for R&D despite 55 per cent claiming they invest in it. (2021b: 133)

The absence of tax relief for R&D in the arts might be a factor that discourages theatre companies from engaging in these practices. But Bakhshi, Breckon and Puttick's research also suggests a further consequence: that even where these practices do take place, they are made less visible due to the lack of formal reporting and budgeting, rather than due to a lack of commitment and support within arts organizations. The case studies in this book aim to bring to light a range of R&D practices that form part of the cultural and creative life of the subsidized theatre sector. Given the absence of support for R&D in the arts via tax relief, and the ways in which spending on R&D in organizations can be obscured as a result of how this work is defined and what it is called, it strikes us as all the more important to make manifest this work and to uncover the practices hidden from view.

## R&D in British subsidized theatre

State funding for British theatre-making might be said to support R&D practices in two main ways: indirectly and directly. The Arts Council England (ACE) provides a number of companies with regular funding for a given (usually four-year) period under the banner of National Portfolio Organisation (NPO) status, through a highly competitive and challenging application process. These organizations represent a significant range of budget and scale, and there are a large number of models by which they support the development of new work through this funding. We might refer to these as the 'indirect' means, as there is a further layer of selectivity, exercised by the NPO itself, which decides which other organizations and individuals receive support. These models might encompass the National Theatre Studio, which under Purni Morell as Head of the Studio (2007–11) had a ring-fenced budget of around £1 million and which scouts and recruits writers, directors, designers, actors and other creatives to form partnerships, acting as a form of laboratory (closed-door) feeder organization for the (English) National Theatre. On the other hand, ACE funding might be allocated by the NPO to formal mentoring schemes, such as that offered by Third Angel's BOOST programme. Some NPOs – such as Talawa – provide 'research and development opportunit[ies] for emerging theatre makers [. . .] offered up at various times through the year' (Talawa 2024), which might for instance comprise literal space as well as mentoring from more experienced theatre-makers: 'one week in the Talawa Studio, with tailored support from our team' (ibid.). In some cases, the offer of subsidized or fully funded R&D 'space' also extends to accommodation, as in the nine artists' bedrooms under the roof of Battersea Arts Centre, allowing artists in residence to live and work at the theatre during their residency. At the other end of the scale, smaller organizations might offer some facilitation work, time with actors or simply a room in which to develop ideas.

Alongside institutionally filtered support of the kind sketched above, state-subsidized theatre also offers more direct funding routes for R&D activities. These other avenues are particularly relevant given the fact that 71 per cent of the UK theatre workforce are self-employed freelancers (DCMS 2023). While freelancers may of course access R&D support and other opportunities (such as employment as actors in the National Theatre Studio, for instance) through state-subsidized theatres and other funded theatre companies including the NPOs discussed above, the Arts Councils of England, Wales and Northern Ireland and Creative Scotland have also developed specific funding schemes to support such activities directly.

In 2018, Arts Council England introduced the 'Developing Your Creative Practice' (DYCP) scheme. DYCP is distinct from ACE's Project Grants in that applications are not designed to lead to an output that needs to be specified at the point of application; nor, in fact, is an output required at all. Recent guidance states that '[w]e don't expect you to use your grant to make public facing work, but you should think about how a grant will help you reach audiences in the future' (ACE 2024a: 26). DYCP is a competitive scheme with four application points per year. The fund offers grants of between £2,000 and £12,000 (an increase to the maximum, from £10,000 to £12,000, was announced in 2023 in response to the UK's cost of living crisis). Successful applicants need to spend the funding within a year of the award. The fund 'supports individual cultural and creative practitioners ready to take their practice to the next stage through things such as: research, time to create new work, travel, training, developing ideas, networking or mentoring' (ACE 2024b). It is aimed not at companies and organizations but rather is a specific fund to support applications from 'an individual, or [. . .] a small group of practitioners who usually collaborate in their work' (ACE 2024a). According to an independent evaluation of the fund in 2022, which looked at the first eleven rounds of DYCP funding, the vast majority – 94 per cent of applications – were for R&D (SQW 2022: 57). The fund is formidably competitive and oversubscribed, as Pearson's chapter later in this volume makes clear, based on her personal experience (p. 109). SQW's evaluation records that since its creation, the fund 'received over 18,000 applications, of which 3,713 (20%) were successful, receiving £33m across 3,670 individuals' (2022: 1). ACE has stated that it will invest £14.4 million per year until 2026 on the Developing Your Creative Practice scheme, which represents 2.25 per cent of ACE's total investment in the arts.

Arts Council Northern Ireland has a very similar fund to DYCP. Their 'Support for Individual Artists Programme' (SIAP) allows individuals to apply for grants of up to £15,000 and is designed for 'artists who are ready to develop their practice. This fund offers opportunity for research, [and] supports you by providing time to create new work, to train, to develop fresh ideas, to receive mentoring and to travel' (ACNI 2024). In 2022–3, of the £21.89 million that ACNI invested in the arts, £1.35 million (6 per cent of the total) was distributed to 361 artists via the SIAP scheme.

Arts Council Wales handles this slightly differently and has a 'Research and Development' category within its main 'Create' funding stream. Again, they explicitly decouple R&D from any predetermined outcome:

> We want to support research and development projects that will provide an opportunity to develop concepts, test ideas, research new markets and build new partnerships. Because of the nature of research and development work, we won't always expect there to be a defined outcome. (ACW 2024)

The 'Create' scheme is separated into 'Small Create' (for funding up to £10,000) and 'Big Create' (for funding between £10,000 and £50,000), though, as recently introduced schemes, data is not available about what proportion of ACW's £29.6 million funding was awarded in these ways.

Creative Scotland's fund for R&D falls under the 'Open Fund for Individuals' scheme. The scheme funds projects between £500 and £100,000 but is limited to £5 million annually (constituting 3 per cent of the £152 million total of grant support in 2022). The scheme is designed to 'support creative activity such as a specific project, production or a period of research and development. It can support an individual's time where this is related to specific creative outcomes' (Creative Scotland 2024: 7). Like the other comparable schemes, Creative Scotland explicitly states that this work does not need an immediate output:

> We will ask you if your proposed activity involves directly engaging other people as audiences or participants. [. . .] If your project is focused on your own work – such

as research towards a future work, or some training for you in a particular area of your practice – then you can select no for this question. (2024: 11)

In England, ACE has also joined forces with other funding organizations in the service of supporting R&D arts projects. For example, in 2011, the Digital Research and Development Fund for Arts and Culture drew together ACE, the Arts and Humanities Research Council (the AHRC, a government-funded organization supporting research and postgraduate study in the arts and humanities) and Nesta (a National Lottery-endowed independent charity focusing on innovation and social good) for a £500,000 pilot project supporting eight cultural organizations to extend and expand their work with digital technologies. On the basis of the success of the pilot project, the Digital R&D Fund for the Arts (2012–15) was established: a £7 million fund supporting a further fifty-two R&D projects, again with a focus on digital technologies, and emphasizing collaborations between arts and cultural organizations, technology companies and academic researchers. One of the key findings of the Fund's report was that the projects '[o]pened up a sector-wide conversation [. . .] on the role of R&D in the arts, and on risk, collaboration and innovation' (ACE 2017b: 15). In a document responding to the report, the three partners (ACE, AHRC and Nesta) confirm funding for Elizabeth Lomas 'to propose definitions of R&D in the arts and culture that can be used to inform public policy in an area which is conventionally restricted to science and technology' (ACE 2017a: 2), leading directly to the above-mentioned work conducted by Lomas with Bakhshi in 2017. Following these calls, we wish to amplify the importance of funding R&D in the arts as a way to foster 'risk, collaboration and innovation', even if (or especially as) Lomas and Bakhshi's important work on definitions has not yet produced the desired change in terms of incentives for artists.

National Lottery Project Grants also provide a key source of funding for theatre R&D. The published data for 2023–4, for instance, include a range of projects listing some variation of 'R&D' as a key activity. Drawing from publicly available information only, and based on the 928 applications categorized as 'theatre', 150 mention R&D within the activity name, totalling £3,651,989 of the £31,526,204 allocated to theatre. That is, approximately 15 per cent of theatre applications and 11.6 per cent of allocated funding in this category name R&D. Interestingly, while the 'theatre' category covers 31 per cent of all funded applications in this period, theatre represents 65 per cent of all R&D funding. This suggests more demand for this avenue of R&D funding among theatre artists than those working in dance, visual arts, music, literature, museums or libraries, which further supports the case for more streams of funding for R&D in the sector.

It is clear, therefore, that these organizations, all of which distribute central governmental and National Lottery funds, acknowledge R&D as an important component in the cultural life of the countries they represent. They all recognize that R&D should be funded in its own right, rather than as a step towards a predetermined, tangible output. Several of the chapters in this study explore R&D practices undertaken using funding from such schemes. However, it is equally clear that competition is fierce and the available funds are limited, with appetite within the industry far outstripping the levels at which R&D is currently funded and incentives, such as the tax relief offered in other industries, currently lacking.

## R&D: A utopian ideal within a dystopian context?

Across the following chapters, this study will explore examples of innovation and experimentation in a range of R&D structures and contexts. As above, we want to make visible how these innovations came about and how we might begin to understand the rich variety of R&D practices across the sector. The book is devoted to investigating the enormous value that lies in the exploration, play and open-ended experimentation that the best R&D processes have at their centre. However, we are also aware that R&D can, at its worst, be an exploitative model of development. Through R&D schemes, for instance, underrepresented artists can find themselves included in data regarding the diversity of artists with whom theatres collaborate but with little tangible support actually forthcoming from the organization. As our artist collaborators remind us across the chapters and long-form interviews which follow, R&D periods frequently involve unpaid and out-of-hours working. This means that precariously employed artists can find themselves working on a project with little or no payment, associated with a theatre – indeed beholden to that theatre for future hopes of a commission – with no contract or meaningful commitment from the organization itself. This was experienced variously by those we spoke to: some acknowledged and frequently leant in to this extra expending of their time, energy and goodwill, prioritizing the R&D over their own resources. Shamira Turner from the theatre company, She Goat, for example, told us, 'I will practise guitar or write a song in the evenings to delight Eugénie and then see what she makes of it and adds to it [the next day]' (p. 30), while playwright Alecky Blythe commented that 'we were doing a lot of work outside the room too before we got the commission and it would be nice to get paid!' (p. 84). In addition to questions of overwork and underpayment, there is also a crucial question of where new ideas come from and how that thinking time might be funded. As Lillian Henley puts it:

> as an artist and musician [. . .] I have to offer an idea that relies on my time and my expertise in order for the idea to be pitched. So, whilst it is important to be paid for the time you put into a project, you've also put a great deal of time and thought into the project before it is commissioned. There are so many unpaid hours! I don't know how this can be recognised, but clearly the time taken to develop an idea into a proposal is central to developing new forms of theatre and storytelling, and yet somewhere in the timeline of generating an idea, we put no fee value on it. (pp. 96–7)

No matter how inclusive, supportive and well-paid the R&D period might be, a freelance theatre-maker is almost guaranteed to spend their own time creating a project plan or initial idea. Without this they can't even begin to complete the application for funding or approach a theatre.

Our study, therefore, explores and probes contested ground. The joy of collaboration, the dizzying experience of creative discovery and the nervous anticipation of experimentation are juxtaposed with the uncertain and precarious context in which such innovation takes place. Given our belief in the ultimate value of such travelling into the unknown – through our own creative practice, our teaching and our research into the work of a wide range of theatre-makers – this book aims to strengthen the case for a re-evaluation of industrial policy, in which R&D in the arts sits alongside the sciences as a recognized way to nurture innovation and enrich lives. This, in turn, will require a review of how to adequately support such work. To return to Bakhshi, Breckon and Puttick's call:

> There needs to be a greater recognition and awareness of the breadth of activities and disciplines captured under R&D by policymakers, funders and industry, including AHSS [Arts, Humanities, and Social Sciences]. This system change will require a coordinated response and will not happen overnight, but it is essential if the UK is to maximise the contribution that R&D can make to innovation and productivity growth. (2021b: 141)

## About this book

The contributions to this book take two forms: essays and interviews. In exploring the breadth of R&D practices across the work of different theatre-makers, we have structured the book so that each chapter is paired with an interview. Although each essay and each interview stands alone, taken together they analyse R&D from the position of key creative roles: actors, directors, movement directors, playwrights, composers and designers, as well as makers (like Selina Thompson, Alex Kelly and Rachael Walton) who work across a number of these roles. While acknowledging that some of the distinctions between these disciplines are purposefully collapsed in R&D, it was key to our work that we did not implicitly suggest that R&D is the province of only certain members of the creative team. Each pairing also includes a short 'Questions and Prompts' section, encouraging makers to consider how they might explore their own R&D work. Some of these sections raise particular thoughts for discussion, some offer hints and tips and some indicate suggestions for practical work. Many of the questions and prompts cross-pollinate and proliferate across sections, useful reminders that questions of time and money, openness, collaboration and failure thread through R&D processes at all levels of experience and across different ways of making. We have shared these sections because they articulate the value we see in ongoing generative dialogue and conversation around this subject. In particular, we hope that they will be useful to those who pick up this book looking for answers to the sorts of questions we hear again and again from our students: What exactly is R&D? How do I know if I'm doing it right? When does R&D stop and rehearsal begin? Can I get paid for doing R&D? How do artists generate ideas? As this book will show, responses to these questions are multiple, contextual and contingent. The most experienced professional practitioners we have spoken to note that R&D is different every time, on every project, with every new group of people. We therefore urge anyone reading this book to sit with the slipperiness of this part of the theatre-making process, trusting that a lack of certainty is an unignorable part of R&D work.

## References

ACE (2017a), 'Digital R&D Fund for the Arts: Evaluation – Response from Arts Council England, Nesta and the Arts and Humanities Research Council'. https://www.artscouncil.org.uk/sites/default/files/download-file/RDFundPartnerResponseV4.pdf (accessed 19 January 2024).

ACE (2017b), 'Digital R&D Fund for the Arts: Evaluation'. https://www.artscouncil.org.uk/sites/default/files/download-file/Digital-RD-Fund-for-the-Arts-Evaluation.pdf (accessed 26 July 2024).

ACE (2024a), 'Developing your Creative Practice Guidance for Applicants'. https://www.artscouncil.org.uk/dycp/dycp-how-apply (accessed 26 July 2024).

ACE (2024b), 'Supporting Individual Creative and Cultural Practitioners'. https://www.artscouncil.org.uk/developing-creativity-and-culture/supporting-individual-creative-and-cultural-practitioners (accessed 26th July 2024).

ACNI (2024), 'Funding for Individuals'. https://artscouncil-ni.org/funding/funding-for-individuals (accessed 19 January 2024).

ACW (2024), 'Research and Development'. https://arts.wales/research-and-development (accessed 19 January 2024).

Bakhshi, H. and E. Lomas (2017), *Defining R&D for the Creative Industries*, London: NESTA. https://webarchive.nationalarchives.gov.uk/ukgwa/20170721170200/http://www.ahrc.ac.uk/documents/project-reports-and-reviews/policy-briefing-digital-r-d/ (accessed 26 July 2024).

Bakhshi, H., J. Breckon and R. Puttick (2021a), *Business R&D in the Arts, Humanities and Social Sciences*, London: Creative Industries Policy and Evidence Centre and Nesta. https://pec.ac.uk/policy-briefings/business-r-d-in-the-arts-humanities-and-social-sciences (accessed 26 July 2024).

Bakhshi, H., J. Breckon and R. Puttick (2021b), 'Understanding R&D in the Arts, Humanities and Social Sciences', *Journal of the British Academy*, 9: 115–45. https://doi.org/10.5871/jba/009.115 (accessed 26 July 2024).

Bird, G., H. Gorry, S. Roper and J. Love (2020), *R&D in Creative Industries Survey – 2020*, Kent: OMB Research. https://assets.publishing.service.gov.uk/media/5f6483a5e90e0759fdaaba44/4565_-_DCMS_RD_in_Creative_Industries_Survey_-_Report_-_D8_PDF.pdf (accessed 26 July 2024).

Blain, M. and J. Turner (2020), 'The Good, the God and the Guillotine: Insider/Outsider Perspectives', in M. Blain and H. J. Minor (eds), *Artistic Research in Performance through Collaboration*, London: Springer: 205–228.

Burnett Bonczek, R. and D. Storck (2013), *Ensemble Theatre Making: A Practical Guide*, London: Routledge.

Colin, N. and S. Sachsenmaier (2015), *Collaboration in Performance Practice: Premises, Workings and Failures*, London: Palgrave Macmillan.

Cornford, T. (2021), *Theatre Studios: A Political History of Ensemble Theatre-Making*, London: Routledge.

Creative Scotland (2024), 'Open Fund for Individuals Application Guidance'. https://www
.creativescotland.com/data/assets/pdf_file/0011/88382/CS-Open-Fund-for-Individuals
-D1.pdf (accessed 19 January 2024).
DCMS (2023), 'Economic Estimates: Employment in DCMS sectors, April 2021 to March 2023'. https://view.officeapps.live.com/op/view.aspx?src=https%3A%2F%2Fassets
.publishing.service.gov.uk%2Fmedia%2F65143a24b1bad4000d4fd8fa%2FEconomic
_Estimates_Employment_DCMS_Sectors_A21_M23.ods&wdOrigin=BROWSELINK
(accessed 19 January 2024).
Department of Business, Energy and Industrial Strategy (BEIS) (2017), 'Industrial Strategy'. https://assets.publishing.service.gov.uk/media/5a8224cbed915d74e3401f69/industrial-strategy-white-paper-web-ready-version.pdf (accessed 19 January 2024).
Department of Business, Energy and Industrial Strategy (BEIS) (2021), 'R&D People and Culture Strategy'. https://www.gov.uk/government/publications/research-and
-development-rd-people-and-culture-strategy (accessed 19 January 2024).
Department for Science, Innovation and Technology (2023), 'Science and Technology Framework'. https://www.gov.uk/government/publications/uk-science-and
-technology-framework/the-uk-science-and-technology-framework (accessed 19 January 2024).
Department for Science, Innovation and Technology and Department for Business, Energy and Industrial Strategy (BEIS) (2020), 'UK Research and Development Roadmap'. https://www.gov.uk/government/publications/uk-research-and
-development-roadmap (accessed 19 January 2024).
Govan, E., H. Nicholson and K. Normington (2007), *Making a Performance: Devising Histories and Contemporary Practices*, Abingdon: Routledge.
Harvie, J. and A. Lavender, eds (2010), *Making Contemporary Theatre: International Rehearsal Processes*, Manchester: Manchester University Press.
Heddon, D. and J. Milling (2005), *Devising Performance: A Critical History*, London: Palgrave Macmillan.
HM Treasury (2021), 'Build Back Better: Our Plan for Growth'. https://www.gov.uk/
government/publications/build-back-better-our-plan-for-growth (accessed 19 January 2024).
HMRC (2023), 'Research and Development (R&D) Expenditure Credit'. https://www
.gov.uk/guidance/corporation-tax-research-and-development-tax-relief-for-large
-companies (accessed 19 January 2024).
Lain, M. and H. J. Minor (2020), *Artistic Research in Performance through Collaboration*, London: Springer.
Marsden, R. (2021), *Inside the Rehearsal Room: Process, Collaboration and Decision-Making*, London: Methuen Drama.
Oddey, A. (1994), *Devising: A Practical Guide and Theoretical Handbook*, London: Routledge.
OECD (2015), *Frascati Manual 2015: Guidelines for Collecting and Reporting Data on Research and Experimental Development*, Paris: The Measurement of Scientific, Technological and Innovation Activities, OECD Publishing. https://doi.org/10.1787
/9789264239012-en (accessed 26 July 2024).
Radosavljević, D., ed. (2013), *The Contemporary Ensemble: Interviews with Theatre-Makers*, London: Routledge.
Rough, E., G. Hutton and C. Housley (2023), *Research and Development Funding Policy*, London: House of Commons Library. https://commonslibrary.parliament.uk/research
-briefings/cbp-7237/ (accessed 26 July 2024).

Simonsen, B. (2017), *The Art of Rehearsal: Conversations with Contemporary Theatre Makers*, London: Bloomsbury.

SQW (2022), 'Arts Council England's Developing Your Creative Practice programme: Independent Evaluation'. https://www.artscouncil.org.uk/dycp/developing-your-creative-practice-independent-evaluation (accessed 19 January 2024).

Syssoyeva, K. M. and S. Proudfit, eds (2016), *Women, Collective Creation, and Devised Performance: The Rise of Women Theatre Artists in the Twentieth and Twenty-First Centuries*, London: Palgrave.

Talam, E., G. Pugh and J. Fairburn (2022), *A Review of the Potential of R&D Tax Policy to Support the Creative Industries*, Staffordshire: Place Based Economic Recovery, Regeneration and Resilience Network (PERN). https://eprints.staffs.ac.uk/7526/1/A-review-of-the-potential-of-RD-tax-policy-to-support-the-creative-industries_PERN.pdf (accessed 19 January 2024).

Talawa (2024), 'FAQs'. https://www.talawa.com/faqs (accessed 26 July 2024).

The Team (2024), 'About the Company'. https://theteamplays.org/about-us/ (accessed 26 July 2024).

# 1

# Warped virtuosity and wobbly visuals

## Skill-learning in R&D

### Karen Quigley

*A flute solo soars above the rhythm and bass of a jazz ensemble.*
*An original verse of iambic pentameter bubbles to an actor's lips.*
*A performer loops her own voice by pressing buttons on a sound controller, while extending her hand to lift a waiting keytar from its stand.*
*A woman on stage fluidly ties a chest protector around her body, and advances towards another woman, both with swords outstretched: parry, riposte, failed parry, riposte, touche, points.*
*A camera lucida projects an audience member's face onto paper, which a performer traces with pencil and builds into a portrait.*

This chapter explores how R&D processes offer time and space to learn new skills, beyond the conventional rehearsal-based learning of lines, songs or choreography, or the development of performance skills via training or short courses. The skills described above (playing jazz flute, writing in iambic pentameter, using a sound controller, fencing with a partner, drawing a portrait) were all learned by theatre-makers during R&D processes. As this book's introduction indicates, R&D is often distinct from rehearsal in its decoupling of theatre and performance work from specific productions or outputs, aiming instead to develop a particular approach to theatre-making or ensemble practice, or to expand the craft of the makers involved. To understand skill-learning in R&D, therefore, is to more deeply understand the function of R&D as separate from (though frequently intertwined with) devising or rehearsal processes. Situating this learning within R&D also animates the distinction between learning a skill and rehearsing the appearance or choreography of a skill. Conversely, in contexts where an R&D process will be followed by periods of devising and/or rehearsal, learning a skill may be something that needs to happen before the next stages of making can commence. Skill-learning in R&D thus sits in its own field of vulnerability and uncertainty for makers and for theatre-making structures, and this chapter will explore some key tensions I have identified in this regard, using interview material from professional and student theatre-makers to discuss a variety of R&D

processes in which skill-learning takes on different forms and functions, with a range of different consequences.

Contextualizing skill acquisition in theatre contexts, Robert Crease and John Lutterbie identify that learning a particular skill to a reliable level allows the performer to 'put it in the service of some other performance [e.g. a production], using it to deliver us to a situation where a new kind of performance ability – a new kind of interplay with phenomena – becomes possible' (2010: 166). In other words, being proficient at a new skill means that the performer can stop focusing on the skill itself, and instead work towards what the skill is *for* in the context of a performance and its goals. Enacting a learned skill on stage therefore amounts to really doing the thing, while also serving the scene or production. In one of the examples above (and to be explored in more detail below), the performer has learned how to play jazz flute and can now find her place in a jazz ensemble, understanding its structures and rules, and can furthermore play as part of that ensemble in character in order to tell a production's story. Simultaneously, as Crease and Lutterbie continue, the learning of a particular skill, and how that learning sits in the performer's body, remains important as we watch a performance, 'for we still have to have some appreciation of what goes into it' (166). Lutterbie notes elsewhere that, in these cases, the effort of what has been learned by the actor isn't sublimated to the performance, and the skills on display are still 'thick [as distinct from transparent], we never lose sight of them completely' (2011: 133).[1] So, as audience members at the theatre, we want to take pleasure in watching skilled actors doing their job well, even as these well-learned skills might appear effortless or easy to those who have mastered them.

This interrelation between a skill and how we watch that skill being performed recalls tensions between phenomenology and semiotics, well-trodden ground in the fields of theatre and performance studies. Phenomenology and semiotics are both concerned with how our experience of something (in this case, a performance, or more specifically a skill being performed) functions. However, while phenomenology deploys 'embodied, situated and relational' tactics for making sense of a performance, semiotics is interested in how performance is made up of multiple signs or sign-systems, all signifying various meanings (Sherman et al. 2015: 1). Returning to Crease and Lutterbie's analysis above and invoking this tension between phenomenology and semiotics, a skill on display at the theatre is really happening, and an audience is experiencing it, but it is also happening because the performance demands it, so at the same time it is signifying something. Bert O. States offers the concept of 'binocular vision', where one eye sees a performance (or the world) in phenomenological terms and one eye sees the same thing in semiotic terms, further enmeshing these two approaches to audiencing, experience and interpretation (States 1985: 8).

Taking this understanding of how skill functions in performance a step further, Carrie Noland observes how the learning and performance of skills can operate not just

---

[1] Lutterbie does not specify, but I assume he is drawing connections with Clifford Geertz's anthropological methodology of 'thick description' (a phrase borrowed from philosopher Gilbert Ryle), in which actions or behaviours can be described in great detail (or 'thickly') and placed in broader interpretive contexts. In theatre and performance contexts, 'thick' descriptions can also be built from embedded or embodied experiences.

paradoxically, but even as a manifestation of 'highly charged and ambiguous' resistance to fixed ways of thinking or modes of representation (2010: 214). For Noland, primarily writing about dance, gesture and physicality, '[s]killing and deskilling are processes through which we are given an opportunity to confront a gesture as contingent' (2010: 214). In other words, the development of a skill can allow us to understand skill itself as something beyond the functional or aesthetic, or beyond sequential acquisition, but as something that encourages consideration of how a particular skill can propel a performer towards thinking and working in a variety of new ways. Building on this, and speaking to the examples shared above and below in this chapter, in learning a new skill, a performer might feel the pressure of a new set of rules (gypsy jazz has *these* particular soloing structures; a fencing bout *must* pause after three minutes; a line of iambic pentameter *only* has ten syllables), but also achieves a new sense of power and control (I can play a flute solo while the rest of the band supports me; I have the stamina and physical fitness to keep fencing for three minutes; I can improvise a whole verse of iambic pentameter). Returning to R&D processes specifically, these new understandings via skill acquisition may be contextual and relevant to a future rehearsal period or production, but are not necessarily taking place with those particular creative outputs in mind.

This chapter's thinking is supported by semi-structured interviews drawn from two particular groups. I interviewed professional performance practitioners Eugénie Pastor and Shamira Turner, who have worked as members and associates of various (primarily devising-based) British theatre and performance companies, most significantly via a long-standing association with Little Bulb Theatre. Pastor has a parallel solo practice and academic career, Turner has a parallel acting, music and producing career, and together they have formed the company She Goat, which blends devised performance, music, live and recorded sound 'with radical co-operation and extravagant multi-tasking' (She Goat 2023). The interview took place in April 2023, and key productions referred to include *Orpheus* (2013) and a currently untitled work-in-progress R&D (both Little Bulb), *DoppelDänger* (2017) and *The Undefinable* (2020; both She Goat), alongside Turner's work with the performance company 1927 and Pastor's solo performance *Pube* (2016).

I also interviewed a group of four student theatre-makers studying BA Theatre: Writing, Directing and Performance at the University of York and working on the Independent Group Production Project module described in this book's introduction. In particular, the focus here is on the module's four-week R&D period, in which students work with the support of their supervisor to explore their chosen project prior to rehearsals. The group in question elected to work towards staging *Athena* by Gracie Gardner (Gardner 2021) for the festival in June 2023, and its membership consisted of two co-directors (Ciara Southwood and Dan Sinclair), three actors (Georgia Firth, Abi Baker and Nadia Bartlett), who would go on to play Athena, Mary Wallace and Jamie, respectively, in the final production, and a designer (George Robertson). The interview (with Firth, Robertson, Sinclair and Southwood) took place in March 2023, midway through the R&D period for *Athena*.

As the book's introduction notes, our ongoing explorations of R&D as a contemporary theatre-making methodology initially grew from our teaching work and our developing understanding of R&D as a pedagogical tool. With this in mind, it felt apt to give voice in this chapter to a student group, returning us to the book project's origins and centring the experience of newcomers to R&D processes alongside those of mid-career theatre-makers. Equally, hearing Pastor and Turner as they discuss a range of professional productions taking places in a variety of contexts over the past decade is a valuable reminder that skill or technique acquisition remains in the trained and training body, and that a theatre-maker can use skills learned in R&D processes to build an ongoing set of approaches to performance.

Reading across the relationship between theatre practice and skill-learning reveals a number of key themes and trends. Drawing together understandings of actors developing actorly skills and actors developing other specific skills, it is clear that the literature takes up various positions in relation to what a skill is, who has learned it, the reason(s) for learning it and how it performs or is performed on stage (or screen).

In theatre studies contexts, there are outlines of various actor training techniques and skills available in practitioner-centred guides, how-to manuals and practice-as-research analyses (e.g. Adler 1988; Curpan 2021; Donnellan 2005; Kapsali 2021; Lecoq 2020; Spatz 2015; Stanislavski 1936), while a wide range of fields explore the transferable and applicable nature of theatre practice skills to medical, legal, teaching, mental health and therapy settings (e.g. Goldingay et al. 2014; Ørjasæter and Ness 2017; Neelands 2009; Shah et al. 2015; Tang et al. 2020). In both cases, the focus tends to be on explaining precisely how a skill works and how it can be applied, or on how actors can maintain and enhance their skill sets as their careers develop. In performance studies, the 'cognitive turn' in the early 2000s saw scholars using cognitive science to understand theatre and theatre-makers using their practice as a way of responding to research questions. Speaking specifically to this chapter's concerns, the former approach led to analyses of what happens in the brain when a new performance skill is learned and how neuroscience can support skill-learning in actor training contexts (Blair 2008; Lutterbie 2011; Kemp 2012). Skills in this context are therefore understood as doing something specific in and to an actor's brain as well as their body, building towards a sense of skill-learning as a vital component in our developing understanding of the relationship between what an actor is doing and what they are feeling. Across the board, the above literature tends to imply that skills should be acquired either in general training contexts or in actors' independent study time (i.e. not in rehearsals for a specific production), and there is no sense of R&D processes operating as part of this landscape.

In screen acting, discussions around actors learning particular skills for particular projects surface frequently in reports of film and television production, from gossipy articles online, to interviews with actors, to performers' published diaries or reflections on their work. In these contexts, the focus tends to be on actors playing people in biopic-style films, and the achievement of learning a new skill in a relatively short period of time, alongside the believability of the actor portraying the person in question. For example, in the 2018 film *Green Book*, Mahershala Ali played the jazz pianist and composer, Don Shirley, and learned basic piano skills ahead of filming taking place (Shaw Roberts 2019). Similarly, Margot Robbie played the figure skater Tonya Harding in 2017's *I, Tonya* and trained for four months in order to evoke some of the figure-skating routines shown in the film (Van Der Meer 2017). This approach is, of course, part of the publicity machine surrounding the release of commercial films, but its guaranteed appearance when a film features a character's profession suggests an ongoing interest in and appetite for glimpses into the relationship between a skill and the person doing it, even if, unlike in the theatre, actors like Ali and Robbie will have professional pianists and figure skaters working as their stand-ins and doubles for particular kinds of shots.

In theatre practice, there is a long history of actors doing 'real actions' on stage (sometimes referred to as 'stage business'), such as smoking, drinking or food preparation. Some of these actions will be innate, and some may need to be learned during rehearsals, in order to skilfully coordinate them with movement and speech, making the actions look 'natural' when they have been pre-rehearsed. However, once the required skill set moves beyond the recognizable business of day-to-day human life, the value of R&D space and time to learn a new skill becomes more apparent. One of the most prominent examples of this in contemporary British theatre is a company of performers learning how to use a range of specialist technical equipment for Katie Mitchell's production of *Waves* for the National Theatre in 2006, the first example of the 'live cinema' form that has become synonymous with Mitchell's practice ever since. In order to stage Virginia Woolf's 1931 novel *The Waves*, and to 'come up with a form to communicate [the unspoken] thoughts [of the characters] and the experience all the characters had of being inside their own heads', members of the company experimented with Katie Mitchell in R&D workshops for two years (largely taking place at the National Theatre Studio and funded by a grant from the National Endowment for Science and the Arts), followed by rehearsal periods in collaboration with video designer Leo Warner and sound designer Gareth Fry (Lease 2020: 254). These R&D workshops explored various approaches to sound effects and video design before the company 'ended up using live filmed close-ups of the characters' faces alongside amplified voices (representing the characters' thoughts), with sound design and live Foley sound effects', all of which involved actors wielding cameras, microphones and various sound-making objects, to the extent that they have been described as 'performer-technicians' as their skills in this domain have evolved (Lease: 254; Cornford 2020: 190).

In what I have encountered, there is relatively little engagement with precisely *when* skills are learned in the context of an R&D, devising, rehearsal and/or production process and thus what this skill acquisition might mean, look like or feel like to artists. This chapter is concerned with all of these things, articulating R&D periods as opportunities for the learning of new skills, and acknowledging that this learning takes place both during and around demarcated R&D times and spaces, while observing the benefits to the ensemble of learning together and the extent to which a given skill needs to be 'really' learned.

## Feeling real, looking real and idiosyncratic virtuosity

In considering the particularity of live bodies performing skills, theatre and performance scholarship continues to be drawn to questions of the real and the imagined. Since Plato's assertion in the *Republic* that all artists should be vilified for their work presenting mere imitations of real-life actions, the theatre has operated in tandem with anti-theatrical suspicions (Emlyn-Jones and Preddy 2014: 391). Discussions of 'the real' in relation to this chapter's aims also bring into view Erika Fischer-Lichte's observations about theatre's 'performative turn' in the late twentieth century, which acknowledged a breaking down of previously held boundaries between art and not art, between performer and not performer and between what something means and how it might be experienced (another articulation of the tension between semiotics and phenomenology, as mentioned above). As Fischer-Lichte puts it, moving on from a primary concern with the text and how its meanings could be semiotically understood, 'the focus of interest shifted to the processes of making, producing, creating, doing and to the actions, processes of exchange, negotiation and transformation' (1999: 168). Thus, she suggests that scholarship in theatre studies retrained its gaze onto what bodies on stage were actually doing in any given moment, offering a new paradigm of performativity and performance analysis, rather than prioritizing the referential nature of performance.

In this section, I am specifically focused on the difference between performing a skill on stage (e.g. playing the piano; frying an egg) and performing the appearance of a skill on stage (e.g. miming playing the piano while an expert plays offstage; pretending to fry an egg). The skill being performed approaches representations of 'the real' (frying an egg is a real skill) while troubling our uncertainty around performativity (but is it acting if it's a real skill being enacted?). Returning to the tension between phenomenology and semiotics is useful here too: playing the piano well on stage is really happening, while also happening due to the demands of the production – we are experiencing it *and* it is signifying something. The kind of work done during an R&D process is thus crucial to the way we ultimately read this skill on stage. In a way, the distinction between the skill itself and its choreography demarcates the space of R&D as one of possibility (where learning a skill could take a performer, company or project in a number of directions) and the space of rehearsal as one of necessity (where learning the choreography of a skill is required for a scene to work).

## Feeling familiar

As She Goat, Pastor and Turner offered examples of some of these differences in reference to their R&D process for *DoppelDänger* in 2017. This piece, devised and performed by Pastor and Turner, combined live and live-recorded multi-instrumental music and singing (original work and cover versions), sketches, dance routines and image work drawing on a wide history of visual art, including 'gender-defying' costumes combining Victorian wrestling gear with Renaissance headpieces (She Goat 2017). Playing on the co-creators' experiences of being mistaken for each other, and exploring a range of influences from Gothic storytelling to Baroque music to pop anthems, *DoppelDänger* leaned into the weirdness, silliness and danger of doubling and doppelgangers. One of their starting points was inspired by paintings and other images of various duos or pairs, particularly these postcards of Victorian wrestling, because [we] couldn't tell what kind of engagement was going on, it's like a hug and it's like a struggle. It's one and the same. It's like puppies playing. You can't really tell. It's quite a liminal experience. (Turner 2023)

In R&D, Pastor and Turner used these images of Victorian wrestling to create physical representations of the poses with their bodies and to extrapolate movement sequences from the still visuals. However, they found that it was impossible to easily move from one position or pose to another and realized that 'neither of us had any experience of wrestling logic or wrestling movement' (Turner 2023). With this in mind, they went to an open wrestling class in London, 'which was just a bunch of giant men doing roly-polys [. . .] we learned loads from being in that atmosphere', and then trained with a professional wrestler who taught them to use their bodies in 'a completely new way for us' (Turner 2023). For She Goat, developing the skill of wrestling as distinct from movement sequences that looked like frozen images of wrestling 'gave us the kind of movement vocabulary, and confidence to be the way we are with each other on stage' as they R&Ded, devised, rehearsed and performed what became *DoppelDänger* (Turner 2023). Although not trying to convince an audience that they were 'real' wrestlers, the level of skill required was about 'real' familiarity with a different type of physical expression and about safely engaging with each other's bodies as they enacted different routines.

## *Personalised skills*

Later, in R&D for their 2019 performance *The Undefinable*, She Goat prioritized learning skills related to accessibility. Through their previous work together, Pastor and Turner had identified a shared aim to enable their work to be inherently accessible to visually impaired communities, and, because audience headphones were beyond the reach of their budget, they decided to learn audio description as a way of embedding this access into the performance 'from scratch'.[2] During the R&D for *The Undefinable*, they centred the development of their own form of live audio description, conceptualizing the ongoing work at that stage as 'a mixture of being a radio host and being extremely caring of one another' (Turner 2023). As can be typical in R&D contexts, this aim suggests an intention to do or learn something but without knowing quite how – an end without an initial means.

*The Undefinable* was ultimately structured as a radio show happening amidst its own off-mic, behind-the-scenes context, with Pastor and Turner playing hosts, integrating live music and dialogue throughout. However, the mere fact of the live performance being a radio show did not make the production automatically fully accessible to those with visual impairment. As the show moved into rehearsal and production, Pastor and Turner worked with Maria Oshodi, Artistic Director and CEO of Extant (a theatre company of visually impaired and blind artists), to bring their audio description skills from R&D into relation with the theatre space and some of its more ocularcentric

---

[2] See Mark Love-Smith's chapter in this volume for a broader unpacking of this term in British theatre.

conventions. In an interview for the Auralia Space project, Pastor and Turner have referred to She Goat's particular approach to audio description, developed in R&D for *The Undefinable*, as *'creative* audio description' (Radosavljević et al. 2021: 6, my emphasis). Though they do not specify, this appears to mean audio description that goes further than the norm in describing sensations, and also harnesses the possibilities offered by the fact that the audio description is being done by the show's performers, rather than another person who has been employed to deliver this.

For example, at the beginning of *The Undefinable*, 'the theatre goes dark *for everybody*' (Radosavljević et al. 2021: 6, my emphasis). Following this blackout, She Goat created 'enhanced [verbal] notes' for the audience, describing the stage aloud as it became slowly illuminated: 'you get the layout of the set, our costumes [. . .] and it's all done in character, so it feels like it comes from the host setting the scene for you' (ibid.). The creative audio description skills honed in R&D thus imbued every part of the show's content and form and enabled the rooted accessibility of what became *The Undefinable*, which began a national tour with Arts Council support in 2020. Following the first national Covid lockdown in March of that year, She Goat (like many other artists) had to cancel their tour and pivot to a different performance context when in-person theatre became impossible. Although this was not a design feature of the original R&D, She Goat reimagined and reshaped *The Undefinable* into a six-part podcast, and thus an audio-only format, using the same skills and deepening their already existing creative audio description work to include Foley sound and evocative descriptions of movement sequences.

Having learned the skill of audio description and made it their own through a sequence of R&D and rehearsal processes, She Goat have continued to draw on this as an integral part of their performance language. Turner observes how this experience has even informed their relationship outside of the work they make together:

> the first time we met up in person after the pandemic, we were in a café, and I could hear us going, 'Oh, shall we have some of this cheesecake? Yes, I can see one here, and it's a lovely yellow colour, isn't it?' and we were just chatting away, and I was thinking, this feels like us, this is She Goat hosting a show and this is us audio describing as we go [. . .] the world of *The Undefinable* has infused the relationship, and the relationship infuses the work, and they constantly feed back and in [to each other]. (Turner 2023)

Crucially, the space and time of the R&D process meant that the work of audio description in *The Undefinable* was not layered on to a finished product or bought in from an external source, but was delivered by the artists themselves deep in the context of the production. The only way for this particular approach to embedded accessibility to be achieved was for She Goat to learn the skill themselves to its fullest possible extent, which required more time (to practice) and creative headspace (to generate ideas) than a conventional rehearsal process allows.

## *Choreographing 'for real'*

Meanwhile, for the student group working on *Athena*, a similar drive to do something to the fullest extent possible yielded very different results. In the context of the module, students are asked to prepare a written document outlining plans for their R&D period, and as lecturers we offer 'experiments, workshop ideas, ways of exploring research questions' as prompts for how they might structure these plans. On reading Gracie Gardner's play about American high school students training to be competitive fencers, and starting to design their R&D in November 2022, the students noted 'How can you stage *real* combat or sports on stage?' as a research question and suggested that

> [a] lot of the R&D period will be taken up by researching and practising fencing, and experimenting with the movements it involves. We want to conduct movement workshops [. . .] alongside fencing lessons for the entire production team and cast. (Sinclair 2023c; my emphasis above)

When I interviewed them during their R&D period, they reflected that 'for our R&D, we had to immerse ourselves in the [fencing] world, physically [. . .] learn the rules, and get good at it to a point where we could either build off [i.e. generate choreography based on] the basic movements or do actual fencing' (Southwood 2023). The company took part in an intensive R&D period of fencing classes with the University club, personal and group fitness training, watching live and recorded fencing matches and documenting long conversations they had with other students who were competitive fencers. Following this process of research and the beginnings of skill acquisition, the students, through their own growing competence with fencing, began to notice fencing and other swordplay in theatre productions they were watching online and to understand these in a different light. In particular, they reflected on rewatching the 2018 filmed theatre production of *Hamlet* (directed by Robert Icke for the Almeida Theatre and starring Andrew Scott). As they observed,

> that's not fencing. That's choreographed [. . .] no one knows the rules. It's very clear that they've watched fencing, because they know what the buzzers look like, and they know the right colours, but their footwork is completely off, their backs aren't straight, they're not protecting their bodies with the foils. Just from going to the classes and speaking to actual people [who fence], their technique's completely off. (Southwood 2023)

In other words, via noting that a skill on stage might not always be what it purports to be, the student group began to realize through their R&D work the difference between the appearance or choreography of a skill on stage and a deeper embodied learning of the skill itself. Thinking onwards from R&D and towards their rehearsal process for *Athena*, the group's R&D experience with fencing empowered them to deepen their thinking about how they would present fencing on stage and how the physical work of fencing might sit with the demands of the play's dialogue. A gap thus opened up between the skill of fencing and its depiction on stage as part of their project. In interview, they acknowledged (pre-rehearsal) that a choreographic approach could be a better choice for the performers physiologically as distinct from aesthetically, because 'you're not exerting so much energy, [so] you can get back to normal talking [more quickly]. Whereas for us, even if it's only a couple of points, we're going to be out of breath for the next while [. . .] sweating [and] panting' (Sinclair 2023a). With this in mind, during R&D they tried a range of approaches to staging fragments of the text, and '[w]hen we tried to choreograph the fencing a bit, it felt not right. It might look good, but didn't feel right' (Firth 2023). Moving into rehearsal, the group reflected that

> the thing we need to bear in mind is [that] we're not going to be performing the show for an audience of fencers [. . .] we'll probably end up doing a mixture of choreography and actual fencing, and the classes have given us the scope to do that rather than having to make a decision from lack of skill. (Southwood 2023)

Here then, the R&D process offered the student company time and space to delve deeply into learning a particular skill, with the additional dimension that their embodied knowledge of fencing started to reveal the gap between the playtext and the sport. This new skill made a fundamental intervention into the group's work on *Athena*, giving them choices about how to proceed with their staging of the play, which, speaking personally, is precisely what staff teaching the module hope R&D processes can offer in this context. R&D is again revealed as a theatre-making methodology that reaches beyond the immediate needs of the project at hand. The student group realized through their R&D work that a balance between choreography and fencing 'for real' (in order for it to 'feel right') was important. In this context, R&D empowered performers with new skills, opening up their future rehearsal and staging options and allowing them to make later aesthetic decisions from a position of strength rather than limitation.

## Idiosyncratic virtuosity

Of course, it is also possible to hold space for a generative middle ground, where a skill learned in R&D might be freed from binary thinking around phenomenology/semiotics, process/product or the sense of a border between the 'real' doing of a skill and a choreographed version of a skill. This midpoint allows for the warped and weird specificities artists encounter as they learn new skills in R&D processes, encompassing tensions between a skill needing to be learned in order for an R&D process to evolve, and the staging of a production relying on the development of a specific skill. Pastor referred to a model of what she calls 'idiosyncratic virtuosity', which embraces the idea of a particular performer learning very specific skills for very specific contexts, or, as she puts it, 'learning to do something in the best possible way *you* can do it. You become your own virtuoso' (Pastor 2023). In her academic work, Pastor has connected this particular sense of virtuosity to Carrie Noland's observation that '[t]here is a first time for *my* body to perform what other bodies already have learned to do. And there is a first time for *my* body to perform the gesture in an idiosyncratic and potentially subversive way' (Pastor 2014: 155). As part of her 2016 solo one-on-one performance *Pube*, Pastor drew a portrait of each participant 'and I'm not a particularly good drawer, especially in under five minutes' (Pastor 2023). In order to speedily develop the skill she needed for the performance, the R&D for *Pube* involved the creation of a 'weird system of mirrors to project an image of the person [onto paper, which Pastor then traced with pencil and sketched on top of], and that was my version of it, my weird camera lucida, and the skill arrives as [a way of] problem solving' (Pastor 2023). Thinking ahead to the performance, Pastor used the R&D process to figure out how to do what was needed for the encounter with the audience member (draw a portrait in five minutes), rather than learning the details of the general skill (training in portraiture). In other words, the particular skill needed to be idiosyncratically learned in order to make progress in the R&D and subsequently towards the performance.

Turner offered the example of working with 1927, a theatre company whose productions frequently involve video animation projected onto a screen with which live performers interact. Turner noted that, for this performer-screen interaction to happen effectively, the company discovered through R&D that 'your body needs to be incredibly close to the screen, but never touching it, so it doesn't wobble the visual' (Turner 2023). Here, the R&D process included the deeply technical work of the actor's body experimenting in order to evoke a particular stylistic choice in the context of the production. However, Turner observed that the learning of a specific vocabulary of performance, though it is 'generally going to build up your skills base as a maker', tends to feel 'illogical to apply to any other performance I do', emphasizing the idea of production-specific skills-learning in R&D processes (Turner 2023). Pastor and Turner further suggested that the specific skills learned in R&D contexts can feel 'warped' at times (Pastor 2023). The example they shared was about She Goat's approach to learning how to use the sound controller and mixer Ableton Push, a physical electronic instrument connected to advanced audio software. Pastor and Turner didn't learn how to use the hardware (or software) itself in its entirety but

> we basically learned to play Ableton in a way that made sense to us and made sense to what we needed it to do for a specific set of songs. So we learned those skills, but I would be unable to do a DJ set on that thing, even though that's what it's mostly used for by music professionals. So, in a way, you acquire very idiosyncratic skills that are also a bit of a superpower, because the way we've organised this machine makes sense only to us. (Pastor 2023)

As Pastor notes, all of the Ableton Push features they have figured out how to use probably have 'a shortcut that would make it easier or more sensible', but the idiosyncratic virtuosity she and Turner have found with this instrument in R&D means that they can write the songs they want to write for the productions they want to make, 'rather than becoming Ableton wizards' (Pastor 2023). I suggest that this work on Ableton Push alongside the work with the screen for 1927 and the portrait-drawing for *Pube* all represent specific limited use cases of one kind or another, all of which might be termed idiosyncratic skill-learning. In these contexts, the focus is not on learning a skill the same way someone specializing in that field would do, or learning the choreography of what a skill looks like, but learning enough of the skill to employ it for the purposes of the performance, in the time available.

## Vulnerability and uncertainty in (paid and unpaid) ensemble practice

Theatre relies on collaboration of various kinds. Ensemble-building lies at the heart of successful collaborative practice. Learning of all kinds and in all contexts requires a degree of vulnerability. Drawing on these fundamental observations in relation to the context of this chapter, I suggest that learning something new in R&D enhances collaboration, encouraging makers to come together in their vulnerability with an unfamiliar skill. Maria K. McKenna and Edward J. Brantmeier note that a 'pedagogy of vulnerability' allows members of a group to 'connect across differences, to speak from the heart, and to add an emotional and spiritual dimension to the learning experience that honours interdependence and deep difference' (2020: 4). They observe that educational philosophers including Paulo Freire, bell hooks, Nel Noddings and Peter McLaren situate vulnerability at the heart of their learning practices. More broadly, the researcher and podcast host Brene Brown has popularized vulnerability as a key driver in our human desire for self-knowledge and connection, and her TED talk 'The Power of Vulnerability' has been viewed over 84 million times (between YouTube and the TED website) as I write this chapter.

Pastor and Turner described the R&D period for Little Bulb's 2013 show *Orpheus*, which took place at Battersea Arts Centre and focused on the new (to all but one member of the company) skill of gypsy jazz, a

> light and dry quality of playing, where the band hold down a song, and the song structure allows for people to take solos over the top of the chord progressions, [so we had to learn] how to trade solos, how to solo, what a solo sounds like in this Django Rheinhardt style of gypsy jazz. There was so much to learn. (Turner 2023)

Although the company members were already well-versed in various musical instruments and had worked together for a number of years, learning how to play in a different genre and style found them feeling 'like gypsy jazz for babies at the beginning' (ibid.). The ensemble developed an R&D process of not only 'sitting around and practicing [. . .] steadily getting better together' during the day but also sitting in on open mic nights at local Battersea jazz club Le QuecumBar (ibid.). In this setting, the company members found themselves gradually growing in confidence with the genre, eventually performing a song one night and over time starting to gig as a gypsy jazz band named The Hot Club, connected to but distinct from work on the show that became *Orpheus*. As Turner evokes, learning a new skill during the R&D period

> gave us the identity of a jazz band together. We had that shared language which can really only happen from the R&D time in the room together. You need time to make mistakes, to figure out what works. I don't know how we could have been a genuine jazz band together, a company, if we hadn't had that sort of time to learn to build up that skill and that history together. (Turner 2023)

For the company, learning a new skill together and having time to be vulnerable while 'figuring it out' was a key element of ensemble-building, even for a company with a lengthy and rich history of collaborative devising practice. Referring to She Goat's work on *DoppelDänger*, Turner reflected that 'there's something about going through the learning process together as complete novices that helps you to build up the robust world of the show', and referred to their wrestling learning as 'an incredible bonding experience for us' (Turner 2023). Here too, the vulnerability attendant upon learning something new nourishes the ensemble as much as the content of the work being produced.

For the *Athena* group, learning the new skill of fencing during their R&D period and feeding that knowledge back into their deepening understanding of the play brought members of the group together, particularly the two principal actors in the company (Bartlett's role of Jamie was much smaller). As Firth observed, their two approaches to fencing bouts were very different:

> Abi [her fellow actor] starts so strong and is very fluid throughout, and for some reason I'm not very good at all at the start, and then get so annoyed that I'm losing that I have to bring it back [. . .] and [mapping this onto the playtext] there's so many moments in the play where Athena gets worked up that she isn't winning. (Firth 2023)

These differences in approach between the two actors (and the overlaps between actor and character) led to a long discussion in a particular R&D session about the group's experiences of female friendship, 'and everyone had these really traumatic stories growing up of bullying, and girls being vicious. That's separate from fencing, but it made us closer' (ibid.). In this context, the skill learned in the space and time offered by R&D encouraged the ensemble to make themselves vulnerable to each other, allowing a deeper ensemble connection to arise from the specific, detailed skill work with which the group was engaged.

## Unpaid labour

It is an industry-wide problem that theatre-makers frequently work beyond their contracted hours, and this book articulates how R&D as a particular aspect of theatre-making is under unique pressure in terms of how it is funded and how its hours operate. While celebrating the collaborative possibilities arising from shared vulnerability in the learning of new skills and how this work strengthens the R&D itself and any future devising/rehearsal/production processes, I also acknowledge the tension between the ensemble-building to which I refer and the normalization of unpaid time and labour attached to these processes. As a number of other practitioners across this volume observe, some of the individual research work of R&D happens beyond paid time or standard work hours. Rachael Walton refers to 'the book you read on the bus [on the way to R&D]' (p. 166) and Alexander Kelly to watching relevant films in the evenings in order to prioritize practical work together in the space during paid R&D time

(p. 167). Alecky Blythe notes that 'we were doing a lot of work outside the room too before we got the commission and it would be nice to get paid!' (p. 84).

Pastor described a recent R&D period with Little Bulb Theatre which saw the company learning how to write in iambic pentameter. She notes that

> once you start, it's very addictive [...] on the Tube you spend your time thinking in iambic pentameter. It's not just something that you leave at the door of the rehearsal room when you go home, and sometimes that's a pleasure, and sometimes that's a bit of a sword above your head where you feel that, 'Oh, I must work outside of working hours, because otherwise I won't be at the standard I would like to be'. (Pastor 2023)

As Pastor implies, this drive to practise a new skill outside of paid hours can be read positively in terms of ensemble-building, and something that artists find themselves doing for each other's enjoyment and excitement, as well as how it contributes to the work being explored in R&D. As Turner continues, during She Goat R&D periods 'I will practise guitar or write a song in the evenings to delight Eugénie and then see what she makes of it and adds to it. [I do it] for that communal discovery' (Turner 2023).

However, it is also clear that these makers are not being paid for the time they spend learning and perfecting their skills beyond the R&D space. Indeed, Pastor and Turner referred to the *Orpheus* R&D period described above as 'luxurious by today's standards' and reflect on the model of 'immersive' R&D periods with Little Bulb, where it had been possible to spend R&D in full-time residency mode, allowing for evening jazz club sessions alongside daytime R&D sessions. In this context, Little Bulb lived and worked together for periods of up to three weeks in accommodation provided by Battersea Arts Centre, who also paid small relocation rates, but no artist fees were paid (either by BAC or by Little Bulb). In short, 'luxury' and 'immersion' here refer to time, rather than money. A tension thus opens up between getting better and better at the new skill, strengthening the ensemble through shared learning, and the amount of unpaid work and time that is required to make these things happen to the highest level. While R&D offers some space and time for the learning of new skills, this is frequently being topped up from artists' own calendars, homes and pockets, and the kind of model possible for *Orpheus* subsequently becomes impossible when family or caring commitments come into play.

The *Athena* group found that their £425 production budget for the module could not fully accommodate the fencing classes and travel to matches that had become such key aspects of their R&D process. Thus, they made a decision as a group to partially self-fund these activities, 'leaving us out of pocket, but better fencers for it' (Sinclair 2023b). They also folded their growing awareness of the financial privilege attached to fencing into their R&D explorations of the play and its themes and characters. As Sinclair observes, some of the group's previously held stereotypes about the typical demographic of university fencing and fencers were confirmed, and their understanding of the play's two main characters was further bolstered:

> It's like there's no smoke without fire. It is very elitist, the kit is expensive. Even doing the training for us is quite expensive to go every week. And I think that's

the biggest thing I've learned from going to the training and being in that world, seeing the other people at fencing and thinking, 'That's something Athena would do, that's something Mary Wallace would do'. (Sinclair 2023a)

According to Sinclair, then, the imperative time and money structures of the *Athena* R&D process were rebranded and reframed as a dramaturgical aid, though I am wary of further normalizing (or even valorizing) self-funding in this way. That said, it is an important reminder for the university and training sectors that, even as our students embark on the beginnings of their first R&D journey, there is already a perception that their production budget should not be spent on R&D when it could be spent on the production itself (which is usually what is assessed), a clear trend in the theatre industry, too. As we foster the next generation of theatre-makers, it is worth reflecting on how these perceptions can be contextualized and what kind of change may be needed in further and higher education.

This section has aimed to show that the overspill of time and labour in R&D relates to both attaining a desired standard in a skill, and a sense of loyalty and shared endeavour among collaborators. Alert to the vulnerability of unpaid time and labour for artists, I am also drawn to the ways in which learning something new encourages theatre-makers to come together in their vulnerability with an unfamiliar skill and to enhance their togetherness as the skill is learned by the ensemble. However, this suggests that in some cases artists are *paying for* the enhanced sense of collaboration described above. An obvious conclusion is that, as this book attempts to illuminate throughout, R&D is under-resourced in contemporary British theatre at every level, and artists are giving of their own time and money in order to continue making the work they want to make, in the way they want to make it.

Moreover, this chapter has found that learning a new skill in the context of an R&D process is, much like R&D itself, different every time. While the *Athena* group have spoken above about their first ever R&D process, and Pastor and Turner refer to multiple R&Ds over the past decade or more, the contingent nature of skill-learning is clear across the board. As mentioned above, learning something new opens up an uncertain space of vulnerability, change and growth. As such, a key factor emerging from my understanding of how skill-learning has functioned for the practitioners to whom I have spoken is that it is deeply needed, and deeply rooted in contradictions, questions and tensions. How real does the skill need to look on stage? How real does the skill need to feel in the body? How much time do we have to learn this new skill? Can we find some extra time anywhere? Is this skill ever going to be useful in any other context? Does that matter? What does learning the skill now enable us to do? What has this skill-learning been for?

Responding to that last question, the notion of 'idiosyncratic virtuosity' identified by Pastor not only leads to a sense of ownership over the specific skills that the performer has learned in particular (or even 'warped') ways in R&D but also allows performers to modify their practice depending on the context. As Turner notes, '[i]t's like, yeah, I play all those instruments, but in really specific ways, and I still don't read music' (Turner 2023). Pastor cannot spend four years at art school training in portraiture when her commissioned production's opening night is in three months' time. The *Athena* actors cannot become nationally ranked fencers in four weeks. However, the skills they have gathered through their R&D processes give them options, opening up possibilities for where the work can go next. Turner reflects that 'we've all got our own very specific details of how to learn and adapt in our scrappy little notes in our notebooks [. . .] you end up going on a journey [. . .] and that learning puts you into a state of curiosity and discovery that's really essential for R&D' (Turner 2023).

# References

Adler, S. (1988), *The Technique of Acting / Stella Adler; Foreword by Marlon Brando*, Toronto; London: Bantam Books.
Blair, R. (2008), *The Actor, Image and Action: Acting and Cognitive Neuroscience*, London: Routledge.
Cornford, T. (2020), 'Katie Mitchell and the Technologies of the Realist Theatre', *Contemporary Theatre Review*, 30 (2): 168–92.
Crease, R. P. and Lutterbie, J. (2010), 'Technique', in D. Z. Saltz and D. Krasner (eds), *Staging Philosophy*, 160–79, Michigan: University of Michigan Press.
Curpan, G. (2021), *In Search of Stanislavsky's Creative State on Stage*, London: Routledge.
Donnellan, D. (2005), *The Actor and the Target*, Rev. edn, London: Nick Hern.
Emlyn-Jones, C. and Preddy, W. (2014), *Republic / Plato*, Cambridge, MA: Harvard University Press.
Firth, G. (2023), Unpublished interview with the author, 8 March.
Fischer-Lichte, E. (1999), 'From Text to Performance: The Rise of Theatre Studies as an Academic Discipline in Germany', *Theatre Research International*, 24 (2): 168–78.
Gardner, G. (2021), *Athena*, London: Methuen.
Goldingay, S., Dieppe, P., Mangan, M. and Marsden, D. (2014), '(Re)acting Medicine: Applying Theatre in Order to Develop a Whole-systems Approach to Understanding the Healing Response', *Research in Drama Education*, 19 (3): 272–9. https://doi.org/10.1080/13569783.2014.928007.
Kapsali, M. (2021), *Performer Training and Technology: Preparing Our Selves*, London: Routledge.
Kemp, R. (2012), *Embodied Acting: What Neuroscience Tells Us about Performance*, London: Routledge.
Lease, B. (2020), 'Interview with Katie Mitchell', *Contemporary Theatre Review*, 30 (2): 253–9.
Lecoq, J. (2020), *The Moving Body (Le Corps Poétique)*, Rev. edn, London: Bloomsbury Methuen Drama.
Lutterbie, J. (2011), *Towards a General Theory of Acting: Cognitive Science and Performance*, New York: Palgrave.
McKenna, M. K. and E. J. Brantmeier (2020), *Pedagogy of Vulnerability*, Charlotte: Information Age.
Neelands, J. (2009), 'Acting Together: Ensemble as a Democratic Process in Art and Life', *Research in Drama Education*, 14 (2): 173–89. https://doi.org/10.1080/13569780902868713.
Noland, C. (2010), *Agency and Embodiment: Performing Gestures/Producing Culture*, Massachusetts: Harvard University Press.

Ørjasæter, K. B. and Ness, O. (2017), 'Acting Out: Enabling Meaningful Participation among People with Long-Term Mental Health Problems in a Music and Theater Workshop', *Qualitative Health Research*, 27 (11): 1600–13. https://doi.org/10.1177/1049732316679954.

Pastor, E. (2014), 'Moving Intimacies: A Comparative Study of Physical Theatres in France and the United Kingdom', PhD thesis, https://pure.royalholloway.ac.uk/en/publications/moving-intimacies-a-comparative-study-of-physical-theatres-in-fra (accessed 27 July 2023).

Pastor, E. (2023), Unpublished interview with the author, 3 April.

Radosavljević, Duška, Pitrolo, Flora, Salazar Cardona, Juan Felipe, Shamira Turner, and Eugénie Pastor, (2021), *LMYE Laboratory #5: She Goat – The Making of The Undefinable (2019–2020)*, Auralia. Space, Royal Central School of Speech and Drama. https://doi.org/10.25389/rcssd.14061716.v1 (accessed 27 July 2023).

Robertson, G. (2023), Unpublished interview with the author, 8 March.

Shah, S., Wallis, M., Conor, F. and Kiszely, P. (2015), 'Bringing Disability History Alive in Schools: Promoting a New Understanding of Disability Through Performance Methods', *Research Papers in Education*, 30 (3): 267–86. https://doi.org/10.1080/02671522.2014.891255.

Shaw Roberts, M. (2019), 'Did Mahershala Ali Really Play the Piano in *Green Book*?' *Classic FM*, 26 February. https://www.classicfm.com/discover-music/periods-genres/film-tv/did-mahershala-ali-play-piano-in-green-book/ (accessed 27 July 2023).

She Goat (2017), *DoppelDänger: The Making Of*. https://vimeo.com/189444924 (accessed 19 February 2024).

She Goat (2023), *She Goat*. https://www.shegoat.co.uk/about (accessed 27 July 2023).

Sherman, J. F., Bleeker, M. and Nedelkopoulou, E. (2015), *Performance and Phenomenology*, London: Taylor & Francis.

Spatz, B. (2015), *What a Body Can Do: Technique as Knowledge, Practice as Research*, London; New York: Routledge, Taylor & Francis Group.

Stanislavsky, K. (1936), *An Actor Prepares* [translated by Elizabeth Reynolds Hapgood], London: Bles.

Tang, S. X., Seelaus, K. H., Moore, T. M., Taylor, J., Moog, C., O'Connor, D., Burkholder, M., Kohler, C. G., Grant, P. M., Eliash, D., Calkins, M. E., Gur, R. E. and Gur, R. C. (2020), 'Theatre Improvisation Training to Promote Social Cognition: A Novel Recovery-oriented Intervention for Youths at Clinical Risk for Psychosis', *Early Intervention in Psychiatry*, 14 (2): 163–71. https://doi.org/10.1111/eip.12834.

Sinclair, D. (2023a), Unpublished interview with the author, 8 March.

Sinclair, D. (2023b), Email to the author, 23 June.

Sinclair, D. (2023c), 'Option Form', TFT00084H: Independent Group Production Project. University of York. Unpublished Google Form.

Southwood, C. (2023), Unpublished interview with the author, 8 March.

States, B. (1985), *Great Reckonings in Little Rooms: On the Phenomenology of Theater*, California: University of California Press.

Turner, S. (2023), Unpublished interview with the author, 3 April.

Van Der Meer, E. (2017), 'Margot Robbie Reveals the Gruelling Training She Underwent for *I, Tonya*', *Grazia*, November 2017. https://graziamagazine.com/articles/margot-robbie-training-i-tonya/ (accessed 27 July 2023).

2

# Interview with Selina Thompson

**Selina Thompson** is an artist and performer. She is Artistic Director of Selina Thompson Ltd, which makes and supports political, ambitious and experimental art that actively works towards the creation of a just society. Selina's work has toured and been critically acclaimed internationally. She was featured in The Stage 100 Most Influential Leaders 2018 and awarded the Forced Entertainment Award in 2019. Other credits include BBC Radio, the National Theatre Studio and the National Theatre of Scotland as well as theatres across the UK, Europe, Brazil, North America and Australia.

Selina's practice is intimate, political and participatory with a strong emphasis on public engagement, which leads to provocative and highly visual work that seeks to connect with those historically excluded by the arts. Over the past decade, that work has included *Chewing the Fat* (2013); *Pat It & Prick It & Mark It with a 'B'* (2013); *It Burns It All Clean* (2014); *Dark & Lovely* (2014–15); *Race Cards* (2015–); *The Missy Elliott Project* (2017–); and *salt.* (2016–20), a filmed version of which was broadcast on BBC Four in 2021.

In this conversation, we talk about R&D processes across Selina's career, looking in particular at how reading-based research gives way to rehearsal room explorations, the generative power of uncertainty in R&D and how funding is structured for Selina's R&D processes. Selina also reflects on the R&D for a new piece called *Twine*, which was ongoing at the time of the interview and provides a key example of how the R&D period allows for the early enmeshing of design with Selina's work as writer, lead artist and solo performer.

*How does an R&D process tend to unfold as part of your artistic practice?*

The starting point would be something I was bothered about, or angry about or curious about, and I would want to explore it in a way not dissimilar from the way that I imagine a documentary filmmaker would work. So for me the strands of R&D are:

Reading – we as a company spend a bunch of money on books; we have a massive library. Lots and lots of academic reading. What I'm usually trying to do is make my way to where the most up-to-date research is. It feels like being a bit of a detective, following bibliographies and Twitter accounts, until you figure out where the symposiums and the day-long workshops and things are. So there's that: what are academics and experts by education saying about it?

Then you want to find experts by experience. That usually involves connecting with somebody . . . for example we're doing a project about adoption at the moment [*Twine*]. So we want to speak to retired social workers, adult adoptees, people who have had their children taken into care and adopted against their will, parents who have adopted. Usually we'll be working with a charity, or something like that, to find people directly impacted by the subject matter and to interview them.

Then the third and most exciting strand is what I call 'Louis Theroux-ing', which tends to be me trying to create a transformative experience for myself, where I can learn about this thing by doing. That's what's usually going to form the narrative backbone of the work. In *Chewing the Fat*, what I brought was a lifetime of dieting, and then actively going on various diets. For *Dark and Lovely* it was working in a series of Black hair and beauty shops in Leeds. For *Race Cards* it was the performances themselves, being in that room for 24 hours and trying to write those [1000] questions [about race]. For *salt.* it was much more explicit: going on that voyage. We're doing another project right now, making a VR work around Missy Elliott and dance and race, and I think that what we're going to be doing for that is going to a series of nightclubs and club nights, asking people to teach me (as somebody who's currently walking with a stick) a dance. It's always those three things: what do experts by education say, what do experts by experience say, and what can you experience on your own terms. And then it's tumble drying those into something. Running parallel to that, there's also R&D around the form. I always want to know what work has already been made. If someone's already said it, I don't need to say it again, or if I do end up doing something which has already been done, I can work with it as a reference or a homage, rather than 'shit, I copied them and I didn't know it!' For example, with *Twine*, we're working with trees as material, and it really makes sense to look at other work about family structures and adoptions that have used the physical emblem of a tree. So I spend a lot of time in the Live Art Development Agency's (LADA) study room or I will go to Lubaina Himid's Making Histories Visible archive up in Preston. With this, I'm also trying to get better at looking at the Black cultural archive and trying to excavate what has already been done by Black artists.

Because so much of that work isn't archived *well*, but it *is* archived, you just need to know where to look for it. Especially with this project, we wanted to look at work that Black activists in the UK have already done around enforced adoptions. For the first time we've employed a researcher to look into those archives for us which is really exciting. We also use long tables and round tables where we can.

And also, you have to be in conversation with a bunch of other artists about what you're doing. I always try and have a creative team in place as early as possible, and I try to have them involved in the initial R&Ds as well. Because I want them to have the same thing that I have: time for an idea to grow and develop over time. I feel like if you just bring them in at the end, when the idea's been made into a play, then their work isn't necessarily a part of the *thought*. I want what my designers are doing to also shape the writing and everything else. It's sometimes sort of mortifying, because it means that you've got to speak to someone who you feel you should be giving clear instructions to, and instead you're just giving them '*feelings*'!

*How do you communicate all of the individual research you do to the rest of your team?*

Working with the researcher on *Twine* has been somebody else doing that for the first time. We're in the middle of that process, so I can't yet tell you how it works; ask me in six months! But one of the things that's been really interesting about that has been having to say 'this is how I want the information presented' and also knowing that you have to trust somebody else to figure out what's interesting.

Previously it's been very solo and very much led by me. I don't tend to ask everybody in the team to read the things I'm reading, but in conversation I will reference things. If there's a really important solid idea at the centre of something, I'll try and make sure they understand what that is. But I wouldn't want to set my teams the masses of academic reading that I set myself, a) because they're freelancers, and they're busy; b) because not all of it is relevant. But there will be a 'hero book' on almost every project. So with *salt.* it was definitely *Lose Your Mother* by Saidiya Hartman, and if anybody had wanted to read anything I would have said that. With *Twine* it's probably *Abolish the Family* by Sophie Lewis. And then there'll be a big folder, usually two or three lever arches of photocopies by the end. There will always be a Dropbox or a Google Drive which is full of images and scans and bits of text, and people can dip into that and read as little or as much as they want. I try and be really open with all of the bits of the process. All of that stuff is there and it's open source from me. But this is the lead artist thing: it all comes through the prism of me.

*What happens next?*

How we get from the reading into bodies in space and moving around, getting the work made, really varies. The body in space is just my body, so it's all happening at the same time, and it comes together quite haphazardly, because I think it's hard to rehearse solo work, and you can't really tell anything until an audience is there.

Generally, we take a bunch of things out of the lever arch and go 'that bit of writing was compelling, that was interesting, definitely want that in'. And there'll be placeholders. Then it's all sort of stitched together. We put it up in front of the audience, rewrite, do it again the next night, rewrite. That first version of a show is always agonizing and difficult. But the offer I make to designers and partner venues, and what I always say my process is, is that we'll get a first version up, then we'll go away and ignore it for a year, to let things percolate and grow and develop, and to get distance from it. And then go back and refine it. And *then* you're working in a much more traditional way, because you have a script, you have a thing that happened. The production manager will be the person that gets a script from me. Because I work in the independent sector, the production manager is the stage manager and the DSM. And they'll need a script because they need cues, so that will always be the imperative to turn it into something that's like 'this will happen then this will happen'.

Something like *Chewing the Fat* was made at university and was very scrappy. In the morning I would have the list of props I wanted, and bits of poetry and stuff I wanted to try out, and I would usually ask a mate to sit in the corner, and just do something else – they didn't have to pay any attention to me, they just had to be another person in the space. I would try bits and pieces out and see how they felt, and then refine them and try again. And then there would be a big sewing together of the pieces.

I always know what my big object will be. Usually very early on I've this big central thing that I need, and we'd have drilled down into what [that] is, and then the visual designer is off working on that. By the time they come back with the big central thing, there's a script. With *Dark and Lovely*, before there was a script, I knew I wanted everything to happen inside a giant ball of hair that we were going to call a 'tumbleweave'. So the designer was off working on that, and she and I were having conversations about that. Meanwhile I would write for fifteen minutes and then sit and stare into space for a bit, go on the internet, feel guilty . . . and then write for another fifteen minutes.

*salt.* was really different, because I'd done the journey. So we went into rehearsals a month before the show went up, and the first three days were just me telling the story of what happened to everybody on the creative team, over and over and over again, so they all knew the story and the ins and outs of the shapes as much as I did. And it was shaped by being in dialogue with them.

With every new project, I always sit down and go 'this will be the one where I just sit down and turn into, I don't know, Mark Ravenhill or someone, and a script just happens'. But that's never what it's going to be. It's always going to be lists and weird bits of poetry and letters or fragmented images that I want to create or a bunch of prayers or fairy tales and things like that. And my job in the R&D is to just try and not police myself. To try and give myself as much space as possible to write, and for it to not be good. But to remember a) that it's not good. So not to think that something is good just because I've written it. And b) that it's OK for it to not be good. Because the really important bit is the editing.

In January 2023, I was on a week of R&D in Cambridge, and I was working with just my designer and an access assistant. There is no script in place. There's one lever arch, and bits of poetry. We know that the main object is going to be a broken tree which is transforming through the show. And what I love about designers is that they immediately want to move to the practical in a really beautiful way. So they ask 'how's it getting from looking like that to looking like that? Can you try and imagine the scene change for me? Can you try to imagine what needs to happen narratively for that tree to transform in that way?' And then my designer will give me a series of model boxes or a series of paintings of the states, and they'll go up in the studio. Now I have this real clear sense of what my worlds are and how I'm moving through them. And that in itself is shaping the story. And I know that there's a section at the end that is all sung, the last bit is sung but without any language. And I'm stuck, can't get any further with it. And I know it's because I need to do some R&D with my composer.

*Staying with this recent R&D for a moment, did you have a sense of how far you hoped to travel during the week or where you hoped to get to? And did you get to where you wanted to, or did you get somewhere else entirely?*

It's so hard to remember. Because now we've got to where we've got to, I feel like we were always there. We'd had one Skype together where we'd sat down for an hour, and

I'd said 'I think the work is in four chapters. This is what I think the work feels like in each of those four chapters. And I think this happens and maybe this, and maybe that . . .' And then Sascha Gilmour, my designer, said 'it sounds to me like what we need to do is create some of this stuff physically, so it can go from being here to being tangible, and in your hands. So that's where we'll start, that's what we'll do.' I remember we kept trying to talk about where we wanted to get to by the end of the week, and every now and again we thought we should try and work backwards to figure out where we needed to be. But it didn't work, because there isn't a script yet.

We stopped trying to figure out where we wanted to get by the end of the week, and instead focus on tasks that we wanted to do. The first task was to just go through each of the sections and create a series of different options of what it could look like, some of which were painted, some of which were in the model box. The other thing that we wanted to do was to talk about the realities of working with these materials and what the ethics of working with a tree are. That actually ended up taking us all week. The way that it would work is that we would talk. Usually, one of us would be asking a bunch of questions or presenting something which the other one would respond to. Then we'd go off in our separate bits of the rehearsal room, and Sascha would continue to make and I would continue to write little bits and pieces, or read little bits and pieces. By the end of the week, where we had gotten to wasn't radically different. It wasn't like the four chapters had really changed. But I felt like my understanding of them was deeper, and richer, and also more practical, like 'OK so this isn't going to be X, it's going to be Y, so that it can do Z later on in the script. And actually this bit needs to look like this to match the writing, which needs to feel like this. And this idea that I thought was cool is nonsense, let's get rid of that.' I feel like the project is in a place where it's really turgid – way too many ideas, way too much stuff it wants to do. There's this big kind of thinning that needs to happen, working with somebody else speeds that process up. Vastly. Also, you have to demystify things, because you have to explain them to somebody else, and if they don't understand it maybe you don't understand it either. So you leave with fewer ideas, but the ideas that are left are so much richer.

What I feel I probably would like to get out of the next R&D with my composer is a sense of the audio world that we're in. The instruments we're working with. And how that song at the end is something which, when the audience leaves and looks back on the work, they realize they always knew was coming, that it was implanted in the work in a very deep, meaningful way. The reason I want to work with the designers so early on is that as much as possible I want the work to feel like it's all coming from one understanding. Which takes time. You can't rush that.

*How do your R&D processes tend to work in relation to funding?*

We try to buy a lot of time for R&D. *Twine* and *Dark and Lovely* have both been funded in very similar ways, which is that four or five partners, all based around different parts of the country, each fund two weeks of R&D at their venue, and they're credited as part of the creation of the work. One of those venues will have put in a little more money than the rest, and that venue will be the venue that gets that first, scrappy version in front of an audience for a three or four night run, and we'll have invited the partners and other potential venues to come and see that. Hopefully, one of those new venues will give us a bit more money, and we'll redevelop the work. And then we will tour it back to the venues that helped to make it.

*salt.* worked differently, because it won a commission, and then we did a fundraiser. It was a very specific process and way of working. We had this initial, very intense making period in Bristol. Then we ignored it for a year. I did a two-week R&D at BAC with a writer, where she was talking me through dramatic structure and the hero's journey and we were working through *salt.* in that way. Then I think somebody paid me 50 quid to do a reading of this new version. I did a six-week R&D with National Theatre Studio. The first three weeks of that were just me writing, and then I invited my designers in to figure out what we wanted to redo and retry. And then we had a week at ACCA [Attenborough Centre for the Creative Arts] in Brighton for the designers to get it to look how we wanted it to look, and sound how we wanted it to sound. So there's this combination of the company and its big arcs for the year, but also little things that I was applying for as a solo artist that then inevitably feed into it.

*How do you find the relationships with those funding partners usually work?*

With the partners we choose, we are left to work however suits us, and we manage expectations. I've been doing this for ten years now, and *salt.* was a successful work, so I think people leave me alone a bit more than they used to. When I was starting out, people would be really on you, and not in ways that were always helpful, but it felt like they didn't really trust you. I'm not sure how certain venues and partners I worked with felt leaving a young, Black, working-class girl in a rehearsal room to get on with it. But ten years ago we didn't speak about race in the arts the way that we speak about race in the arts now, and now I'm allowed a lot more space and I feel more confident to demand that space.

I also think – I hope – I'm better at talking about my work, at sitting down with a producer or an AD at the end of the week and explaining what we did and where the work's at. I'm not afraid to say that I don't know yet, but that I will know when I need to. That sort of conversation usually serves three purposes. There's a real practical purpose – they're always going to [want to know] if they as a venue and a host did everything that they could have done, and if I as an artist and a guest did everything I should have done. Secondly, the conversation is between two people who love art, talking about an artwork. When that's offered without consent, it can feel really stressful. But when you're in the right frame of mind, these are people that probably see the most art in the country, and sitting down and speaking with them about your ideas can be really helpful. The third thing is selling. Are they going to be interested in the piece when it comes back? How do you make it sound exciting? If you're a venue in Newcastle, and the work that you've invested in is going to premiere in London, how do I make it sound delicious enough that you think it's worth getting that train to come and see it? So that conversation at the end of the week is really important, but also complicated! Some of those instincts are in conflict.

*Finally, I'd like to return to what you said about giving yourself the freedom for the work not to be good in R&D so that you will keep writing. If those are the freedoms offered by an R&D process, what are the (helpful or otherwise) constraints?*

Let me try and talk you through what's happening in my head. Are we talking here about the constraints that I set for myself? Is R&D something that you've got to show up for, you've got to be in the room every day? But that's not true for me, that can't be true for me because I'm disabled, so it doesn't always work that way. Is it that at the end of it all you've got to make something? Is that the constraint? But that's not true, because you can decide to walk away – artists do R&D and walk away from the work all the time.

I don't know if constraint is the right word for this, but I guess I will always have to have a compass. I had really bad writer's block with this new piece for ages, for a bunch of reasons that I think are very understandable: pandemic, massive changes to my body. Feeling about *salt.* like 'oh my god, don't ask me to make another one of them, I can't. I made that, that's enough.' But then I went back to my really early folders on *salt.*, and my only aim for that work was that I wanted to make something that was about the history of the enslaved that didn't depend on the abjection of the Black body. And that I wanted to be a better writer at the end than I was at the beginning. That was my only set of goals for *salt.* And I thought those were such simple goals! I think I have a similar thing with *Twine*, which is that by the end of it I want to feel confident to call myself a playwright. There's a certain expectation *I* have of this script, and that means that I can't make a solo show that I'm in. In terms of content, I think the only thing I really care about with this work is that we make it in a way that feels sustainable. The way that we made *salt.* wasn't sustainable. I couldn't perform it, it really hurt me, in really deep ways. And I think it was a difficult process for Rochelle [Rose, who took over from Thompson as the performer in *salt.*] as well. I would like to make *Twine* in a way that isn't damaging for me or my team. So those are the constraints. This show is not about the breaking of self for the consumption of audience. That is guiding everything we do and every decision we make, and how we work with this material which is really live and raw and painful. So the constraints in the R&D room are the ethical demands that I make of myself and my company. That we want to be committed to care in deep, embodied ways, that our health comes before our show, that we seek to learn more about disability justice and embed that in everything that we do, that I don't think 'well now that I'm not in it, we don't have to have any fat actors, and we don't have to have any disabled actors'. That we're always maintaining these ethical and political commitments. Because if they're not there in the R&D, they will not be there in the final work. You can't add them in at the end in a panic, they've got to be built in from the foundations.

30 January 2023
Interviewed by Karen Quigley

## Questions and Prompts #1

- Do you think you might want/need to learn a new skill as part of your R&D? If so, how can you carve out time during R&D to focus on learning and practising this skill? Could this form part of the collective experience of R&D, perhaps with the group spending the first and last hour of each day on the skill?
- If appropriate for your ensemble, is it worth exploring how you can practise this skill outside of the R&D space? For example, if you're learning a new musical instrument or musical style, is there a local open mic night at which you could perform? What R&D practice happens outside of the rehearsal room? Does this need to be recognized in funding/payment?
- Who can help? Can you frame this as peer learning? Or can you access local expertise to help you develop this skill? For example, if you want to be able to peel a pile of potatoes very quickly on stage, could a nearby restaurant or café offer advice or tips?
- In the context of your own process, what would it mean to immerse yourself in *learning* a particular skill versus *choreographing* a particular skill?
- How can you create an atmosphere in the R&D period so that everyone feels supported in learning something new, rather than exposed by their lack of expertise?
- What are you angry about? What are you curious about? How could your responses to these questions generate some ideas for your R&D?
- What kind of research do you need to do? Is there a relevant archive of material or a particular reading list you could put together? How can you divide this reading across the R&D project team? How will you share what you've learned with each other?
- Who are the experts (e.g. on a particular topic; other artists working on similar-scale work) you need to talk to about this project? How can you access them?
- How do you get from a reading/talking research stage to being in the space? Who might you need with you in the room in order to start trying things out practically?
- Would your R&D project benefit from an anchoring object or material item of some kind? Can you find/make an approximation of this object in order to test it out?
- How can you offer yourself space to make work during R&D that isn't necessarily 'good'?

3

# R&D in public

## Scratch at Battersea Arts Centre

Mark Love-Smith

## Introduction

The 'scratch night' is by far the most broadly accessible and widely familiar form of research and development undertaken by theatre-makers in the UK. Its history in this country can be traced back to the Battersea Arts Centre under the successive artistic directorships of Tom Morris (1995–2003), David Jubb (2004–19) and David Micklem (joint artistic director 2007–12). However, exact attributions vary in their specifics, and no in-depth account has yet been made of the development of the idea of 'scratch'. Like R&D more broadly, the relative lack of academic attention belies the depth and breadth of the adoption of the practice by theatres and theatre-makers across the UK. Many theatres have instigated some form of the 'scratch night', sometimes linked to a broader programme of artist development. Nationally and internationally, companies make use of residencies, workshops and one-off or time-limited public 'sharings' to support the development of new work, and the word 'scratch' is used liberally in descriptions of these, often without further explanation or elaboration. Beyond the 'scratch night' lies a whole 'scratch culture' as a shorthand for describing a version of R&D which centres on bringing audiences into contact with snippets of new work at stages when the work is openly, avowedly – and crucially – unfinished.

This chapter sets out to establish the particularities of the environment that enabled scratch to take root at the Battersea Arts Centre (BAC). It also argues that scratch practice is emblematic of a turning point in British theatre-making at which international (predominantly Continental European) ensemble and body-based practices became more widely shared and understood in mainstream domestic theatre-making, in a challenge to assumed models of actor/writer/director/audience relationships. I approach the subject through research in the BAC archive held at Wandsworth library, and both new and archival interview material. My central thesis is that 'scratch' is what happens when R&D occurs in the public sphere, and that it is best understood as an ecosystem, not a performance structure. I finally draw upon analogies with the theatre studio to characterize the qualities (and in some cases tensions) of the scratch ecosystem.

## Scratch nights: A brief definition

A 'scratch night' as frequently organized in the UK consists of a number of different, unconnected short performances, often offered for free, for little cost, or as 'pay what you can'. These are billed as 'work-in-progress' performance extracts and tend to be ten- or fifteen-minute scenes or excerpts intended as the first draft of a longer piece in development. They are usually curated by a producer through invitation and/or applications; rarely would they be open to all comers on the night (setting them apart from 'open mic' events, for instance). Audience responses are often sought through a combination of discussions chaired by the producer, the use of questionnaires or post-it notes which attendees are invited to complete in an interval or post-show moment, and less formal post-show discussions (usually in the theatre's bar).

The literature on 'scratch' is somewhat piecemeal. Diana Damian's interview with David Jubb is insightful in laying out the essence of the scratch night, and Jubb himself has written a number of blog entries on the subject (Damian 2013; Jubb 2024). Liz Tomlin (2015a) has considered scratch within the context of avant-garde creativity, as I examine later in the chapter. Teresa A. Fisher (2014) mentions scratch in the context of post-show feedback mechanisms.

I situate scratch as part of the broader set of R&D processes common within the current UK theatre industry because both are developmental opportunities which hinge on an experimental approach to certain performative questions. In our interview in Chapter 4, Gilly Roche places the distinction between 'scratch' and 'R&D' in the necessary presence of a *public* audience (as opposed to an invited audience of theatre producers/representatives/insiders). Furthermore, Roche points to the 'closed' nature of the feedback processes that drive scratch as relative to R&D: a successful scratch event will tend to be driven by specific rather than open-ended questions for input from the audience and may in fact deliberately *not* open up a more general feedback or talkback session.

The final key element of any scratch event is its compendious nature: several different companies or artists will present work one after another, facilitated by a host whose role it is to ensure that the audience has any necessary context, that the artists are supported in receiving audience input, and that the process is a mutually beneficial one for performers and audience. Some scratch events will be organized around a theme or particular provocation to the artists. However, such organizing principles can end up loosely adhered to and are less common than 'open calls' or the curation of artists whose work is more generally of interest to the producer or producing team.

Those involved in the early days of what became known as 'scratch' are keen not to put a specific starting point on it: the collaborative and iterative nature of the R&D process is reflected in their reluctance to ascribe definitive authorship or ownership of the concept itself. Tom Morris and David Jubb both credit multidisciplinary theatre-maker Kazuko Hohki, one of a constellation of artists who congregated around BAC in the 1990s, with the coining of the word 'scratch' for the process that was emerging at the time. Trying to work out what to call this evolving process of supporting work-in-progress, Hohki suggested it was like 'scratching at' an idea. BAC advertising around their scratch nights certainly leaned into the idea of the 'creative itch' as well as the smaller scale of the work being presented (one event was entitled 'Just a Scratch'). The phrase also holds connotations of putting together something new from ad hoc ingredients (a 'scratch meal' of whatever people bring, or 'scratch team' made up of whichever players turn up on the day); of creating something from nothing ('from scratch'); and of the Scratch Orchestra (1969–74), an experimental musical ensemble which emphasized improvization, the democratization of classical musical performance and the embrace of all-comers, whether expert or amateur (Cardew 1969). The aptness of each of these resonances may well have contributed to the catchiness of the designation.

Hohki might thus be credited with the naming of scratch, but Jubb suggests that the concept itself arose – like many ideas – from 'multiple places at once' (Jubb 2023). While he acknowledges BAC as a hub for the evolution of the concept in the UK, there was no one 'place or person who started it':

> I think if it came from anywhere, it came from decades of artists – particularly artists who'd been making work that isn't conventionally scripted, directed, produced in that more conventional model of theatre-making – it really came from them, because actually, artists have been devising, creating work iteratively. They've basically been using it forever. Doing work-in-progresses, having small informal audiences to see the work. Just putting it in front of an audience. (ibid.)

The 'scratch night' is the most public-facing aspect of this work, but this embrace of, and attempt to support, iterative and collaborative creative processes went much deeper than a one-off 'night' suggests. 'Scratch' at the BAC in fact became a shorthand for a raft of artist support mechanisms and institutional policies, some of which predate Tom Morris's arrival as artistic director in 1995 and some of which were developed further following his departure from the theatre. 'Scratch', then, like 'R&D', is a handy container for a bundle of interrelated concepts. The term was applied retrospectively to already-evolving strands of artist development which involved a willingness to present as-yet incomplete work to public audiences. It helped give an identity to this way of working, and shaped the programming and ethos of Battersea Arts Centre from the 1990s onwards.

## A history (and prehistory) of scratch at Battersea Arts Centre

The Battersea Town Hall building was first repurposed as a community arts venue during 1973–4. Since then, under a succession of artistic directors, it has developed a reputation for supporting experimental work and affording space and time for theatre-makers to conduct research and development with an audience-facing element, under the blanket heading 'scratch'.

Many of the conditions for the emergence of 'scratch culture' were established prior to Tom Morris's appointment in March 1995, in particular during the five-year tenure of Morris's predecessor, Paul Blackman. Surveying the situation at the point when Morris was taking the reins, the chair of BAC's board wrote that, under Blackman's leadership, 'audiences have nearly doubled and BAC has acquired a national profile as a centre of new writing and new ideas at the cutting edge of the fringe as well as the major arts and entertainment venue in south-west London' (BAC 1995: 2). Blackman shifted the venue's focus away from the established model of the community-centric 'arts centre', which involved a significant proportion of amateur performance as well as community arts and crafts events. Instead, BAC started to emphasize its role as a hub for new professional theatre work, programming touring productions and starting to co-produce more performances.

Blackman also instigated a 'pay what you can' scheme for specific dates, with Tuesday night performances offering a recommended (but not mandated) ticket cost from as early as 1991 (Anon. 1991). Crucially to this discussion, Blackman reflected on how 'the whole Tuesday night audience is a different mixture and the rapport between actors and audience is always stronger on that night' (Blackman in Lister 1993). 'Pay what you can' is often viewed primarily as a mechanism to make theatre more accessible for audiences – and thus to increase attendance. Contemporary reports on this then-novel phenomenon in the UK theatre industry (such as Lister, cited above) observed that theatregoers would attend on the Tuesday, paying one or two pounds for a ticket, and if they enjoyed the show they would return to a full-price performance later in the run – possibly also bringing friends – in order to support the performer. But beyond the benefits for audience engagement, this deepened 'rapport between actors and audience' should also be viewed as the seed of the comprehensive artist development support work that Morris set about growing during his time at BAC. 'Pay what you can' is fundamentally a reinvention of the audience/performer/venue relationship. This shift in ticketing arrangements itself alters the interaction between audience and performer, introducing an element of audience choice and value to the exchange. The invitation of 'pay what you can' is unlike that when a ticket has a fixed price agreed up front: each audience member is invited to consider what the performance might *mean* to them, thus introducing the notion of audience evaluation into the exchange. The claim that audience members would return in order to pay more than their original outlay is doubtless based on relatively rare cases, but even if it was largely wishful thinking, it shows how the venue sought to invite audiences to change the way that performances were valued.

Despite the positivity around the growth in audiences and the venue's reputation as 'a bustling megavenue which programmes 1,000 events a year' (Armitstead 1995) and 'one of the best fringe theatres in London' (Rutherford 1995), Morris inherited an organization whose finances were in a dire state. With staff costs and operating charges totalling nearly a million pounds annually, and the failure of several grant applications in the period running up to Morris's appointment, the company's deficit nearly doubled between 1994 and 1995, to £82,308 (BAC 1995: 7). Morris's proposed solution to this was to set about positioning the theatre as an incubator of new work with a focus on the role of the audience. This was the 'gap in the market' that he perceived, with audience agency becoming part of 'a vivid story about the programme so that people would notice it' (Morris 2017). By 1998, the theatre was describing itself as 'a foundry for consistently dynamic new work': importantly, one where '[a]udiences have an unparallelled [sic] opportunity to not only take a passive observatory role but an integral part in the development of the work' (BAC 1998).

In the mid-1990s, BAC saw numerous applications for funds to support artist development programmes rejected. As a result, Morris and his team's evolving approach attempted to make the most of the resources they had, in terms of space (BAC is a large venue, relative to other fringe spaces in London), support from producers and contact with audiences. A later codification of BAC's 'vision and model' explicitly references 'the finite resources of BAC – time, space and money' and the aim of marshalling these cannily to offer 'artists, staff and audiences an environment in which new ideas can flourish' (BAC 2011). This emphasis on audiences being an active part of the creative environment was in many ways, then, a response to ongoing financial imperatives. Blackman's earlier moves to reposition BAC away from the traditional arts centre model he had inherited stemmed in part from his anticipation of a deprioritization of funding for arts centres in England. Morris reaped the benefits of this foresight as he continued Blackman's work in establishing BAC as a champion of new (professional) theatre artists.

Blackman especially built relationships with a range of companies working visually and physically, establishing BAC as one of the regular host venues for the British Festival of Visual Theatre, showcasing 'work that has come out of the theatre and is edging towards the gallery' (Blackman in Gardner 1993). In 1995, very early in his tenure, Morris also instigated an opera strand to the programming (BAC Opera), aiming to combat the perception of that artform as inaccessible and reliant on huge budgets. This became a regular late-summer festival at BAC, in which intimate, low-budget stagings of works from the operatic repertoire jostled side-by-side in the building with promenade performance by musician-performers such as Clod Ensemble, new musical works, and improvisatory shows from Opera Circus. Moreover, by 1998, BAC was experimenting more and more openly with audience involvement in the creative process, through the staging of an 'opera in a week', which started rehearsing on the Monday and held open rehearsals through the week, for audiences to observe and pose questions of the cast, before the opening night on Friday. The 1998 festival also included 'Grace Notes': 'ideas not yet at the stage of full production, the sort that sometimes get locked away in a laboratory environment'. This was the opportunity for opera '[to show] its guts to audiences' (Anon. 1998). So Morris built the image of BAC as featuring eclectic programming, the opening up of apparently inscrutable creative processes, and frequent mini-seasons of work involving creative collaborations and collisions.

Further feeding into this picture of diversity and unpredictability was the work Blackman had done, and which Morris continued, in making BAC a home for alternative stand-up comedy. Blackman had set up the annual 'Short BAC and Sides' festival, offering an environment where comedians and cabaret acts heading to the Edinburgh Fringe could develop and test new material, and highlighting the growing overlap between stand-up, theatre and performance art. Morris later recognized the links between this and scratch, and the value of '[s]howing unfinished work to an audience': 'Good stand-up comedians develop their work in dialogue with the audience. [...] Lots of theatre-makers think they don't need to' (Morris in Logan 2003). The immediacy of the performer/audience relationship in stand-up comedy and the way that comedians hone an act, and their craft in general, in direct interaction with live audiences are key elements of scratch. It is unsurprising that the earliest break-through success of BAC's scratch culture was created by two comedians, Richard Thomas and Stewart Lee, in the form of *Jerry Springer: The Opera*. This had its first twenty-minute scratch performance in 2001, evolving through audience participation in which Thomas sat solo at a piano and shared rough-sketched material, directly asking audience members for their suggestions as to what might be included in 'an opera about Jerry Springer' and rewarding them with 'a beer for an idea' (Slater 2003). When the show returned to BAC for a later run in a more fleshed-out format, the piece was credited: 'Written by Richard Thomas & Stewart Lee; Improved daily by the company and the audience; February 2001 – February 2002' (BAC 2002[?]). This highlights the key role played by both artists and audience, over a longer period than the scratch 'night' would suggest.[1] The eclectic melting pot of ideas and instincts, tastes and infrastructure outlined above became an environment in which nascent work could thrive and evolve.

While these approaches to opening up the creative process were being explored by Morris at BAC, David Jubb was also separately working with structures that facilitated short sharings of works-in-progress. From 1998 to 1999 he ran the Lion & Unicorn, a pub theatre set up by Central School of Speech and Drama with a view to supporting artists as they began their careers. Morris went to see a show by the Shunt collective at the Lion & Unicorn, and it became clear to him that the two venues had a shared modus operandi. As Jubb puts it, 'all the artists I was interested in programming and working with there, none of them had a show. They all had an *idea*' (Jubb 2023). At the time, the most common model for theatre in London was that of the three-week run, so theatre-makers at these early stages – of their careers and of the development of their work – were unable to find a slot or to attract a suitably sizable audience to fill such a block of time. Jubb saw programming shows for shorter (often three-*night*) runs in this smaller venue as making economic as well as artistic sense. But the 'true origin of it' was, he insists, the artists themselves. 'Artists had been using [that model of sharing early work], and then places like the Lion & Unicorn and Battersea simply just started to create – I suppose *adapt* – their programmes to enable that way of working' (ibid.). Jubb and Morris entered into discussions about the Lion & Unicorn operating as a 'feeder venue' for BAC's main programme, resulting in 'the Lion & Unicorn Night of Glee' in 1999, which was essentially the template for a scratch night, albeit a rough and ready one. 'It went on to about midnight. It was terrible – everything took too long, and there were dozens of artists, it was massively overprogrammed. But it was wild and exciting' (ibid.). When a job as a Development Producer came up in 1999, Jubb officially joined the team at BAC.

---

[1] *Jerry Springer: The Opera* grew from a scratch into a cultural phenomenon. It also helped establish a connection between Morris and the National Theatre under Nicholas Hytner; in 2003, Morris left BAC for a role at the NT as associate director, and it was 'all Jerry Springer's fault' (Cooper 2004).

It is worth sketching here the national environment in England at the time with regard to support for theatrical development. The Arts Council (England) published a *Green Paper on Drama* in the year Morris joined BAC, in which the distinction was starkly drawn between 'new writing' and 'experimental theatre'. As Ben Payne argues, 'it implied that the latter only had validity as a "laboratory" for the "mainstream". [...] The paper was, almost by its author's own admission, the means by which the funders decided who to cut and how' (in Deeney 1998: 30). 'New writing' was emerging as a vibrant, organized industry which had greater success in attracting funding pots than 'experimental' (non-text-based) work. This was largely thanks to the collective, grassroots actions of writers who, through the 1970s and 1980s, came together to form unions lobbying for more formal funding and management structures. The result was that support for new writing exploded in the 1990s (see e.g. Bolton 2012). In parallel to this (though following some distance behind) was a growing recognition (for instance by Lyn Gardner; see Gardner 1997) that theatre-makers interested in developing their work physically, visually, collaboratively or otherwise away from a 'script-first' approach also needed avenues of support. While aspiring writers might send scripts to literary departments, join a playwrights' network or (by the end of the 1990s) apply to the Royal Court Young Writers programme (see Love 2015 and Haydon 2013: 68), those who worked collectively or sought to develop ideas physically or visually tended to congregate at one-off festival events, at the Edinburgh Fringe and, increasingly, at Battersea Arts Centre. BAC's hosting of the British Festival of Visual Theatre doubtless helped position it as a venue of choice for these artists, as did, from the mid-1990s onwards, Morris's tastes as a theatregoer. But as Gardner put it at the time, 'how can you nurture your work if [...] your only income is from gigs? [...] The fact is, there are fewer support systems for artists who make their own work than for those who write it' (Gardner 1997). The scratch culture that developed under Morris and Jubb presents itself as an attempted answer to Gardner's question.

Scratch, then, is not simply a one-off opportunity for artists to share works-in-progress – in other words, it is not just a 'one-night stand'. The 'support system' of the scratch culture at BAC was characterized by Morris as a 'ladder of development'. In the early 2000s, particularly following the huge success of *Jerry Springer: The Opera*, this, like 'scratch', became common parlance, referenced in reports on the theatre and laid out in BAC documentation as follows:

1 SCRATCH NIGHTS.
2 TWO OR THREE NIGHT RUNS OF SCRATCH PERFORMANCES.
3 TWO OR THREE NIGHT RUNS FOR FINISHED WORK, PRESENTED IN THE CONTEXT OF ONE OF BAC'S THREE ANNUAL FESTIVALS.
4 TWO, THREE OR FOUR-WEEK RUNS OF FINISHED WORK.
5 THE WORK MOVES ON. ARTISTS EXPLORE NATIONAL AND INTERNATIONAL TOURING POTENTIAL FOR THE WORK. (BAC 2014)

Across 2001 and into 2002, after a flurry of one-off scratch nights which established the concept, the programming pattern started to develop into this 'ladder'. At this point, the word 'scratch' began to be used in the second sense above, referring to short runs of stand-alone or double-bill 'scratches' (as opposed to compilation events). Companies and performers such as Toby Jones, Ridiculusmus, Sound and Fury, Sinéad Rushe & Jenny Boot, and Spymonkey all had nascent work programmed under the 'scratch' banner during 2001/2. At the same time, 'BAC Artists scratch nights' started being held regularly on the first Sunday of every month, on a 'pay what you can' basis.

Across all of these formats, scratch consistently contained an invitation to the audience to provide feedback in dialogue with the performers. Some scratches, such as the aforementioned *Jerry Springer: The Opera*, were overtly interactive, with audience/artist dialogue involved directly in the performance. In feedback gathered by BAC from the artists who shared scratch work, many performers commented on the value of simply putting work in front of others, which helped them assess which aspects were worth pursuing and which were not. In the earliest days of scratch at BAC, other audience feedback mechanisms were extremely informal and revolved around the audience and artists meeting to chat in the bar after the event. However, another common thread in artists' comments preserved in the BAC archive from this era is the observation that the feedback received in this way was less helpful and often hard to elicit. Many found it socially awkward and suggested more structured ways of managing these interactions, such as a producer-hosted discussion in the performance space itself. By 2003, BAC producers had instigated the use of written feedback forms which audience members were invited to complete following each piece.

The idea of 'scratch' became a permanent fixture throughout BAC's programming at this time, and successfully captured the attention of both theatre-makers and audiences. Around May 2001, a BAC Scratch Night information sheet for theatre-makers explained:

> We are beginning to establish an audience for Scratch Nights, but since feedback is key, we ask performers to bring along as many friends as they can muster to form an audience. The audience could comprise anywhere from 10 to 70 people. (BAC 2001a)

This may sound like a somewhat desperate appeal for performers to bolster audience numbers. However, by July of that year, the BAC management was deciding that '[t]he Studio [their smaller black-box space] is no longer big enough to hold Scratch Nights' (BAC 2001b), and they started programming some nights in the Main House, seating 150. Scratch had expanded beyond the scope of the smaller rooms at BAC, both in terms of audience sizes and in its impact on the venue's programming more broadly.

## Not a ladder but a pyramid: Scratch and its discontents

Liz Tomlin (2015a) is one of the few to submit the idea of scratch to sustained analysis. She hails the positives of the scratch night model in the broad possibilities that are opened up for participation for more theatre artists nationwide. But she has reservations regarding claims of innovation in the work that results. In Tomlin's conception, scratch is inherently anti-avant-garde. It subjects creative ideas to the logics of the marketplace at too early a moment in development: in a scratch, unfinished work is put up for assessment (and, implicitly, institutional judgement as to whether to invest further in the work) early, rather than allowing longer development and eventual exposure to larger audiences. This mechanism, Tomlin argues, tends to stifle or homogenize radical thinking, leading to fewer real risks being taken.

Tomlin's argument is, effectively, that the ladder of development in fact represents a 'pyramid'. In her framing, there is a broad base of grassroots creativity which rapidly narrows as independent producers and venue programmers select the practice they will support, based largely on the market logics which deem only some limited avant-garde practice worthy of 'consecration' (Tomlin 2015a: 268) within the broader cultural sphere. This system, Tomlin argues, has far more losers than winners, and the winners tend to be those most in tune with the pre-existing and prevailing market conditions: the scratch model means 'each new generation of vanguard practitioners now risks being yoked to the demands of the market itself at the very earliest stage of development' (2015a: 275).

It is hard to find fault with this structural analysis, nor to find ways to propose any alternative, short of radical overhaul of the systems of funding for the arts in the UK.[2] The 'ladder of development' proposed by Morris, Jubb and others at BAC has the scratch night as the lowest 'rung' offered by BAC, with higher ones offering longer and longer runs of works-in-progress, then the presentation of completed work at one of several BAC-hosted festivals. One risk of scratch, then, is that it can look like a cut-throat competition to keep your practice progressing up through an increasingly precarious system. However, it is important to note that BAC's producers sought always to find the best 'rung' at which to share a given piece of work – not for every show to begin at the bottom and advance from there. And rewards other than possible future funding might also be witnessed in the community of the scratch culture and the way that feedback (not only approval or disapproval) can be sought through such performance opportunities. This was always offered by producers but was also provided by peers – sometimes like-minded and sometimes enlighteningly different in outlook. Below, through specific examples at BAC, I propose an alternative framing by which to assess these wider structures and offers of scratch.

Tomlin rightly points to some other possible limitations of the scratch night format, in that it may exclude longer engagement and 'non-theatregoing audiences' (2015a: 278), primarily appealing to those already possessed of the cultural capital of theatrical insiderdom. But then, it is difficult to imagine similar concerns being raised about an R&D practice which periodically invites in other theatre-makers of diverse backgrounds and influences to offer dramaturgical input as 'outside eyes'. Reframing the scratch night as part of the ecosystem of artist support – as an ongoing R&D process,

[2]  Morris has himself proposed some form of this. In 2003, he wrote an article calling for a 'New Deal for Theatre Artists' (after the model of a 1999 New Labour initiative called the 'New Deal for Musicians'). This would be open to '[a]ctors, writers, designers, directors and stage managers [who] could sign up for two years; they would be entitled to a stipend and be given a framework within which to assess and record their development' (Morris 2003). In the piece, he laments the passing of the dole (unemployment benefit) as an instrument for the support of radical, experimental work and suggests that a 'New Deal' such as the one he proposes would enable talented theatre-makers to 'establish reputations to connect them with Arts Council funds'.

not a one-night talent show – leads the way to an appraisal of scratch which does not lead inevitably to the assimilation (Bourdieu's 'consecration') of the avant-garde. While I acknowledge that, institutionally, scratch nights can be presented as means for the handy, low-commitment and cheap showcasing of multiple companies and artists for the delectation of those who hold the purse strings, this is not an intrinsic feature of the model. Scratch at its best is about interaction rather than selectivity: conversation, not consecration.

The model on which Tomlin focuses, where the purpose of scratch is for producers to select work from the snippets on offer, to offer them financial support and development opportunities, is, it must be acknowledged, unquestionably one manifestation of the scratch night. This conception perhaps also sees scratch nights *only* as the physical/visual/live art practice equivalent of the workings of a theatre's literary department, where complete scripts are (often cursorily) assessed by expert readers, and conversations about full productions begun on that basis with a select few. Tomlin presents 'showcases' such as those funded by BITE (Barbican International Theatre Events), the British Council at the Edinburgh Fringe or London International Festival of Theatre as the end goal of the scratch night: the apex of the pyramid. This implies that the purpose of scratch, at the base of the pyramid, is as a shop window of products more or less ready for touring. On the other hand, development processes in which work intersects with audiences through invitations to sit in on R&D processes require an extreme level of insiderdom and exclusivity. The scratch night is one outcropping of broader R&D cultures which in fact bridges the gap between these two extremes: inviting somewhat expert audiences into a development process and facilitating conversations with others, of whom funders may be part but are not by definition the focus.[3]

Crucially, the BAC model of scratch is *explicitly* an R&D process, not a presentation of completed work. BAC's framing of this evolved during the early 2000s, but from the outset it was a prerequisite of the artists' applications for inclusion that they provide a framework for audiences to consider in responding to the performances shared. The freesheet distributed to audiences included brief descriptions of the performers as well as tailored questions for each piece: 'Is the balance right between musicians and actors?', 'Would the prospect of 75 minutes of this thrill or horrify you?', 'Can a ghost story be unsettling when all the mechanics are performed by the actors and on full display?', 'How did the work affect you?', 'In what ways does the use of silence and stillness heighten or diminish the impact of the piece?' (BAC 2005). These range from open to very specific, but all are examples of the kinds of dramaturgical questions which frame an R&D process; here, they are being posed directly to the audience. BAC's producers took pains to emphasize this developmental rather than competitive aspect, explicitly stating to artists that scratch was 'not a showcase to get programmed at BAC' (BAC 2001a). Tomlin's core argument is that these public feedback mechanisms involve an introduction of the logics of the marketplace (and hence of capitalism) at an increasingly early stage of artists' development. But scratch evolved at BAC in the

---

[3] This artist perspective, and what R&D and scratch is for from a development perspective, is also examined in detail by Deborah Pearson in Chapter 7.

1990s–2000s from *anti*-capitalist impulses – pay what you can; communities of interest – and from experimentalism with performance forms which can *only* be developed by exposure to audiences.

Indeed, scratch can be seen to have developed most rapidly at a time when increases in public subsidy permitted a less product-oriented approach to theatrical research and development, while also showing resilience in times of greater constraint. There are parallels to the national political situations early in Morris's tenure (in 1995-7) and as Jubb and Micklem codified and expanded the uses of scratch (especially from 2010 onwards). In both eras, arts budgets in England were contracting, deprioritized by Conservative or centre-right coalition governments placing emphasis on the need for cuts and financial caution. But it is noteworthy that the concept of scratch gained a name and a coherent identity at a time of almost total reversal in governmental arts policy under New Labour after their election in 1997. In the late 1990s, investment in the arts expanded hugely (see Hesmondhalgh et al. 2015: 71–73), and Lottery funds were distributed, via initiatives such as 'Arts For Everyone', to arts organizations that could evidence 'growth' and 'return on investment' in the 'creative industries', especially where those organizations could demonstrate their commitment to incubating new talent. Clearly capitalist logics are at play in the neoliberal framing of how funding should be distributed. But these policies left BAC particularly well-placed, and its financial outlook started to look much more secure. From the early 2000s, the venue regularly reported annual profit, enabling Morris and company to plan more thoroughly for ongoing support for artists. Hence it would be wrong to see scratch as purely a pragmatic financial solution to a shortfall in funding, bringing in audiences at lower cost than a main-house show. As Tomlin argues elsewhere (2015b: 59), it represents a partial shift of power away from Arts Council selectors and towards creative producers who are closer to the grassroots creative artists who are developing the work, and also closer to audiences. Hence scratch as it was manifested in the late 1990s and early 2000s at BAC may be seen as enabling BAC to *shelter* artists from the market forces acting through the competitive funding system – at least for slightly longer.

## Marketplace, ecosystem, studio?

Lastly, I wish to reconsider the economic narrative of the above conception of scratch and reposition BAC as an ecosystem rather than a marketplace. Moreover, I make the case that the venue, through its embedding of a scratch *culture*, might be analysed as a theatre *studio*. While depictions of scratch (including mine so far) emphasize the changed artist/audience relationship explicit in its offering, here I look more closely at the relationship between artist and institution/producer. A figure such as Morris or Jubb – and more broadly the network of producers in the institution they lead – is central to scratch. They curate everything from the contents of any given scratch night to the venue's programming, to discussions about the future direction of development for particular performers and companies. This relationship makes scratch culture as evolved at BAC not merely a 'marketplace of ideas' but an ecosystem that seeks to provide the conditions for continuous R&D.

As discussed above, scratch processes provide performers with feedback both through post-show discussions and audience questionnaires, and via the in-the-moment, embodied feedback of a live audience's responses. There is also a third form of feedback, based on longer-term relationships and dialogue. Soon after his arrival at BAC, Morris set about building a network of 'development producers' employed by the venue. His own role was a model of this way of working – emphasizing the creative producing side of his work, rather than a role as a director (though he did also direct or co-direct some shows). David Jubb was first taken on as a Development Producer and was part of a team including the likes of Louise Blackwell and Kate McGrath (who subsequently set up the influential independent production company Fuel).[4]

Following each scratch night, the in-house producing team would meet and draft a formal report summarizing each performance and agreeing next steps for the development of the scratch format. This might include assessing the most appropriate space to host the next event or thinking through alternative mechanisms for gathering useful audience feedback. They would always follow up, in person or via email, with each performer or group. The questions posed for each were: 'What did they do?', 'Why did they do it?' (in the artists' own words), 'What was the result?' (describing the audience response and feedback, noting, for instance, 'Audience began by appearing confused, but ended up laughing and interacting') and 'What are the next steps?' (BAC 2001b). This last question is crucial to an understanding of a scratch night not as a one-off cabaret but as part of an ecosystem of artist support. In almost every case preserved in the BAC archive, a specific member of the BAC producing team was nominated to talk to the artist in question. At times, where the work might not be a good fit for further development at BAC, another possible venue might be suggested as a connection for the artist. And quite often, the producers would consider work 'too polished' and hence 'out of place at a Scratch Night' (BAC 2001b). A survey of these post-scratch-night reports suggests that 'scratch culture' aimed to offer a venue for work at various stages of development, but 'scratch nights' were intended to engage with artists as they were beginning the development of a piece rather than polishing (or promoting) one that had already had a good deal of development time. The producers also sought feedback from participating artists, asking about their expectations, why they got involved in a scratch night, how useful it was and what audience responses they had received on the work. So feedback was not one-way but a loop. For example, one report recommends the 'next steps': 'Talk to [the artist] to see *if they got what they wanted out of it*. Ask about their next steps and *whether they want more from BAC*' (ibid.; my emphases). What comes through most strongly is the sense that conversations and interpersonal connections are crucial to the conception of scratch culture under the lead of the likes of Morris, Jubb, Blackwell and McGrath.

Through the provision of space in which to develop and share performances repeatedly and iteratively in a public forum, and through conversations both on the night and subsequently, BAC offered support for theatre-makers whose work could not

---

[4]   See Tomlin 2015b: 56–9 for more on Fuel and the emergence of the 'creative producer'.

express itself clearly through a script or be developed through new writing programmes. Taken as a whole, these offers constitute a developmental ecosystem: a web of relations between different but interdependent organisms. As a metaphor, the ecosystem speaks to a vision of scratch as a culture extended in time (ongoing), grouped in space (localised) and comprised of mutually developmental interpersonal, inter-company and inter-practice relationships through one-to-one and group interactions. Battersea Arts Centre's scratch programme, while shaped by Morris's curatorial perspectives, is certainly not contained by any one mindset or approach.

Certain characteristics of this particular ecosystem might be observed, and they position BAC at the forefront of physical, visual and devised work in the UK in the 1990s onwards (see also Tomlin 2015b: 97). Companies such as Théâtre de Complicité and Kneehigh and performers such as Toby Jones and Marcello Magni regularly developed productions through work-in-progress sharings at BAC. These were emblematic of the burgeoning influence of Continental European (especially French and Polish) training practices as they flowed into the country through such theatre-makers' experience of the teachings of Lecoq, Gaulier, Kantor, Grotowski and the Gardzienice group. What these practices have in common is a training grounded in iteration, ensemble and responsiveness to live audiences: an improvisatory alertness to the live moment. The Lecoq system of *autocours*, for instance, is an iterative, self-guided form of artist development based on the repeated sharing of short performance excerpts: it 'replicated the stage/spectator relationship as a strategy to enrich the actors' understanding of how an audience interpret and invest meaning' (Callery 2015: 4). This approach to performance is 'about the quality of interaction between you and the audience and your fellow performers' (Pemberton in Murray 2002: 33).

In Lecoq's training, then, the audience is pre-eminent. The same is true of scratch. As discussed above, Jubb argues that direct audience contact – 'just putting it in front of an audience' (Jubb 2023) – is usually much more useful to a performer than anything received via questionnaires or discussions. Scratch allows feedback through the direct experience of an audience's response, however subtle:

Ridiculusmus [for example] would very rarely listen to audience feedback! But they'd already had it. They *do* listen to it because they'd had it in the space. I mean, obviously with their work, it is about humour, but equally, you know when something's kicking off in a live space. You can feel it. And you know when it's dying on its arse and it's really failing. [. . .]

Perhaps in the way that scratch got rolled out, it was understood as much more about what people wrote on the feedback forms. And actually, I think we didn't always find ways of articulating and valuing the feedback the audience gives in the space, which is just the electricity that does or doesn't emanate from them as they're watching it. (ibid.)

Repeated performance-based feedback, informal group and one-to-one discussions with peers from a range of related practices, and social and working connections developed over a length of time are hallmarks of a studio system. This, then, is the conceptual framework by which some of the contradictions of the scratch environment can be reconciled. As Bryan Brown argues:

> While the cultivation of the individual is an important goal for the studio, it is to be attained within, and through, the collective. The studio archetype, then, is constituted by the bonds of its members. (Brown 2019: 47)

The members of a scratch culture are the artists, the audience members and the producers, all bonded through the studio-like ecosystem of the institution itself.

In considering the history and politics of the theatre studio, Tom Six (publishing as Cornford) traces the lengthy but broadly unsuccessful line of attempts to establish a long-term ensemble-led, studio-based form of theatre-making in the UK (Cornford 2021). He contrasts this with the more fully realized studios of Anton Stanislavski, Michael Chekhov and Michel Saint-Denis, while remaining careful not to romanticize those also imperfect guru-led models. Moving beyond the ladder or the pyramid, we might instead see Battersea Arts Centre as one of the most influential and successful UK theatre *studios* of the late twentieth and early twenty-first centuries – perhaps the closest the British theatre has come to fulfilling the model of studio practice. It is no coincidence that those who took to the offer of scratch, and contributed to its early development, were often those trained in practices where repeated presentation of work in progress was expected or indeed crucial to the pedagogy.

There was a more literal pedagogical objective to some aspects of the scratch ecosystem. Alongside the practice of ongoing artist support, at this time BAC housed a Young People's Theatre as well as a Development Theatre Company. The latter was a resident troupe of theatre-makers generally aged between twenty and thirty, who were aged out of the youth theatre but who received training through workshops and projects with more established theatre-makers and companies such as Frantic Assembly, Ridiculusmus and Toby Jones. In company correspondence in the early years of David Jubb's artistic directorship, the concept of the Development Company sharing a work-in-progress at a BAC scratch night is already well-established. The point is not that BAC hosted a youth programme and resident ensemble of developing theatre-makers – many mid-scale theatres do similar – but that this was fairly seamlessly integrated with the wider system of scratch nights and other support for and from artists associated with the venue. In this way we see BAC's scratch culture as a developmental one with a pedagogical, or perhaps mutually educational, aim: a training and developmental ground, rather than merely a testing ground or showcase for completed work. Asked what he was most proud of, artistically, during his time at BAC, Morris responded: 'Creating an atmosphere in which artists inspire each other and take risks' (in Anon. 2003).

Cornford identifies unifying characteristics of studio practice under Stanislavski, Copeau, Granville-Barker and others as one with an 'implicit politics' of commitment – albeit inevitably imperfectly – to collaboration and 'to a process of continually revising their work through experimentation' (2021: 6). This 'technique of creating your own technique [. . .] refuses to consign the past to the past, but keeps it in the room, and subjects it, continually, to the rigours of the present' (ibid.: 17). Put another way, studio practice, like the scratch environment, is *iterative*; it involves the weaving of disparate temporalities into a single space where 'pragmatic intelligence [. . .] develops within the sphere of action' (Dewey cited in Cornford 2021: 19). As Morris has formulated it, scratch also centres on 'iterative uncertainty' (in Haydon 2019: 86). Scratch, then, can also be seen as itself a form of training which occurs through iterations of shared performance (the action) within a defined (but changeable) theatre ecosystem (the sphere).

Through its focus on continual self-reassessment through contact with others, Cornford's analysis identifies the theatre of studio practice as 'not a series of commodifiable products [. . .] but rather a place of work'; '[e]mphatically the social art' (Cornford 2021: 20). Morris, too, situates theatre as a social art, emphasizing the affordances of the BAC building in embodying this:

> It's very important for me that we have no green room here. [. . .] Artists and audiences here come in through the same door, they drink in the same bar, they eat in the same cafe and that's very important from the point of view of the nature of collaboration I want artists and audience to have. (Morris 1997: 56)

Using the analogy of the studio serves also to bring into focus one particular tension inherent in scratch: that scratch culture positions its theatre both as a place of work *and* as a series of products. This, perhaps, is at the heart of the critique of the scratch night exemplified by Tomlin's arguments above, given its implicit qualities as marketplace or (apparent) showcase. Scratch aspires to the status of a studio practice emphasizing processual, relational and collective work, but it also contains, at least *in potentia*, the neoliberal imprint of the competitive marketplace, as Tomlin argues, through the integral interaction with *paying* audiences. That scratch culture as evolved at BAC ended up spreading deeply and broadly beyond these monetized points of contact (scratch nights); that it developed within an institution where 'pay what you can' was already embedded; and that it thrived in a context where increased state subsidies relieved some of the financial pressures to increase audience sizes, all speaks to the possibility that a scratch culture may, at least in theory and given a prevailing wind, resist capitalist pressures through a model of R&D in the public sphere.

## Conclusion: BAC and beyond

As the notion of a scratch culture became embedded more deeply in BAC, David Jubb and his co-artistic director David Micklem elaborated on their circular, iterative vision, one where an ecosystem – an 'ecology' – was ultimately explicitly referenced as the desired model for the organization:

> Rather than describing a single goal, the new mission describes an ecology in which one aspect of the organisation feeds another. Our purpose is to nurture this ecology. (Jubb 2015)

David Jubb's mission during his time as artistic director of BAC was one of continual refinement of the notion of scratch. Aligning with Tomlin's argument about the risks of scratch, Jubb was mindful of the possibility that a focus on scratch nights would tend towards commercialism and product-focused work. In his development of the idea he has striven instead for a focus on process, as part of his ongoing attempts to resist this capitalist gravity. He also began abstracting the notion of scratch, advocating for the dissemination of scratch processes into all areas of an organization. Jubb and Micklem evolved the core purpose and mission of BAC, from 'to invent the future of theatre' (BAC 2011) to a circular set of interlinking aims: 'TO INSPIRE PEOPLE -> TO TAKE CREATIVE RISKS -> TO SHAPE THE FUTURE -> TO INSPIRE PEOPLE' (Jubb 2018). They spoke of scratching meetings, scratching tendering processes, scratching job interviews and, memorably, a scratched response to the gutting fire which devastated the beautiful main hall in 2015. Their devotion of space in the building for bedrooms where artists could live and work together again brings to mind a studio-based, long-term commitment to artist development with prolonged co-presence at its core. Jubb and Micklem sought ever more deeply embedded iterative artist- and audience-focused processes of management and programming throughout the organization, which resulted, paradoxically, in the falling away of the focus on the scratch 'night'.

The study of scratch cultures is, in this and many other ways, a squaring of circles. Iteration stands in contradiction to the fixed deadline of the scratch night. Artist development clashes with the display of their wares (the aspect of 'training' against the aspect of the 'shop window'); attempts to grow an audience clash with the sense that attending a scratch night requires some level of insiderdom; artists participate in scratch nights to elicit feedback, yet the feedback offered verbally might often be the least useful to that artist.

Through the 2010s, the notion of scratch culture became further expanded and entrenched in BAC's ways of working, while the idea of the scratch night spread rapidly through the UK, with iterations taking root across the regional theatre landscape, in Glasgow at The Arches, in Birmingham through the regional Pilot Nights scheme, in Leeds, Manchester, Coventry and many more towns and cities. These programmes varied widely in terms of their longer-term engagement with artists and audiences, the nature and quality of the compering, the ways that feedback was elicited. And it must be remembered, when engaging with scratch as it has come to be understood, that the 'night' is only one outcropping of a deeper model for artist support and R&D. In response to local critique of Battersea Arts Centre's tendency to provide work for theatrical insiders rather than what the local community 'really wanted' from an arts centre, the then artistic director Bill Hutchinson responded presciently – in 1977 – 'Where industry has its research labs, art has also got to have them' (Porter 1977).

# References

Anon. (1991), 'Back Stage (Arts pages)', *The Independent (London)*, 3 April, 15.
Anon. (1998), 'Untitled', *Time Out*, 12–19 August, in the BAC Archive, n. p.
Anon. (2003), 'Inbox: Tom Morris', *Total Theatre*, 15 (3): 4. http://totaltheatre.org.uk/archive/features/inbox-tom-morris (accessed 16 July 2024).
Armitstead, C. (1995), 'Fringe Free-For-All', *The Guardian*, 8 February, T4.
BAC (1995), 'Annual Report', 31 March, in the BAC Archive.
BAC (1998), 'Home page'. https://web.archive.org/web/19980121073858fw_/http://www.bac.org.uk/bac/welcome.htm (accessed 16 July 2024).
BAC (2001a), 'Scratch Nights' information sheet, May[?] 2001, in the BAC Archive.
BAC (2001b), 'Report on BAC Scratch Night, July 1st 2001', in the BAC Archive.
BAC (2002[?]), *Jerry Springer: The Opera* freesheet, in the BAC Archive, no date.
BAC (2005), 'Freshly Scratched' freesheet, 2 July, in the BAC Archive.
BAC (2011), 'Vision and Model'. https://web.archive.org/web/20111226033444/http:/media.bac.org.uk/media/pdf/Vision_and_ Model.pdf (accessed 16 July 2024).
BAC (2014), 'The Ladder of Development'. https://artsandculture.google.com/asset/the-ladder-of-development-battersea-arts- centre/aAFNkQcr7jJElQ (accessed 16 July 2024).
Bolton, J. (2012), 'Capitalizing (on) New Writing: New Play Development in the 1990s', *Studies in Theatre and Performance*, 32 (2): 209–25.
Brown, B. (2019), *A History of the Theatre Laboratory*, Abingdon: Routledge.
Callery, D. (2015), *The Active Text: Unlocking Plays Through Physical Theatre*, London: Nick Hern Books.
Cardew, C. (1969), 'A Scratch Orchestra: Draft Constitution', *The Musical Times*, 110 (1516): 617–19.
Cooper, N. (2004), 'Just Remember This Way Up . . . and Handle with Care', *The Herald (Glasgow)*, 16 March, 17.
Cornford, T. (2021), *Theatre Studios: A Political History of Ensemble Theatre-making*, London and New York: Routledge.
Damian, D. (2013), 'Interview: BAC Artistic Director David Jubb talks to Diana Damian on all things Scratch', *Run Riot Website*, 15 May. http://www.run-riot.com/articles/blogs/interview-bac-artistic-director-david-jubb-talks-diana-damian-all-things-scratch (accessed 16 July 2024).
Deeney, J. (ed.) (1998), *Writing Live*, London: New Playwrights' Trust.
Fisher, T. A. (2014), *Post-show Discussions in New Play Development*, New York: Palgrave Macmillan.
Gardner, L. (1993), 'Let's Get Physical', *The Guardian*, 22 September, Features, 5.
Gardner, L. (1997), 'The Unsung: Faces for Spaces', *The Guardian*, 25 October, Features, 7.
Haydon, A. (2013), 'Theatre in the 2000s', in D. Rebellato (ed.), *Modern British Playwriting 2000–2009*, 40–98, London and New York: Bloomsbury Methuen Drama.
Haydon, C. (2019), *The Art of the Artistic Director: Conversations with Leading Practitioners*, London: Methuen Drama.
Hesmondhalgh, D., K. Oakley, D. Lee and M. Nisbett (2015), *Culture, Economy and Politics: The Case of New Labour*, Basingstoke: Palgrave Macmillan.
Jubb, D. (2015), 'The Complexity of Our Ecology Has Fed in to Our Most Interesting Projects', 25 May. https://davidjubb.blog/2019/09/02/battersea-arts-centres-new-purpose/ (accessed 16 July 2024).

Jubb, D. (2018), 'We Have Let Product Rule Over Process', 22 March. https://davidjubb.blog/2019/09/02/we-have-let-product-rule-over-process (accessed 16 July 2024).

Jubb, D. (2023), Unpublished interview with the author, 27 March.

Jubb, D. (2024), Personal website. https://davidjubb.blog (accessed 16 July 2024).

Lister, D. (1993), 'Theatre Thrives on "Pay What You Can"', *The Independent*, 7 January, 6.

Logan, B. (2003), 'A Song and a Dance; Theatre Special: Jerry Springer – The Opera', *Time Out*, 2 April, 13–15.

Love, C. (2015), 'A Culture of Development: The Royal Court and the Young Writers' Programme', *Theatre Notebook*, 69 (2): 113–24.

Morris, T. (1997), 'The Pirate Zone', in D. Tushingham (ed.), *Live 5: My Perfect Theatre*, 46–56, London: Nick Hern Books.

Morris, T. (2003), 'Sign on for Stardom', *The Guardian*, 4 January. https://www.theguardian.com/artanddesign/2003/jan/04/artspolicy.artsfeatures (accessed 16 July 2024).

Morris, T. (2017), 'Theatre Deli Podcast: Tom Morris interviewed by Roland Smith on 17 July 2017'. https://www.theatredeli.co.uk/blog/podcast-tom-morris (accessed 16 July 2024).

Murray, S. (2002), '"Tout Bouge": Jacques Lecoq, Modern Mime and the Zero Body. A Pedagogy for the Creative Actor', in F. Chamberlain and R. Yarrow (eds), *Jacques Lecoq and the British Theatre*, 17–44, London and New York: Routledge.

Porter, C. (1977), 'Does Battersea Arts Centre Give Value for Your Money?', *South London Press*, 18 November, 6.

Rutherford, M. (1995), '"Dangerous Corner" and "Suzanna Andler" (reviews)', *Financial Times*, 1 February, Arts section, 13.

Slater, E. (2003), 'Climbing the Ladder', *Total Theatre*, 15 (4): 9. http://totaltheatre.org.uk/archive/features/climbing-ladder (accessed 16 July 2024).

Tomlin, L. (2015a), 'The Academy and the Marketplace: Avant-Garde Performance in Neoliberal Times', in K. Jannarone (ed.), *Vanguard Performance Beyond Left and Right*, 264–82, Ann Arbor: University of Michigan Press.

Tomlin, L. (2015b), *British Theatre Companies 1995–2014*, London and New York: Bloomsbury Methuen Drama.

# 4

# Interview with Gilly Roche

**Gilly Roche** is Head of Interdisciplinary Practice at Guildhall School of Music and Drama, London. Prior to that, they were New Work Producer at Leeds Playhouse from 2015 to 2019 and also worked as a producer at National Theatre of Scotland and freelance with the Citizens Theatre and Southside Studios, Glasgow.

As a producer, Gilly has over ten years' experience supporting artists to develop new work and creating multidisciplinary spaces for artistic exploration. They have been instrumental in establishing initiatives providing support for new work across several institutions, including the Furnace programme at Leeds Playhouse, an ongoing artist development scheme for local theatre artists.

In this interview, Gilly explores the development of their work with artists across their career, and in particular the scratch night sharings of work that Gilly helped create, paying particular attention to how to support R&D through careful instruction and the creation of an inclusive environment for audiences and artists alike.

*What does scratch mean to you as a producer and in your current role in an educational setting?*

The thing that's always interested me is how you create spaces that nurture and allow for risk and failure. Because if you want to innovate, if you want to make work that changes the world, then it has to be new, and in any newness there's always risk.

You have to create a space where the artists can *obviously* fail. They're totally allowed to just get up and fuck it up. I would say that to the artists who were scratching at Leeds Playhouse. My responsibility as the producer is to create a space where you can fall flat on your face, and the audience will still go 'nice try! We celebrate you!'

In Leeds, we invited all of the artists to ask one or two questions – focused questions – that they wanted feedback on. We asked them to be succinct in those questions. They were then written up on a piece of paper and put on the wall. So the context is clear for the audience. We have a visual reminder of why we're all in the space in the first place. Then the audience used post-it notes to put their answers to the questions, immediately after each piece. The post-it notes I like because it means that the audiences have to think about what they're writing. Because they're going to be demonstrably putting it up on a piece of paper in front of people. I've been to scratch nights in the past where everybody's sitting behind a massive A3 piece of paper and shuffling it, and it creates this weird wall of paper that feels so bizarrely administrative – and you can also just write

'I hated it, you're shit', and nobody will know because it's anonymous. And you would hope that people don't do that, but I know for a fact that people do write 'rubbish!' on those forms. Whereas with the post-it notes there's something about 'I'm going to be *seen* putting this up there, so I'm going to have to write something that's considered'.

And then the artist just takes it away at the end of the event – they take it off the wall and take it away. I've also known scratches where the producer then has to go away and type them all up. That again just distances – there's something one removed that for me doesn't feel useful. So the artist just takes it away.

We did that for the first time here at Guildhall last year with the students who are now in their third year. Those students are currently making fifteen-minute solo performances. They're working with a dramaturg called Elayce Ismail. And Elayce told me the other day that one of those actors, as a starting point, brought in all these post-its from a scratch he'd done in year two. That was sort of amazing to me that they had kept them. It felt very much like they were an important resource in the evolution of that piece of work. So that's the most obvious use of scratch in my current role. It serves the maker, because it's direct feedback from their peers, and it helps the audience, who are their fellow students, by developing their criticality and helping them hone how they read and respond to new work.

At Guildhall, I also set up and run a programme called *undisciplined*. This is loosely modelled on the Furnace programme which I helped set up in Leeds, and is similar to other artistic development programmes that exist around the country. It's designed to be a sandbox where students can try stuff out. It's an extra-curricular programme of funding, workshops, residencies, social events and talks. Students can apply for up to £2000 every term. The only rule is that there has to be a collaboration with at least one other student from at least one other department, so an actor and a musician for example. We will fund basically anything as long as it's a genuine and meaningful collaboration. At the moment, because it's only just over a year old as a programme, most students are applying for shows. They just want to do a show, whereas I think I want more students to apply with weird collaborative experiments. The thing I say is 'if you want to bake a cake together we'll pay for the ingredients'.

And the name is intentionally a bit provocative in the context of a conservatoire and relates for me to Queer theory. The name 'undisciplined' is taken from Jack Halberstam's *The Queer Art of Failure*. There's a bit in that book, a subheading called 'Undisciplined'. And I remember reading it when I was coming up with the programme and I was like '*that's* the word'. I was revisiting it recently and thinking about how the principles that Halberstam sets out in that little section apply to the programme. Undisciplined in his context means we should 'privilege the naïve or nonsensical', and 'resist mastery', and 'suspect memorialization'. And all of those things feel quite radical within the context of a conservatoire. Any context. 'Suspect memorialization' – what canon are we repeating? What knowledge are we reproducing? What are we memorizing? What are we reenacting? 'Privilege stupidity, privilege the naïve', prioritize nonsense – encourage the fuck ups – it's great! So like I said, I feel like I'm smashing into – making this kind of big soup of – everything I learned about scratch, and learned from reading David Jubb's blogs, mixing around with Halberstam's *Queer Art of Failure* and Queer undisciplining.

The *undisciplined* programme isn't credited, it's not assessed; it's entirely extra-curricular. And as a result, the people who *want* to do it *are* doing it. No one's forced to do it. And it's totally self-regulated learning. The students determine their own measures of success. Which again feels really intrinsically linked to me with ideas of R&D. And one of the reasons we ask them to think of specific questions in scratch is because within R&D it shouldn't matter if the audience *like* your piece. In a way their opinions of it at that point don't matter. I remember when Charley Miles was first developing [her play] *Blackthorn* [2016], the question she wanted to ask in scratch was 'is it annoying to see grownups playing children?' Because she wanted to open the play with that. And she asked that and then she made them do it even though she really wasn't sure at all if it was any good – she made the grownup actors perform as kids, and she got great feedback on it. And was like 'cool, let's put that in'. I'm sort of undoing my point there because 'is it annoying' is very much about the audience's subjective opinion. But it was very targeted. There's something about the specificity of 'I just need you to answer this. Your job as an audience is *this*, and only this. Enjoy it if you want to – or don't! I need you to do *this*. If I'm going to bare my soul to you, this is what I need from you.'

*I wanted to pick up on something there. If for scratch to be useful you have to have focused questions, what to you differentiates scratch from just any R&D process? Because isn't that the definition of an R&D process, really: going into something with questions you want answered through . . . well, you tell me!*

Well. When I talk about scratch I'm talking specifically about scratch events, I'm talking about scratch nights. I'm not talking about the scratch 'engine' that David Jubb and BAC talked about where 'anything can be scratched: meetings, titles, whatever'. That is amazing, but I'm talking specifically about scratch *events*, where a public audience is super important. You wouldn't have an audience in an R&D. But also I don't think that format of asking specific questions, getting answers on post-it notes – it's not open. It's quite closed. Deliberately so.

In academic settings we talk about intended learning outcomes and unintended learning outcomes. There's not much room within a scratch night for unintended learning outcomes. Whereas I think an R&D process is *all* about unintended learning outcomes. So you think you're going in with this question, but then actually whoops, you've gone over here or over here.

*So is it about the specificity of questions you're going in with? You need more specific questions for a scratch, whereas an R&D might be what happens if I stand here with this microphone and talk?*

Well, again, specifically about scratch nights. They're different from R&D because there shouldn't be an audience in an R&D process. That is a closed space that feels like it's for at least one person, but really the writer or whoever can just be in an R&D process themselves. Basically, the people who are making the thing. They may come in with questions, but the questions might change all the time. And it might take them off in totally different directions, whereas when I talk about scratch I'm talking about an artist asking a very specific question because they've been through the R&D process, and at the end of that process they're like 'this is the thing that we still don't totally know the answer to. Because *we* can't determine whether it's annoying to see adults playing children on stage, because we *are* those adults. So we can't decide on that. We need to put this in front of an audience and we need to ask that specific question of an audience.' What we don't want to do is open the entire R&D process up to the audience because the audience don't have the context. They'll come in and be like "that's a bit weird, I didn't understand why you did that."'

It's all so vulnerable, that space. I've been to scratch events where someone has done something and the host comes and says 'OK, any questions . . .?' You see the artists go 'Brace! Brace!' It's terrifying, because you can really just come and stamp on something, not knowing that you're stamping on it.

*Building from that, then, what are the keys to facilitating scratch events? What do you, as a facilitator, bring to it?*

I'm going to start with David Jubb, then I will talk about me. He did an interview ages ago where he said that five things need to be in place in order for it to be a successful scratch environment. So I'll tell you those things and how I've sort of interpreted and expanded them over the years.

First. Context. The context needs to be clear. That is obvious. Everyone needs to know why they're there.

Second, there needs to be a producer. And I interpret that as somebody who's liaising. There needs to be a contract, there needs to be liaison between the venue and the artist. Basically, everything just needs to feel chill. Because you know you're getting paid, and whether you get a dressing room, or whatever.

Instruction. The host needs to give really clear instruction. Like 'These pieces will be no more than ten minutes in length. We'll have three. Then we'll have a break. If you need to use the loos, they're just along there. The bar is there.' And the audience just go 'ah, ok' and relax. 'I know I don't need to sit here for more than thirty minutes.' And – really, really importantly – they need to be stuck to. Because if you say 'This piece will be no more than ten minutes', even if it's the best thing you've ever seen in your life, if it goes to twelve minutes, that two minutes is the longest two minutes of your life, because you don't know, is it going to be half an hour? How long am I going to be here? I need to get the bus, I need the loo – whatever it is. As an audience member I completely stop being generous towards it. Because I've been *told* that it would be ten minutes. And it then has a knock-on effect on everyone else performing that night – you've poisoned the well.

Environment. Just, like, a nice room. I love spaces that the audience come into and go 'wow'. Because you're already on a win. If your audience feel like they're on a win when they come in the door, then your artists are already so protected. I used to work in a space in Glasgow, an artists' studio called the Southside Studios. I did a lot of scratch events there, a lot of things that were multidisciplinary. It was an amazing space. You'd go through this little door in Govanhill, and then you'd walk through this little corridor, and past artists' studios. So there was something in the architecture that suggested things were in the process of getting made. It was sawdusty and paintery. Theatre audiences would come in and go 'OK, I'm in a space of making'. In order to get to the performance space you had to go through a woodworking shop, a carpentry space – which had an element of danger because there were various saws out – but also you'd walk past artists using the workshop to build and create new stuff that was tangible and *built by hand*. And that handmade thing made it feel less cerebral and kind of esoteric than other spaces which was really useful. And the space that you got to . . . a lot of Glasgow tenements are built around squares. 7:84 used to perform on a flatbed truck in the middle of these tenement squares, and people would chuck pennies down from the windows. We would perform in the back courtyard. We only really did them in the summer, obviously! But you'd go through, and there's a courtyard with trees. And we'd laid out seats, there was music playing, and there was a little bar . . . And people's reaction was just instant. The work could be terrible, you could do the worst theatre in the world and people would be like 'had the best night of my life'. Because the *space* was incredible. So yes, environment. The level of the music, the lighting, all of those things.

And then the last one is food and drink. Again, a similar thing. If you give people a free beer, or a packet of crisps, again they feel like they're on a win. When I was in Leeds we deliberately moved a bar into the Barber Studio when we did scratches, for that reason. Because you want to see refreshments. As an audience member, it engenders generosity. It makes it feel like you're being hosted.

So they're David Jubb's five things that I always try and tick off.

As a 'host', there are two things that I try and model. First, just relentless enthusiasm. Relentless. I feel like I make them clap way too much. I'm constantly encouraging the audience to give a round of applause for whatever reason. And second of all, and this has become more conscious since reading Halberstam, and Queer theories: modelling failure. Being a bit of an idiot. I remember I have also been to scratches where the person hosting is really cool, you know? And you always feel, no matter how cool you are, or anyone is, you feel like you're not cool at all! As host I think you need to try and soak up the nerves of everybody in the space, be a sort of shock absorber.

That doesn't mean comedy falls or anything – but you can just be a bit of a doofus, in a very gentle way. It helps that I *am* a bit of a doofus, when I'm standing up in front of people. I think those things are what I bring. I had a great collaborator at the Southside Studios, an artist and friend called Fergus Dunnet. He would give me great notes when I was hosting events. There's one example I remember: I think I said 'I know most of the people here', or something, when I was on the mic. And he was like 'Don't ever say that again. Because if you're that one person in the audience who *doesn't* know you, you're instantly alienated.' I feel like my 'enthusiastic doofus' act has been refined over the years with the help of lots of people, some brutal notes and lots of fuck ups.

*Can we go back a bit further into history – when did you first start engaging with the idea of scratch? Can you remember where it came from for you?*

Yes, I can. I properly started engaging in it in my first proper professional theatre job, which was as Artistic Assistant at the National Theatre of Scotland. And that job was based within the New Work Department of NTS, and I worked with Caroline Newall, who was the Director of New Work, Frances Poet, who was the Literary Manager, and Vicky Featherstone, who was the Artistic Director. So I learned from this trio of very brilliant women who know a lot about risk and supporting artists.

Because my first job was with NTS and they only made new work, that was the thing that I knew. And I would go as Artistic Assistant to scratches. And I particularly went to The Arches, which was a space set up by Andy Arnold, who now runs the Tron Theatre, in the railway arches underneath Glasgow Central Station. It no longer exists, which is really terrible. But The Arches was particularly known for new work – and quite radical new work. Especially under Jackie Wylie as the Artistic Director. So Nic Green was making stuff there; I remember seeing Taylor Mac there. And because it was also a nightclub – and a great nightclub – and because it was underground, there was a kind of sense that everything was a bit sort of subversive. It was like 'anything can, and probably will, happen here', a kind of hedonism. As a building it was really different to the Southside Studios.

*Well, like you say, at Southside Studios there was a fairy pathway through to an open space . . .*

That's what it felt like to me. Whereas people who went to The Arches didn't see daylight all day! But yes, I saw some *fantastic* scratches there – and I saw some terrible scratches there. And they used the word 'scratch', which is where I first encountered it. And it can't have been much after the BAC started using the word 'scratch' for that kind of event.

I remember one of my favourite scratches I ever saw was by an artist called Jenna Watt. Jenna did a piece that would inform a show called *How You Gonna Live Your Dash*. It became known as 'the apple smashing piece'. She came out and put on these leather gloves, really slowly and deliberately. And then she went backstage, and got a brown paper bag, and she put it in the middle of the stage. And she went back again and she got a baseball bat. And everyone was like . . . Huh?! And she picked an apple out of the bag, threw it up in the air, and smashed it at the audience. And then she just continued to do it, until the bag was empty. Apples were flying everywhere, and hitting people. One hit me in the leg. Staff from The Arches were trying to stop them – shouting 'Stop throwing them back!' Because people were chucking them back at Jenna, and she would just pick them back up and calmly smash them back at people. And I remember thinking, 'this is crazy chaos . . . and so exciting!' I think that apple smashing piece really just totally thrilled me. And it stayed with me so vividly. It was the immediacy of it. She captured a feeling of risk and vitality and danger.

The first scratches I actually produced were at the Southside Studios. That was the space where things started to come together. And they were not the sort of 'ask a targeted question' scratches; we didn't do the questioning. That questioning with the post-it notes, that was Leeds where I first did that. That was the place where everything changed, for me, in terms of R&D. And the idea that you can make a space where artists can fail, and that that felt like the producer's responsibility.

After that, at Southside, we did an event per summer for two summers, where we would stage a play, and an art exhibition, and a gig. We'd just make a thing that had those three parts and then the audience would come and we'd all create a sort of artistic melting pot. Then I applied for money from Creative Scotland and that became a project called Team Effort!, which brought together six artists: three from theatre, two from visual art and one from music. It was effectively professional development. So we got some money and I worked with them as a producer, and said 'what do you want to spend your money on? You've got a pot of three grand or whatever; what do you want to do?' They were all at the bit between 'early' and 'mid' [career]. And there was always going to be a little bit of pressure on them if it had been in a space like The Arches or BAC or something. But this was somewhere that nobody had heard of, it was totally behind closed doors, they could just do whatever they wanted to. And that was great. We did a series of events there which were much more scratchy, much more like 'here's a ten-minute thing', and they were called 'IF'. 'IF' stood for 'Informal Fuck-about'. The whole idea was like 'we'll invite some friends; they'll invite some friends; *they'll* invite some friends; let's see what happens'. They were the first proper scratchy kind of events I did.

Then the National Theatre invited first me, and then both Fergus and me, on attachment. We did a couple of attachments at the NT Studio, under Laura Collier and SJ Murray at the time. I remember being down there with Fergus reflecting on the events we'd done and trying to figure out *what* we'd done – how did we make it feel? What were the things that actually made it feel like a safe space for risk? Because it definitely *did*, but how? Why? And that's when I came across David Jubb's five things I talked about earlier. And I remember reading them and being like 'oh, *that's* how!' We had context, environment, instruction, food and drink, producer – all the things. And it all grew from there I think.

*Can we take the story up to Leeds? One of the things that really stuck out for me in terms of the way you've talked about Furnace previously was that it wasn't all about the Furnace Festival. You were quite insistent that Furnace is an ongoing thing – that artist development is ongoing.*

Yes. We launched that, as an idea, around 2017. Well, that's not true. Amy Letman had come up with the word, and the idea that Furnace was the engine for new work, and did a tonne of work getting it off the ground. But what I did, with Amy Leach in particular, was articulate it as a more holistic, ongoing thing. A rolling programme of artistic development that was where we'd offer professional development for artists, as well as developing new pieces of theatre, both for our own programme and to support the local artistic ecology. Because so often this work, in any institution, is other. Is secondary, or tertiary even. But we wanted to bed it in, for it to feel like the 'main programme', in inverted commas, wouldn't exist without this.

That's what Furnace was. I think it's what it still is. And the great thing about that venue now is it has a studio theatre [the Bramall Rock Void], and it's a great space, architecturally, for new work. It's deliberately . . . bricky!

*Yes, it's that subversive space that you've been talking about.*

It's *made*. You can feel the hands of it, which I love. The first Furnace that I did was in the Barber Studio rehearsal room, when we were still a bit unsure what Furnace would become or where it fit into the bigger picture. In order to get to the Barber Studio at that point you had to go through a door basically into the admin side of the building, then through this uninviting corridor, and then through a weird little dressing room, and then down these clanky stairs . . . So if you were a wheelchair user it was inaccessible that way. There was a lift, but it was mostly used for beer kegs. It was not good. And it didn't do 'environment' – it didn't tick that box. Because you don't come in and go 'wow'. You'd come in and you'd kind of go 'Why am I in this weird shit space?' So one of the first things I did was ask whether we could come in the front door. There was a fire exit door onto the street, which they've now made into the front of the building. We opened that door, basically. And I remember people being like, 'This is wild, I've never come in that door before!' It was such a tiny thing, but it did do something to the space – made people see it anew or something. I'm really aware that I'm talking so much about the spaces and not the actual art or artists – that's interesting.

Another thing that felt important as part of that work was to change the contract for scratch artists. I rewrote it as a letter of agreement, in language that was clear and people didn't have to get a lawyer to understand. And also we gave money to scratch – if you were scratching you get 100 quid. It wasn't much, but it was more than most places offered at the time. And we tried to contextualize it by saying you shouldn't be working for weeks on your ten-minute scratch. The money was more a recognition that the work was of value. It allowed artists to get a taxi to and from the venue or whatever, to buy their lunch and dinner without being out of pocket. And the letter of agreement wasn't massive – just a page, a couple of paragraphs. But it meant the artists understood where they had to be, and why, and how much they would be paid, and what happens if they cancel. So this was trying to do the 'context' thing, in a really small but I think important way.

And we evolved the process of organizing tech for the artists in the scratch. Technically, often, these events – whether it's a scratch night or a piece of new work or a festival of new work – they are often treated as the *other* thing. The main house thing is happening, so we can have some technicians, but you'll need to pay overtime or get freelancers in. OK, but the main house thing has a budget, we don't, so why should we be the ones to pay for the extra technicians? And this energy can mess with the alchemy of it all and sometimes means scratching artists feel like they're being a bit of a pain in the arse, which shouldn't be the case at all. So, to try and do the 'producer' thing, we created a very simple tech pro forma. We were very clear about the fact that you could have a warm wash, a cold wash, a special if you let us know six weeks in advance; you can have up to this many sound cues. And it sounds sort of awful and restrictive in a way – it's the enemy of the apple smashing piece. And I don't know if I'm saying that this is a great thing – I'm actually rethinking it as I'm talking – but there was something about the clarity of it for everyone involved that was useful, especially for Leeds Playhouse where this kind of work still felt quite new.

*Where does R&D and scratch and funding all tie together? Is there anything else that strikes you to talk about getting funding, distributing funding, arguing for funding, for scratch?*

Yes, so many things! It can often feel so piecemeal and precarious, where the artist has to scrabble around to get 500 quid here, a thousand pounds there, and as a result sacrifice an 'in association with' credit, or a 'coproduced by' credit. And the precarity of it, where if a venue pulls their money, or if ACE [Arts Council England] . . . if it can't happen for whatever reason, that show doesn't happen. I got a bit sick of it. If established artists are fighting as hard as they're fighting, then what hope does any of this work actually have? This can't be the way that we do things.

When I left Leeds, I was quite disenchanted with how R&D is funded across the industry generally. How we value risk; how the *industry* values risk, risky work and failure. And that's been talked about a million times by a million people. But I felt myself with a stake in it, as the person who was saying 'well, we've got £500, but we need an "in association with" credit' or whatever. I would work really hard for that. I would try and make it worthwhile, so that they really felt associated with us. But still.

And I know that there are more unhealthy models that exist around the country. I felt like I wanted to change it, either from above or below. So that felt to me like [it meant going into] government, or [going into] education. And this is where I landed.

*You're not standing for parliament then?*

Hell no! I'm glad I picked this.

*What changes have you seen 'from above' – from the Arts Council and the political climate in general – since you started working in the arts?*

I started at NTS I think it was 2008. Gordon Brown was the Prime Minister. And then Cameron quite soon after that and then austerity. Also I started at a company like NTS, where it felt like there was money! There wasn't loads of money but there was definitely money, and it was a national theatre so there was always going to be more money. But that first decade of my career was the decade of austerity. What we saw was just this gradual ebbing away of funding and, as a result, an increase in the commodification of art. That it has to sell in order to be of value. I think it also led to more competition among artists – early career artists in particular – which I felt so keenly in Leeds. And artists framing their work around the questions that they were asked by Grantium [Arts Council England's application platform], rather than about the art that was being made. And it's not their fault, it was just what happened. And it just made me sad.

*Do you think scratch contributes to that air of competition?*

It's a good question. There's so much bad about scratch. There's this whole other argument about how it can be treated as a way for venues to get free work. Oh god, I wish it wasn't. There's something that I'm trying to think about with the students again that comes into all of this new soup of thinking that is about co-operation and communities of practice. And I talk about it all the time, but Brian Eno has this idea of the Scenius, which is the opposite of the genius. The idea that there's no such thing as a singular genius. There's no such thing as one. If you look through history, there's no one who just did it on their own; everyone had a community, or a 'scene' around them, lifting them up, challenging them.

So when I ask the students at Guildhall, 'look around you', I'm also framing it within the context of that idea of the Scenius. This is yours. Look around you. These are the people who will build you up, lift you up. You'll need them. You might still be working with them in fifty years. I think if you can foster that . . . And also just queer the whole idea of disciplinarity up a bit and make space where failure and fluidity and mess are celebrated. And maybe we can question the whole idea of disciplines, like maybe consider that *They. Are. Actually. Really. Not. Real!* It feels like that's how you start to kind of unsettle the idea of competition, that artists are in competition with each other. But money also matters, obviously. Artists and arts workers need to live, need to be able to pay themselves and each other. They need to feel valued and valuable. There's so much more to say!

22 March 2023
Interviewed by Mark Love-Smith

## Questions and Prompts #2

- When is the right time to put your work, or part of it, in front of an audience?
- What specific questions do you need answering in this phase of R&D or scratch? What is the best way to find possible answers to these questions – and how might an audience help?
- Share something before it's ready. Share something before *you're* ready.
- As a producer, how do you create the conditions in which failure is possible and not fatal? How do you 'host' the audience? The artists? The technical staff?
- How do you listen to feedback in the moment of performance? How do you hear feedback after the show, and what do you need to do with it? Does the audience know what questions you're asking? Are you asking the right questions?
- What does your piece of work need (as opposed to what you need)?
- What disciplinary boundaries are you assuming? How can you work across them? What are the affordances and limitations of the different training environments, traditions, cultures in which you and your collaborators have shaped your practices? How do you find shared understandings together – of success and failure, of the languages of practice, rehearsal, performance?
- What are you risking in this R&D or scratch? What would 'failure' look like, and can you embrace that possibility?
- How will you set up the environment in which you are working or sharing work? What kinds of rooms (or other spaces) do you tend to work in, and what effects does this have on the work you do, and the way it is received by others?
- Think about the exchanges involved in sharing your work. What are you offering audiences? What do you ask of them? What do they expect of you or your work? What do you get from it?

5

# R&D at the National Theatre Studio

## *London Road*

Tom Cantrell

## Introduction

This chapter explores the way in which the National Theatre Studio supported the research and development of new projects via the example of one of the most innovative and unusual theatrical productions developed at the National Theatre, *London Road* (2011). *London Road* was a verbatim musical which was developed over the course of four years at the National Theatre Studio under the leadership of Purni Morell. Writer Alecky Blythe recorded interviews with inhabitants of London Road in Ipswich, whose neighbour had been arrested for the murder of five women. The media frenzy around the events and the effect that this had on those living on the road formed the focus of Blythe's interview material. The speech cadences and verbal idiosyncrasies captured in these interviews were then set to music by composer Adam Cork, resulting in a highly distinctive and unusual musical score. Cork's composition and the performance of the spoken testimony combined to create a rich and complex aural world in which, according to Lib Taylor, 'The characters slide almost imperceptibly from speech into song and back again, with almost no apparent hiatus between them' (2013: 373). The play opened on 14 June 2011 on the National Theatre's Cottesloe stage, directed by Rufus Norris. It was heralded as a 'startling, magically original success' in the *Evening Standard* (Anon. 2011), as 'genuinely groundbreaking' by *Time Out* (Lukowski 2011) and as 'one of the most exciting experimental pieces the National has ever presented' in *The Independent* (Coveney 2011). After garnering several five star reviews and a Critics' Circle Award for Best Musical, it was restaged the following year in the larger Olivier Theatre where it ran from 28 July to 6 September 2012. A film version, again directed by Norris and featuring the original cast with the addition of Olivia Colman and Tom Hardy, was released in June 2015. In the National Theatre's televised live show celebrating its fifty years of theatre-making, *Live from the National Theatre: 50 years on Stage* (BBC Two 2013), *London Road* was the only play by a female writer to be included.

This chapter draws on new interview material with those who were key to the play's success: writer Alecky Blythe, composer Adam Cork and Purni Morell, whose four-year tenure as Head of Studio at the National Theatre began with making arrangements for Blythe and Cork to meet and ended only a few months after *London Road* opened. *London Road* has been the subject of several scholarly analyses. Particular focus has been given to the relationship between the musical form and verbatim content (see Whitfield 2012; Zavros 2017; Stamatiou 2019; Garson 2021), as well as the relationship between the verbatim testimony and embodied performance (Taylor 2013). However, research to date has focused on the product of this collaboration, not on the process that brought it into being.

In her research into play development practices in key state-subsidized English theatres, Lucy Tyler interviewed a range of practitioners. She discovered a 'standard process' for working with writers on single-authored plays, which, though flexible, followed 'a pre-determined model that understood playmaking as a journey of improvement from commissioning to production via showcasing and refinement' (2017: 51). However, most relevant to this study, she also identified 'the method of not structuring the development process. This can almost be called an anti-model because its central tenet is an explicit resistance to applying pre-conceived models. Instead, it advocates methodological fluidity and celebrates the importance of finding a bespoke strategy for each piece of art' (2017: 51). In concluding her article, Tyler issued a call:

> It would be interesting to continue this enquiry and to discover whether this celebration of developmental flexibility correlates with the emergence of new forms of work. By prioritising a flexible development model over a traditional single-author development approach, theatres may be contributing to an evolution of form through a conscious broadening of development methodology. (2017: 51)

This chapter responds to Tyler's call. Rather than exploring the content of the R&D periods in detail, the chapter will focus on how the institutional structures within the National Theatre Studio allowed the 'developmental flexibility' that Tyler identifies. It will analyse how R&D functioned in this period at the National Theatre, the largest and most highly funded theatre company among Arts Council England's National Portfolio Organisations. It will explore Tyler's notion of an 'anti-model' and will analyse how Morell's leadership of the Studio was designed to 'advocate methodological fluidity' via its working processes. Through the example of *London Road*, this chapter will investigate the ways in which the Studio's approach facilitated an evolution in the musical theatre form and will consider the wider significance of these methodological innovations.

In focusing on the National Theatre Studio, I am aware that I have chosen an atypical example of institutional support for R&D, as the level of funding provided resources and time that is unavailable to many theatre-makers. This chapter will, therefore, consider particular aspects of the Studio's work that have wider applicability and relevance. These aspects include the matching of resource to need, notions of protection and support, questions of ownership and, most fundamentally, the primary aims of the Studio with regard to the development of new projects. This chapter asks how the Studio deployed its significant resources and analyses both the principles underpinning its work and the practices in conducting it. The challenges, the complexities and the ultimate success of *London Road* will provide tangible examples of these principles and practices in action.

## The National Theatre Studio

Purni Morell was the National Theatre's fourth Head of Studio. The Studio was founded in 1984 by Peter Gill, who was the inaugural Director. It was, as Gill defined it, a place to 'generate new and experimental work through projects, playreadings, and small scale productions; and to provide the NT Company with an opportunity to refine and extend their skills' (Peter Gill's website). In 1990, Sue Higginson took over as Head of Studio having worked under Gill as Studio and Festival Manager. Higginson was followed in 2003 by Lucy Davies. Purni Morell took on the role in 2007 before becoming Artistic Director of the Unicorn Theatre, a London-based theatre specializing in work for young people, in 2011. Morell was replaced by Laura Collier, the last person to the last person to run the Studio in its original guise, as a major overhaul of the structure of the National Theatre's development of new work came in 2015, when the Studio and Literary Department were combined to create the New Work Department.

Given its national importance in the development of new projects, the absence of a book-length analysis of the Studio is a notable gap in theatre scholarship. Rather, research into specific elements of the Studio's work can be found in wider studies, including Peter Gill's work at the Studio (Norris 2014; Cornford 2015), the relationship between new writing and new work in the Studio and physical architecture in which this work takes place (Haslett 2011) and the departure from its original function under Nicholas Hytner (Cornford 2020, explored below). However, by far the most common type of reference to the Studio in theatre research is a preponderance of fleeting acknowledgements of it as the site of development for specific projects. Examples include David Eldridge's *Market Boy* (2007) which was 'a theatrical tour-de-force and the culmination of a four-year process that began with ten actors, Eldridge, and the director Rufus Norris in a room for a week at the National Theatre Studio' (Lane 2010: 92), several analyses of Nick Stafford's adaptation of Michael Morpurgo's *War Horse* (2007) which 'began in 2005 in a short workshop at the National Theatre Studio' (Millar 2007: 18, see also Mermikides 2013a and Kohler et al. 2009), Katie Mitchell's adaptation of Virginia Woolf's *The Waves* (2006) which was devised via a series of workshops at the Studio (Mermikides 2013b; Mitchell 2008) and the work of Frantic Assembly, whose work at the Studio allowed them to 'engage the writer . . . without a particular theatrical end-product in mind' (Evans and Smith 2021: 29). These passing references provide tantalizing glimpses of the breadth of activity at the Studio and the number of projects that started out life there. This chapter is the first to explore how the National Theatre Studio developed new work via the example of a specific project.

Key to understanding the processes of research and development at the National Theatre Studio at this time was the relationship between the Studio and National Theatre. The Studio is housed not in the main National Theatre building on Southbank but on The Cut, a ten-minute walk from the theatre, next to the Old Vic Theatre. The

Studio comprises three rehearsal rooms, five writers' rooms, a piano room as well as meeting rooms and offices. The 'physical division' that Haslett identifies (2011: 365) is a significant factor in what Tom Cornford has called the 'semi-detached' (2020: 308) relationship between the Studio and the National Theatre. Throughout Purni Morell's period as Head of Studio, Nicholas Hytner was the Artistic Director of the National Theatre and Nick Starr was the Chief Executive. Given the string of successes that were developed in the Studio during Hytner's tenure (including *War Horse* (2007) and *Curious Incident of the Dog in the Nighttime* (2012)), discussion about the Studio is curiously absent from Hytner's book on his period as Artistic Director, *Balancing Acts* (2017), receiving only 'scant mention' (Cornford 2020: 308). In my interview, Purni Morell suggested that 'Nick Hytner is not particularly interested in R&D – he doesn't work that way himself but he's happy that other people do it'. This semi-detachment was a mixed blessing for Morell. She recalled that 'when I joined there was a sense that no one in the Theatre fully understood what the Studio did'. This did, however, afford Morell a high level of freedom. As Hytner states:

> The director of the Studio has a large degree of autonomy: she brings in the artists she thinks can use the Studio's resources most productively and she lets me know when I should see work in progress. In turn, I send over to the Studio shows that I think would benefit from unpressured workshop time before they go into rehearsal. (2017: 76–7)

This autonomy, as we shall see, was certainly central to Morell's ability to design the Studio's support for research and development. However, Cornford has argued that Hytner's attitude reduced the remit of the Studio's work:

> For Hytner . . . a studio was not a space either for training, for developing an ensemble, or even for experimentation. Rather, it was dedicated to innovation in the commercial sense: to the development of products in a low-risk environment, from which it is the director's role to select and shape those they consider most promising for the riskier – and potentially more profitable – business of full production. (2020: 309)

While Cornford's claim might be absolutely correct for Hytner's attitude towards the Studio, it may not, in fact, follow that this was true of the Studio's function during his entire tenure. Rather, via the example of *London Road*, this chapter will demonstrate that the Studio was indeed a space for experimentation. Moreover, it will show how projects were deliberately obscured from the Artistic Director's view to support this experimentation.

## Autonomy of the National Theatre Studio

Purni Morell's autonomy extended across the key areas of the Studio's research and development work – choice of projects, finance and scheduling – and her priorities and choices had a direct bearing on the types of support available to theatre-makers in the Studio. With regard to projects, Morell identified three categories of work:

> Firstly, shows that the National instructed me to develop. Second, ideas that people showed up with that I thought might be for the National, and then there were shows people showed up with and that I thought would never be for the National . . . where we were producing to send somewhere else . . . The first category wasn't more than a third [of the total]; I think it was a bit less.

Therefore, although Morell had no control over what 'the National instructed me to develop', she had a high degree of autonomy over the second and third category, which comprised the majority of the Studio's work. Morell controlled and was responsible for the Studio's budget and how resources were allotted for each project. The Studio had an annual budget of around £1,000,000. Half of this funded core staffing, infrastructure and estate costs, and the other £500,000 was, as Morell called it, 'to do the art'. This funding was ring-fenced for the Studio. For Morell, the budget and her control over the Studio's scheduling of work went hand in hand; indeed she saw her financial and creative responsibilities as inextricably linked:

> There seems to be a notion that artistic talent or creativity and producorial skill are different from each other. That notion is embedded throughout our structure of how we run things. We have an artistic director and executive director and it is assumed that the artistic director will read scripts, the executive director will read budgets. I'm a bit of an odd hybrid of those two things because I don't see them as different: I can't imagine making arrangements with an artist without going through the budget with them. When you look at the money, I can see the size of what you're thinking much better than if you just tell me your artistic ideas.

Morell's role at the Studio thus combined skills that are often separate within an organization. As we shall see in the example of *London Road*, this allowed Morell to match the resource to the needs of the project, to carefully time periods of R&D to support the development of the work and to ensure that the whole enterprise stayed on budget. The accountability that accompanied this autonomy was not limited to the budget, however. The Studio had to function as a pipeline for new productions on the National Theatre's three stages. Indeed, in one of her first meetings, Morell recalled that Nick Starr advised her 'What you're always going to be asked is what you are delivering'. To answer this, Morell reported to Nicholas Hytner using the three categories of activity:

> I [kept] really clear pie charts of what money was spent how. I had regular meetings with Nick Hytner and [I] laid out the percentage spent on different areas . . . Divided by money percentage and also by project percentage, which is obviously different. I also carefully tracked pound per head on artists of colour, [and] women.

We can thus recognize that, though there were clear reporting lines and responsibilities both with regard to budget and as a pipeline for new projects, the Studio under Purni Morell had significant autonomy. In Morell's experience, Hytner's attitude towards the Studio only increased her authority to choose projects and to employ a model of developmental flexibility: given the extent of her control over the activities, finances and resources of the Studio, she could respond closely to the individual needs of a project. In this way, we can start to identify Morell's approach as an example of Tyler's 'anti-model' mode of development, demonstrating 'an explicit resistance to applying pre-conceived models' (2017: 51).

## *London Road* and the 'Writers and Composers Week'

Matt Trueman, listing the achievements of *London Road* (including the sell-out run in the Cottesloe and the Critics' Circle Award) in his preview of its 'upgrade' to the Olivier, wrote 'not bad for a project that came about by fluke' (2012). This section will explore the circumstances of the play's inception and analyse the ways in which careful scaffolding provided Blythe and Cork with what Morell has called the 'best conditions' for collaboration. It is my aim here to question the claim of *London Road* being a fluke. This is symptomatic of a wider critical tendency to view the absence of a predetermined outcome as relying on luck or chance. Such tendencies fail to acknowledge the work that goes into designing R&D practices to nurture and support projects, with the result that the nature of these skills and the approach to creating these 'best conditions' are currently obscured and underexplored.

Blythe and Cork were introduced at the National Theatre Studio's 'Writers and Composers Week' which ran from 30 April to 4 May 2007. It was organized by Clive Paget, then the National Theatre's Music Theatre Consultant, whose role included a responsibility to develop new musical theatre work at the organization. The week matched three pairs of writers and composers, giving them space and time to explore possible ways of working together. Purni Morell was appointed a fortnight before the Writers and Composers Week, and one of her first actions was to find a writer to partner Adam Cork. After discussions with Blythe's agent, Giles Smart, they decided that the two would be a good match and that their meeting might be fruitful. The event, which Cork called an 'encounter week', exemplifies a specific mode of R&D: the creation of space and time to bring together individuals with different skill sets and to provide an opportunity for them to explore how their distinct areas of expertise might combine to create something new.

The structure of the week was relatively free: Cork and Blythe didn't have a facilitator, dramaturg or other staff member working with them, nor did the week have a strict, predetermined shape. As Blythe remembers, 'There wasn't really a structure . . . they mainly left us to it for the week.' Blythe is a documentary theatre-maker with a particular approach to staging the interview testimony that she gathers. Rather than editing this material into a written script, Blythe has developed a 'recorded delivery' method in which actors work with headphones, listening to the voice of the person and repeating what they hear, both in rehearsal and in performance.[1] She arrived at the Writers and Composers Week with new interview material:

> [I] was keen to explore verbatim and music. I took my early Ipswich recordings along, not planning that we would necessarily write a musical about that subject but more as clay for us to experiment with. However, by the end of the workshop we discovered that the subject matter was very well served by the addition of music. (Lombardi 2016)

Similarly, Adam Cork, a Tony Award-winning composer and lyricist, didn't enter the week with a specific plan in place:

> I didn't know what sort of writer [Alecky Blythe] was. She explained that she wasn't a writer in the normal sense of the word in that she records real people responding to her questions spontaneously . . . I latched onto Alecky's focus on the 'how' as much as the 'what' of someone's speech. For me, that was one of the musical keys, as you've then got a way of focusing on the rise and fall of the spoken voice that is melodic . . . A lot of our time in that first week was just spent listening to recordings.

The week included informal daily debriefs. Cork remembers that 'we would feed back about what we are doing in teams but also discuss drama and music theatre more generally. It was a bit of a "University of Musical Theatre".' These discussions included Matthew Scott, who was the Head of Music, and Sebastian Born, who was the Literary Manager. At the end of the week there was what Morell called a 'sharing moment' and which Cork called a 'final presentation', again attended by the Music and Literary Departments. Though Morell may have framed this simply as a sharing, Blythe was clear about its function and importance: 'they said there would be a sharing on the Friday to see if you've made any discoveries. So we immediately knew that that was the hurdle we'd have to get over if we wanted to do another workshop.' Their sharing included both songs and verbatim extracts, as Cork reports:

> By the end of the week I had written a couple of songs including fragments that later became 'Everyone is very very nervous'. We all presented our work at the end of the week and I played the songs that I had recorded . . . They said that this is one that we would like to see have another workshop. They were really interested in the musical results that we had come up with and what we might do with it . . . So we put a date in the diary for another workshop around three months later.

It is clear from Blythe and Cork's comments that they felt the week to have been very productive and that by the end of the five days, they had formed the foundation of their work. Indeed, some elements of the final production can be traced back to the

---

[1] For more on the recorded delivery technique, see Hammond and Stewart 2009: 78–102; and Cantrell 2013: 139–68.

very beginning of their collaboration. As Cork remembers, 'It is nice that this Jurassic artefact from the first week of development [the song, "Everyone is very very nervous"] is still there in the finished piece.' The Writers and Composers Week can be identified as an effective mechanism to begin these conversations. The week established a clear ethos for R&D in which discussions, space for experimentation and sharing ideas were prioritized over the creation of an output or product.

## *London Road* at the National Theatre Studio

The National Theatre Studio's decision to arrange a second workshop week for Blythe and Cork, allowing them to continue their development of the project, was a noteworthy milestone from an organizational point of view. It moved their collaboration from participation in a stand-alone R&D event to their work becoming part of the National Theatre Studio's core business: supporting new projects.

The scheduling spreadsheets of the Studio over *London Road*'s four-year development demonstrate both the vibrancy of activity in the Studio at any one time – with three projects simultaneously in development in the three large workshop spaces, theatre-makers working in the two smaller meeting spaces and five writers working in individual offices – but they also record some of the various forms of support that the Studio provided to Blythe and Cork. These included time and space for Blythe and Cork to experiment with equipment, project meetings with Studio staff and small-scale, two-day development opportunities in the smaller meeting spaces. However, the most significant support that the Studio offered the piece were six distinct periods of R&D. These tended to take place in the largest workshop space and were either a week or a fortnight long. The dates and the focus of the six periods of R&D were as follows:

**Period One** (30 Apr–4 May 2007): Writers and Composers Week

*The National Theatre Studio offers further R&D time*

**Period Two** (23–27 Jul 2007): Further foundational work: Blythe and Cork scope ways of working and gather material
**Period Three** (28 Apr–9 May 2008): Dramaturgical work on structure

*The Literary Department commissions the piece*

**Period Four** (19–30 Oct 2009): Further work on structure and actors join the Rehearsal of work in progress.
**Period Five** (18–23 Jan 2010): Nicholas Hytner attends the showing on 23 Jan

*Hytner programmes* London Road. *Rufus Norris confirmed as director*

**Period Six** (22–26 Nov 2010): Norris explores the piece with actors ahead of rehearsals

Blythe and Cork provided a reflection on these weeks in my interviews. In the same way in which the 'Writers and Composers Week' functioned, there was minimal structure to Period Two. Blythe remembers: 'It was just time and space for Adam and me to continue our work, with Sebastian [Born] popping in and Purni taking an interest too.' One of the main resources that the Studio supplied was time to dedicate to the project, which was used by Cork for writing music and by Blythe for recording further material. Indeed, though the Writers and Composers Week had allowed them to develop a way of working, Blythe was aware that she did not yet have enough material from which to create a full play:

> By the second workshop, I knew that the trial was going to be back in Ipswich. All the interview material I had for the first workshop was material for half a play... That was one of the questions from the end of the first workshop: they liked what we had done, but we didn't have enough narrative content to be a full-length play.

Again, the week culminated in sharing the work with Matthew Scott, Sebastian Born and Purni Morell, who, according to Cork, 'said Yes – we like this, let's have another workshop'.

Each of the next four workshops had a distinct focus, identified according to the needs of the piece and Morell's stated aim to support the project to the next stage. This was a key element of Blythe's experience:

> There are different focuses of the different workshops. You can set the focus: what are the needs of the workshop? We had different needs for each of the workshops we did.

The third period of R&D, which ran for a fortnight, took place nine months later. Where previously Cork and Blythe used the time for working on the transcripts and writing the music, Cork noted that 'the bulk of the writing for me took place outside the workshops ... structurally that meant that we had lots of material for the workshops'. This allowed their time at the Studio to become more dramaturgical in its focus. This dramaturgical work, which encompassed the third and fourth periods of R&D, actively involved staff members from the National Theatre, particularly Sebastian Born and Associate Director Tom Morris. Blythe spoke highly of Born's expertise in the development of *London Road*: 'The structuring work was discussed with Sebastian in those workshops ... The expertise of Sebastian was invaluable. He could see how it was coming to fruition through the workshops.' Similarly, Cork noted Tom Morris's work on dramaturgical structure:

> Tom had some very good dramaturgical, structural advice which he added to the advice that Sebastian and Matthew were giving us ... Week 3 was a lot of Tom and Sebastian thinking about structure with us ... Tom was certainly another voice in the room at that point.

After the third period of R&D, the piece was commissioned by the Literary Department. Throughout this process, Blythe and Cork were in close contact with Purni Morell and discussed the relationship between their plans and the resources that were most useful to take the project to the next stage. Cork remembered:

> It was very open to us to use the time in whatever way we wanted. Purni and her team at the Studio were asking, for example, whether we felt it was the right time for them to give us some actors to work with. I think in that third week we might have said no. By the time we got to week four, we were saying yes.

In their fourth period of R&D, almost eighteen months after their previous work at the Studio, Blythe and Cork began to work with actors. Blythe noted that her recruitment of actors departed from the usual process in the Studio: 'Normally in the Studio you don't audition. They try to bring in people who are in one of the shows at the NT as this is cheaper for them.' However, given the nature of the project, both in the exacting musical demands on actors and the 'recorded delivery' headphone technique, Blythe auditioned her workshop actors: 'I've always had meetings and auditions with actors. It's not everyone's cup of tea, so we did have meetings and tried the technique out with them.' Given her care to find actors invested in the process and the technique, it is perhaps of little surprise that two of the workshop actors, Michael Shaeffer and Kate Fleetwood, stayed with the project over the intervening R&D periods and appeared in the final production.

Momentum was building and two months later Blythe and Cork returned to the Studio to prepare their work for Nicholas Hytner to watch with a view to programming the production. The Studio's schedule for this period of R&D notes the personnel involved: '3 creatives, 10 performers, Sat showing'. Cork remembers:

> By this point we spent most of the week rehearsing . . . We didn't want to present anything that was unclear. It is a real shame if you're presenting something that you've laboured over and it has an unclear presentation that makes it seem weak.

Hytner was suitably impressed by what he saw in the fifth workshop and programmed *London Road* for the following year. However, Tom Morris, who had been involved in the R&D of the play, left the National Theatre to run the Bristol Old Vic and Rufus Norris was brought in as director, a decision to which this chapter will return. In November 2010, five months before *London Road* opened, Norris led the final R&D week in the Studio, which provided him with the opportunity to work with actors on the piece ahead of rehearsals.

Cork and Blythe's account of *London Road*'s development invokes Tyler's 'anti-model' of play development, which 'celebrates the importance of finding a bespoke strategy for each piece of art' (2017: 51) as Morell carefully tailored the Studio's support according to the needs of the project. This flexibility was absolutely key for Morell, who stated that 'I think that the more structure you've got around R&D, the worse it is'. This is not to suggest that the support offered could be infinitely malleable – the major periods of R&D were offered in week or two-week blocks, for example – but the resources and organization of the Studio (and the autonomy Morell had over these elements) foregrounded flexibility as the modus operandi.

# The process of development versus the machinery of production

The six periods of R&D can, with hindsight, suggest a smooth, linear process of development in which the Studio supported Blythe and Cork at key moments, offering time, space and expertise to allow them to fulfil their ambitions for the project. The success of the end product is beyond doubt, and Cork and Blythe both fully acknowledge the role that the R&D at the Studio played in this success. However, the path of development for *London Road* was not inevitable but rather a result of Morell's care and her navigation of the complexities and politics of R&D.

Particular support was needed to navigate the tension between the process of development and the machinery of production. The aims of each activity were very different: the latter focused on scheduling, rehearsing and staging plays in specific slots across the National Theatre's three stages. As such, production work is intrinsically concerned with the end product. This distinction was further emphasized by Morell's reference to production activities belonging to the 'main building', again signalling that the geographical separation between the Theatre and the Studio was mirrored in distinct working processes. This production work was outside her control, though we shall see ways in which she navigated the relationship between R&D and production work.

The research and development of new projects was Morell's responsibility. In contrast to the focus of production on the end product, Morell identified that 'R&D is different: it isn't end-gaming the process'. In my interview she described how this focus on process was informed by her key aim: 'What I'm trying to do in my role is to get the thing that someone is working on to be as much the thing itself as it can be.' Morell's articulation of this key aim bears a remarkable similarity to the formulations that Lucy Tyler encountered in her aforementioned research into new play development. Indeed, the title of Tyler's article '"Responding to the thing that it is": a study of new play development in English theatres', uses a quotation from Tessa Walker, Associate Director at The Birmingham Rep. Tyler notes that '"Respond[ing] to the thing that it is" is a sentiment of development that was espoused by everyone I spoke to' (2017: 49). Tyler sounds a note of caution with regard to the suggestion that R&D processes can be infinitely tailored to specific projects: 'While it's possible to take seriously the claim that each piece of work undergoes a unique development, actually, there is a process informing development and that process is, to an extent, determined by where the work has come from, and where the work is going' (2017: 49). The question of 'where the work is going' is germane here, and it is the answer to this question which reveals how Morell was able to create such flexibility.

In my interview, Morell said, 'My opinion on whatever it is is not the point. My opinion as to whether it is itself yet is the point . . . I want it to be the thing itself before it goes into production.' Morell's description of the limited application of her own artistic judgement is complicated here. Clearly, her own judgement was central to her decision as to which projects deserved access to the Studio's development time and resources. To this end, her suggestion that 'my opinion on whatever it is is not the point' underplays her function as a gatekeeper to resources and a key figure in the National Theatre's development of new work. However, it is striking that Morell puts such emphasis on the self-realization of the project. There is a useful distinction to draw in relation to Morell's judgement of the R&D activities at the Studio: she had control as to what was developed at the Studio but not over what was chosen for production. This decision lay with the Artistic Director of the National Theatre, not the Head of Studio. Therefore, to return to Tyler's point, because Morell had little control over 'where the work is going', her focus was solely on the self-realization of the project. Given this focus, one of Morell's key principles in R&D was to see development as a series of stages:

> My job was about trying to figure out what the person actually needs next, not what they need for the whole thing. What's the difference between the idea that you've got and the next thing it could become? How do I support this to get there?

Morell was not, therefore, a passive facilitator in this work. Her response (using Tyler's phrase) 'to the thing that it is', is a *creative* response: her assessment of what the project is trying to be and using her expertise to shepherd it towards realizing this. In this sense, her work was not simply enabling the self-realization of the project but, rather, realizing her appraisal, from close collaboration with the makers, about what it might become.

## 'We're not sharing this with the main building yet': Space and time for risk-taking

Cork and Blythe both reported that one of the significant values of R&D was the opportunity for experimentation. Blythe's description of this opportunity focused on the notion of 'play': 'That is the great thing about workshops. It allowed us to really play: to explore things, try them out, and to find new things and to try things that didn't work. You can't do that in a short rehearsal process.' Cork's sentiment was similar, though he framed experimentation as the ability to take risks:

> One of the most important things about R&D, if not the most important, is the ability it provides to take risks. The ideas that are going to push the form forward, whether it is music theatre or straight theatre, are probably those that seem like a risk in the first instance. If organisations don't fund the time and space to make those discoveries, you are never digging for new minerals. You will always just be recycling the old ones because it is too risky to do anything else. But targeted resource into the digging gives you the chance of striking gold, or to find something you didn't know existed before and which can expand the form.

As Cork and Blythe identify, it is only where time and space are funded that risk-taking can be embraced in the development of a new project, and it is only through risk-taking that new elements and ways of making work can be found. However, creating this space and time was a more active task for Purni Morell than might initially appear. Morell describes the lengths she went to in order to protect the project and afford it the space and time required:

> I realised that *London Road* had real potential and the only way to develop it and support the process was not to tell anyone what we were doing. So I got Alecky and Adam in a lot over the course of the next year or two, which never appeared on any documents. I never told anyone because as soon as I did, the questions would start: What's happening with *London Road*? So part of my work on the development of *London Road* was to do a lot of lying. I kept telling people I was doing one thing but actually doing another. I kept it under the radar as best I could until we had more or less a draft script structure.

Morell's candid comments demonstrate her care for the creative process and her sense of custodianship of the project's development. She resisted the strong institutional pull towards moving the piece from a development process into a production process, informed by her awareness of the danger of this happening too quickly. It is noteworthy that the project moved from 'untitled' to 'Suffolk Project' on the Studio's schedule and only became '*London Road*' for the sixth period of R&D when it had been programmed and Norris was in place as the director. Morell clearly took great effort to protect – and conceal – the process from the machinery of production until it had become 'as much the thing itself as it can be'. The major decision-making point was the showing for Nicholas Hytner on 23 January 2010. His judgement would dictate whether the piece would be staged at the National Theatre. Morell observed that 'at a certain point we decide that this is what we are asking Nick to consider . . . But people always get to that moment too soon'. This is complicated terrain, as naturally the makers of the work want to see it staged. Indeed, Blythe said

> I remember thinking that it was ready to go to Nick, and Sebastian and Purni said 'No, I think you need to do one more turn on it; because Nick's only going to see it once' . . . I was so keen to get him to read and see it sooner, but they said you need a little more work on it. It was brilliant advice, really . . . you have to make it as good as it can possibly be. So I did another draft.

Morell recalled her conversation with Blythe: 'I think the National was about to do things with it, and I think I sat down with Alecky and said . . . say no to it. Trust me. Wait; develop it further. And she did.' With hindsight, Blythe acknowledges the wisdom of this decision, but she was clearly frustrated at the time: 'Purni therefore probably was right that we needed to get it really clear, to make sure it was really ready. I thank them all for being so careful with it . . . I get it now, but at the time I thought "What, another workshop?! Can't we just get on with it now?"'

Morell thus took conscious steps to allow maximum time for experimentation and development, even if this risked frustrating Blythe and Cork. In her research into *London Road,* Sarah Whitfield notes:

London Road does something remarkable . . . It opens a different road for music theatre . . . by demonstrating the possibilities for collaborations between unlikely practitioners, and the benefits of the kinds of institutional support and protection the National Theatre is able to give new work. (2012: 310).

Part of the 'support and protection' that Whitfield identified in her analysis of the success of *London Road* can be seen in Morell's actions. At no point in my interviews did Cork or Blythe suggest that they were aware of the ways in which Morell deliberately obscured *London Road* from view until she deemed it ready to share. However, in their ability to 'play' and 'take risks' they keenly felt the advantages of this protection, even if, at the time, they wanted to move it towards production more quickly. A simplistic view of the National Theatre Studio's function is simply to prepare projects for a Caesar-like moment where the Artistic Director decides whether it will live or die. However, Cork and Blythe's experiences demonstrate how Morell's actions and the care that she took ensured that this wasn't their relationship with the institution and that the Studio focused on the development of the project rather than, as Morell puts it, 'end-gaming the process'.

## 'Whose is it?': R&D and the politics of ownership

There is a complex question of ownership that lies at the heart of this and many other R&D processes. *London Road*, over the course of four years, developed from an idea between a writer and a composer to a production staged by the National Theatre. The journey from an idea being conceived by individuals to a production owned by others is of course familiar and common to most theatrical projects. What was unusual here, however, was that the very first meeting was arranged by the Studio, and resources were tailored by the Studio to support the development of the project before and after commissioning the work, all before it went into production. So where did ownership sit, and what bearing did the question of ownership have on the R&D process?

Formally, the ownership of the project went through three distinct phases. Cork and Blythe were paid the standard weekly rate of £345 for each period of R&D, as were actors and collaborators brought in from outside the organization. In this pre-commission stage, the project was wholly owned by Blythe and Cork: they were under no obligation to continue to develop it at the Studio and nor was the Studio bound to offer its resources. Much of their work prior to commission was unpaid, as Blythe noted, 'we were doing a lot of work outside the room too before we got the commission and it would be nice to get paid!' The second phase of ownership came after the third period of R&D in May 2008, when the play was formally commissioned by the National Theatre. Cork recalls 'Matthew and Sebastian said that they wanted to commission it [. . .]. So at that point something became more real about the whole project. That was turning point number one in an ownership sense.' The commission was paid in thirds: the first payment at the point of commission, the second on the delivery of the full script and the third when the piece was programmed. The commission, therefore, tied the project to the National Theatre, meaning that Cork and Blythe could not take it elsewhere, though it did not require the National Theatre to stage the eventual work; rather they had first refusal on it. The third phase of ownership came in January 2010. As Cork notes, 'turning point number two was Nick [Hytner] coming to watch the presentation and saying "I want to put this on".' At that stage, *London Road* became a National Theatre production. The timing of the decisions which signalled the move to the next phase was set by the theatre: it was the Literary Department's decision as to when to commission the work and, as explored above, the timing of Hytner's invitation to watch the work was made by the Studio staff. Therefore, although they may have had a high degree of creative control in the development of their work at the Studio, Blythe and Cork were working in a context where the key decisions about the future of the project (which clearly had financial, scheduling and workload implications for them), as well as the timing of these decisions, were controlled by others.

In my interview with Purni Morell, it became clear that ownership was something of a vexed issue in the National Theatre's work: 'I think the biggest question is just whose is it? . . . there is a lot of politics behind the development of these plays.' Morell explained how the politics of development manifested when she began her work as Head of Studio:

> Part of the context when I started was that there were a lot of cooks at the Studio. That was very difficult – lots of people wanting to give advice; lots of people who thought the project was theirs . . . There are a lot of people in the building who think that their job is to solve it, to get involved.

It appears that Morell's response to this issue was to avoid having National Theatre staff members who were present throughout or formally attached to the project in its early stages. Rather, Heads of the Literary Department, the Music Department and the Studio were identified as points of contact for Blythe and Cork. These staff members took a close interest in the development process and attended the end-of-week sharings, but as the project was not formally 'owned' by a member of the National Theatre's team the experience of Blythe and Cork was one of space to work by themselves, with a high degree of creative control.

There were two particular decisions that demonstrate the complexities of ownership as the project moved from development at the Studio to production at the National Theatre. First was the timing of a director's attachment to the project. Appointing a director has a profound effect on the direction of the work, as Morell made clear, 'The problem with the Studio is that once you put a director on a project, it's very difficult to get that person off it later because the work grows with them.' This, therefore, gave Morell two options when approaching the issue of who might direct work that the Studio is developing:

> Either we needed someone who's just definitely not going to direct the final production and they can just take it to the next stage, knowing that there's no question they'd be employed to direct that show, or we need to find who is really going to be the right person.

Tom Morris had been a presence in the third, fourth and fifth R&D periods and had prepared the work for Hytner to observe. From my interviews with both Blythe and Cork, it is clear that Morell had succeeded in finding the 'right person'; Blythe commented, 'We loved Tom and we thought he was a very good fit to direct it. He had been our go-to collaborator.' Morris's departure, therefore, was a moment of real concern. In an email a month after Hytner had seen the work-in-progress and had decided to programme *London Road*, Blythe emailed Cork, quoting Sebastian Born's news that Tom Morris was unavailable:

> I trust Tom, he's very collaborative . . . [but] 'Tom is not available until the end of next year so you will have to find another director.' Fuck! . . . I'm thinking . . . now you're asking me to put my trust in someone else who probably has never seen my work.' (Rosenthal 2018: 334)

The choice of director was outside Blythe or Cork's control. Blythe recalled that she was informed that Rufus Norris would direct rather than having any say in the decision: 'Nick just called up and said Rufus will be directing. I wasn't expecting that. He didn't know my work.' Blythe's concern about the appointment of the director is a further example of how ownership switched to the National Theatre once the piece had been programmed. The second decision that signalled this switch in ownership was on the 'recorded delivery' technique. In the work-in-progress that Hytner attended, the actors used headphones for the spoken testimony and took them off for the sung elements. However, Blythe recalls that Hytner had a clear condition for programming *London Road*, 'even when he said yes, there was still a proviso: he wanted us to do it without the earphones. That completely floored me. I hadn't seen it coming at all. I'd always worked in this way – it's why I thought I was there. It was my thing.' Given that all of her previous work had used headphones, this was a sizable intervention by Hytner. Blythe recalls that 'Adam and I discussed it and we came round to realizing that it is such a complicated piece and the NT is one of the few places in the country which is able to offer the expertise and resources we need to pull it off. If this is what they are insisting, then perhaps we go with it.' Therefore, after having a high level of creative control and ownership through the R&D process, a change of director and an instruction to rehearse and perform the work in a quite different way was destabilizing and deeply concerning for Blythe and Cork. Blythe's pre-rehearsal meeting with Norris assuaged some of her concerns, but it is clear that these late changes were difficult for her:

> [W]e met up and he understood where I was coming from and wanted to maintain that authenticity. I trusted that he would. In rehearsals, we worked for three weeks with the earphones and three weeks without them. But that was a big dilemma: a show at the National but no earphones and a director who didn't know my verbatim process. After four years developing the show with them, that was fundamentally challenging.

The shift from R&D into production, and so from the Studio to the National Theatre, was evidently the most significant shift in creative control and therefore a moment of real jeopardy for Blythe and Cork. The care and custodianship that guided Morell's development of the project in the R&D periods stand in stark contrast to the bruising lack of control that Blythe and Cork experienced in the production process. These two significant decisions – the unilateral choice of director and the decision to work without headphones – removed the creative agency that Blythe and Cork had previously experienced. Morell's insistence that her work at the Studio was to make the project 'as much the thing itself as it can be' was countered in the production process by the primacy of the National Theatre's decision-making processes, which were evidently less collaboratively handled. However, it was arguably the care that Morell took to ensure that the project was ready before entering this production phase which gave it a robustness to withstand these interventions; despite these changes threatening to derail the project and compromise the earlier development work, the project had a resilience to sustain these late interventions.

## Conclusion

This chapter has analysed the ways in which the National Theatre, via the Studio, deployed its significant resources to develop new work. In focusing on the development of a single project, this chapter has explored the principles underpinning the design of R&D at the Studio in action. It is clear from this example that there was not only a distinction between development and production but also a real tension between them. *London Road* clearly illustrates the energy that Morell put into protecting the development process from the pull – indeed lure – of production. The pull towards moving the project into production came from both the institution (which was keen to bring this work to its stage and audiences) and from the makers (who were keen to see their work realized in a full production, given the years of work that they had dedicated to its development). The lure of production from the makers was all the more strong due to the financial model underpinning this R&D work: they received their final commission payment when the work was programmed. In this context, Morell's focus on protecting the project until it was fully realized was a significant act and central to the later success of *London Road*. Her care ensured that the 'pull' and 'lure' didn't compromise the integrity of the project, and her concealment ensured that the project wasn't exposed to new creative ideas from a director until she was content that it was 'as much the thing itself as it can be'. It is evident, however, that Morell did not operate in isolation, immune from the institutional pull towards production: indeed, a key aspect of her role was to bring exciting new work to the National Theatre's stages. Her notion that 'R&D is different: it isn't end-gaming the process' should not be taken to suggest that the 'end' isn't important but just how innovative the end product can be if care is taken to provide resources and time to allow its self-realization. The division of decision-making powers was useful here: the fact that Morell, as Head of Studio, did not make the final judgement on the suitability of the project for the National Theatre's stages meant that she could prioritize the journey and focus exclusively on helping the project to move towards the next stage of its development. Likewise, Hytner's focus on production allowed Morell autonomy to develop the work and to only share it when she deemed it ready.

This chapter has uncovered a range of modes of R&D within the National Theatre Studio. The Writers and Composers Week which was purposefully designed to bring together theatre-makers with different skills to see what might happen when they collaborated for a week away from any necessity to create an end product. The R&D process also included desk-based dramaturgical discussions of draft structures with input from the expertise within the National Theatre, practical explorations with actors to see the work-in-progress performed and a series of sharings of the work with members of staff. Each of these was shaped by specific aims, and it was the needs of the evolving project as defined by the makers at the different stages, rather than a predetermined programme of development, that informed how the Studio shaped its support. Ownership during the R&D process sat firmly with the makers. Though they were not ignorant to the fact that they were in a system that may (or, indeed, may not) result in a production at the National Theatre, as there was no member of the National Theatre running the R&D or leading the project, they experienced it as their own: a space in which they could follow their own agenda and hopes for the production. Morell's custodianship manifested itself through the creation of this time and space rather than through creative control. This was Tyler's 'anti-model' in action; this chapter has analysed the way in which Morell 'advocates methodological fluidity and celebrates the importance of finding a bespoke strategy for each piece of art' (2017: 51). *London Road*'s development process was, of course, a product of the significant investment in R&D at the institution; Morell rightly noted that 'It comes back down to a half a million pound budget. It gives you that flexibility.' However, though there are few organizations that could develop a production over the course of four years, the aims that informed this development have wider applicability and her work proposes principles and practices for project development that can be followed.

Tyler's suggestion that 'theatres may be contributing to an evolution of form through a conscious broadening of development methodology' (2017: 51) has been borne out in the example of *London Road*. It certainly evolved the musical form and has re-energized the verbatim musical (with recent examples including *Committee: The Public Administration and Constitutional Affairs Committee Takes Oral Evidence on Whitehall's Relationship with Kids Company* by Josie Rourke and Hadley Fraser (Donmar 2017), *Public Domain* by Francesca Forristal and Jordan Paul Clarke (Southwark Playhouse 2020) and *The Children's Inquiry* (Southwark Playhouse 2024)). R&D, therefore, allowed Blythe and Cork to make a significant innovation in theatre-making, and their work demonstrates the value of R&D as a methodology. It is hard to imagine such innovations being made without the space and time afforded by the R&D process. To return, finally, to the suggestion that *London Road* was a 'fluke'. We can simultaneously acknowledge that there was no guarantee that any of the three pairs invited to the Writers and Composers Week would go on to create a successful new musical and still find such a success story unsurprising, given the National Theatre Studio's creation of the optimal conditions: careful structuring, space, time, care and custodianship for these developments and innovations to take place.

## References

Anon. (2011), Review of *London Road*, *Evening Standard*, 15 April. https://www.standard.co.uk/culture/theatre/london-road-is-an-astonishing-tale-7424497.html (accessed 5 June 2021).

Blythe, A. (2022), Unpublished interview with the author, 16 March.

Cantrell, T. (2013), *Acting in Documentary Theatre*, London: Palgrave.

Cork, A. (2022), Unpublished interview with the author, 26 January.

Cornford, T. (2015), 'Acting, Skill and Artistry', *Shakespeare Studies*, 43: 88–98.

Cornford, T. (2020), *Theatre Studios: A Political History of Ensemble Theatre-Making*, London: Routledge.

Coveney, M. (2011), Review of *London Road*, *The Independent*, 15 April. https://www.independent.co.uk/arts-entertainment/theatre-dance/reviews/first-night-london-road-national-theatre-london-2268140.html (accessed 15 January 2022).

Evans, M. and M. Smith (2021), *Frantic Assembly*, London: Routledge.

Garson, C. (2021), *Beyond Documentary Realism*, Berlin: De Gruyter.

Gill, P. (undated), Peter Gill website. http://www.petergill7.co.uk/studio/nt_studio.shtml (accessed 17 June 2021).

Hammond, W. and D. Steward (2009), *Verbatim, Verbatim: Contemporary Documentary Theatre*, London: Oberon.

Haslett, R. (2011), 'Architecture and New Play Development at the National Theatre, 1907–2010', *New Theatre Quarterly*, 27 (4): 358–67.

Hytner, N. (2017), *Balancing Acts*, London: Jonathan Cape.

Kohler, A., B. Jones and T. Luther (2009), 'Handspring Puppet Company', *The Journal of Modern Craft*, 2 (3): 345–54.

Lane, D. (2010), *Contemporary British Drama*, Edinburgh: Edinburgh University Press.

Lombardi, C. (2016), 'How 'London Road' Became 2016's Most Unique Movie Musical', *Film Independent*, 9 September. https://www.filmindependent.org/blog/how-london-road-became-2016s-most-unique-movie-musical/ (accessed 30 March 2022).

Lukowski, A. (2011), 'Review of *London Road*', *Time Out*, 18 April. https://www.timeout.com/london/theatre/london-road-1 (accessed 30 March 2022).

Mermikides, A. (2013a), 'Collective Creation and the "Creative Industries": The British Context', in K. Syssoyeva and S. Proudfit (eds), *Collective Creation in Contemporary Performance*, 51–70, London: Palgrave.

Mermikides, A. (2013b), 'Brilliant Theatre-making at the National: Devising, Collective Creation and the Director's Brand', *Studies in Theatre and Performance*, 33 (2): 153–67.

Millar, M. (2007), *The Horse's Mouth: How Handspring and the National Theatre Made War Horse*, London: Oberon Books.

Mitchell, K. (2008), 'Directors Give Instructions' interview with Andy Lavender, Central School of Speech & Drama, 14 October. eprints.epwp.eprints-hosting.org/id/eprint/27/1/CEN_KM_journal.pdf (accessed 2 February 2022).

Morell, P. (2021), Unpublished interview with the author, 20 January.

Norris, B. (2014), *To Bodies Gone: The Theatre of Peter Gill*, Bridgend: Seren Books.

Rosenthal, D., ed. (2018), *Dramatic Exchanges*, London: Profile Books.

Stamatiou, E. (2019), 'A Brechtian Perspective on *London Road*: Class Representations, Dialectics and the 'Gestic' Character of Music from Stage to Screen', *Studies in Musical Theatre*, 13 (3): 287–98.

Taylor, L. (2013), 'Voice, Body and the Transmission of the Real in Documentary Theatre', *Contemporary Theatre Review*, 23 (3): 368–79.

Trueman, M. (2012), 'Adam Cork: The Man Behind Theatreland's Oddest Musical', *The Independent*, 24 July. https://www.independent.co.uk/arts-entertainment/theatre-dance/features/adam-cork-the-man-behind-theatreland-s-oddest-musical-7973254.html (accessed 20 December 2022).

Tyler, L. (2017), '"Responding to the Thing that It Is": A Study of New Play Development in English Theatres', *Studies in Theatre and Performance*, 39 (1): 38–53.

Whitfield, S. (2012), 'Two Different Roads to New Musicals in 2011 London: *London Road* and *Road Show*', *Studies in Musical Theatre*, 5 (3): 305–14.

Zavros, D. (2017), 'London Road: The Irruption of the Real and Haunting Utopias in the Verbatim Musical', in G. Rodosthenous (ed.), *Twenty-First Century Musicals: From Stage to Screen*, 212–29, London: Routledge.

# 6

# Interview with Lillian Henley

**Lillian Henley** is a composer, musician, actor and musical dramaturg. She is one of the four founding members of 1927, a theatre and performance company that merges animation, storytelling, live performance and music. Her work with 1927 has included *Between the Devil and the Deep Blue Sea* (2007), which was performed at the Edinburgh Fringe before an international tour. The production won six awards, including a Fringe First, a Herald Angel Award and an Empty Space Award. In 2010, 1927 staged *The Animals and Children Took to the Streets*, which was first performed at Battersea Arts Centre before transferring to the National Theatre and embarking on an international tour. This was followed by *Golem* in 2014, a co-commission between the Salzburg Festival, Théâtre de la Ville Paris and the Young Vic Theatre. The production was filmed and aired on BBC Four in 2018. Lillian's most recent collaboration with 1927 was *Roots* (2019) which opened at the Spoleto Festival, United States, before an international tour. *Decameron Nights* was a reimagining of the show during the Covid pandemic as a three-part series, released on BBC Radio 3's 'The Essay' in 2020 and 2022 for BBC Sounds. In addition to her work with 1927, Lillian has worked as a composer with companies including Regents Park Open Air Theatre, London. She is also a silent film accompanist, working with the Barbican Centre, the BFI, the Cinema Museum, Kennington Bioscope and the Palace Cinema in Broadstairs.

1927's work is created through extended periods of R&D in which storytelling, live composition and accompaniment, and animation are developed simultaneously, and in this interview Henley describes the development of 1927's distinctive aesthetic and how the four core members of the company collaborate in R&D periods to bring story, music and image together.

*1927's website states that '1927 have performed to over 1.5 million people across six continents and we are still experimenting with what happens when performance, live music and animation come together'. I wondered if you could explore how your work with 1927 brought these different components together?*

In every show that we've made, we have explored different storytelling approaches. We're constantly exploring how best to tell the story. And the four of us all approach this question from our different areas of expertise: Suzanne Andrade (co-artistic director) would do this through writing and performance, Paul Barritt (co-artistic director) would do this through animation and Esme Appleton would do this through performance. I approach this question through composition and storytelling with music. I get such a buzz out of playing with musical language, instruments, voices. I didn't train as a musician in a classic setting, but I learnt approaches to listening and responding as an actor. So those skills all fed into the sort of maker I became when I met 1927.

*How did you begin to develop* Between the Devil and the Deep Blue Sea?

Esme and Suzanne had trained together at Bretton Hall, and Paul and Suzanne had collaborated before: they had been to the Edinburgh Fringe in 2006 (the year before we went up for the first time as 1927 with *Between the Devil and the Deep Blue Sea*). Their show had been more static, and they were interested in making it more theatrical. Esme, Paul and Suzanne were thinking about the idea of blending animation, poetry and short stories together. I came on board as they wanted a live musician.

When we first started, in our early workshops and R&D for what would become *Between the Devil and the Deep Blue Sea*, Suzanne would come with a scene or an idea or a few lines of script. In the early days we would sit by the piano; it was the simplicity of playing with the relationship between her words and my music. She might already have had a conversation with Paul and Esme: the best way that I can describe all of our R&D work is that we were all like little satellites, having lots of conversations individually at this really early stage of an idea for a show. This starting point continued throughout all of our work: lots of little conversations, starting with the story or what the show could be about, or what the four of us are interested in. The R&D would bring these conversations together. So Suzanne and I would sit by a piano with a little bit of a story and I would play. It would be really joyful. My way of processing the story would be through music. So she would tell a story and automatically I might play a short tune on the keys, and pick up a theme through which I could express what one of the characters might be feeling or express the mood of the scene. We would have a conversation through the music. I might play a section and Suzanne would suggest it could be a bit wonkier, and gradually we would craft a soundscape to her poem. It felt witty and playful. Through this process, our styles and approaches to making blended. Parallel to this, Suzanne and Paul were having conversations about how to bring the story to life through the animation. In our early work, at the end of 2006/beginning of 2007, Paul animated the stories in a very simple and charming way. Our basic aesthetic consisted of a projector (which provided the light source onto the stage), a large cloth screen hung from the ceiling (to allow the performers to move in amongst the animations) and a piano next to the screen with a light source. Esme and Suzanne would move in amongst the animated vignettes, like moving portraits in a large picture frame. We developed how my singing voice and acting skills could be worked into the short scenes, uniting all of our stage performances into the animations. It became obvious to us all that weaving in the actor-musicians in the interactions of the animated work gave the music more visibility, highlighting that the music was also a key element of the live performance.

*Between the Devil and the Deep Blue Sea* started out being a cabaret of ten short stories. We brought in a range of collaborators to explore how we might tell these short stories in a cabaret setting. So our first experience of research and development was by gigging: we would try things out live in front of an audience, constantly asking ourselves what the showing told us about what made a good story. What made the audience stop drinking at the bar and turn round and watch weird pieces of artwork and storytelling? So all of that playful exploration was happening live in front of an audience. Battersea Arts Centre (BAC) became involved at this stage of the project's development. They gave us a space to perform and try stuff out in. All we needed was an empty room and a piano. I remember that Esme and Paul arrived with a big sheet that they had sewn together and paper illustrations on copper rods and a big projector. So that early R&D time was spent exploring how we play with these elements: how we make stories with limited resources. From this work, BAC offered us a slot in one of their scratch nights. Again, our work was thinking about audiences. Our view was that if it wasn't landing, let's change it. That was one of the main drivers. These early cabaret nights were rowdy and it gave you a real buzz when a weird animation show with a cryptic, witty story and wonky music grabbed people's attention. As we developed on our journey over the winter to spring, we started to discuss the possibility of going to Edinburgh.

*The Edinburgh run of* Between the Devil and the Deep Blue Sea *was a huge success and you won several awards for the production. What were the next stages of development of the show and your work with 1927?*

Following the run in Edinburgh, there were lots of offers of support and opportunities for tours. Jo Crowley joined the team as our producer and she was able to pull the opportunities together. That allowed Paul and Suzanne, the co-artistic directors, to focus on the making. The relationship with BAC continued – their support was amazing. They were very helpful as we tweaked the show during the runs: although the R&D period might have finished, and we had been on the road and performed to lots of people, if something was feeling baggy or wasn't quite working, they would give us space to develop it. In this sense the 'R' of R&D was our research into the audience: which moments weren't working, what felt like it needed attention.

Alongside planning the tour of *Between the Devil and the Deep Blue Sea* we started the R&D for our next show, which became *The Animals and Children Took to the Streets*. We continued the same approach to making our work: we had long R&D phases for all of our shows – a distinct research and development stage. For most of our shows, it takes about three years before they are staged. Two of us, or the four of us when we all came together and we booked a space, would meet to explore how we could expand our ideas out away from the piano and onto the stage. Putting ideas on the stage, actually trying ideas out on stage, starts to inform where the story might go. There are constant conversations between us: Paul taking ideas away to develop in the animation, discussions with Esme about how this might become three-dimensional and theatrical. Looking back on our early work, we were having these initial ideas where we were asking fundamental questions about what we wanted to create. This was always about the specifics: one scene, one character, or a moment in the scene. Then those decisions filtered out into other scenes which Suzanne would write as we went, and my music helped shape the flow and rhythm of the stories.

One of the challenges was our need for space: we had to hire a massive space in Leyton to develop *The Animals and Children Took to the Streets*. This was partly practicalities: the studio space was near where we all lived, but the key thing was the animation studio was in the same space as where we were creating the performance with the projections. This meant we could be in constant dialogue. Again, the process of developing *The Animals and Children Took to the Streets* began with playing. We had a character, Mrs Villikar, and we had lots of scenes that featured her, and I've lots of happy memories of being in this freezing cold studio and Paul being in the animation studio next door listening on headphones. So we could literally develop these elements at the same time in the same space. He could film something in the studio and then we could try it straight away. He set up a stop-motion camera and the three of us were dressed as leopard-print gossip women who live in the tenement block. Paul would create stop-frame characters in animations. He'd reduce us down and put us in the film as background characters for the animation. It was great to see the different layers of the piece developing around you. I loved the free playfulness of the R&D. It was, though, still a very slow process. We were in the cold studio for about six months making *The Animals and Children Took to the Streets* as the animation took so long. Jo Crowley, our producer, once described this as slow-cooking a feature film; it took us a very long time.

Battersea Arts Centre played a big part in our research and development for our early work. Because of our combination of live performance, live music and pre-recorded animation, we couldn't develop the whole play in one go. Rather, we had to focus on short sections. As the company got more skillful in its different areas of storytelling – whether this was writing and storytelling, the animation or the music – we started experimenting with broader brushstrokes. So, rather than building the piece from little moments, we could get the main elements of the story in place and build from there. But the length of time that it would take us to develop a new piece was almost unheard of. It was new for the theatres that commissioned us: we couldn't just do six weeks of rehearsals. We needed all of those experiments beforehand. We would develop the plays moment by moment, using our different skill sets in the room together. But when you are embarking on something that is quite technology-dependent, it can get costly and time-consuming.

*I can certainly see the challenge of bringing together music and storytelling, both of which can be improvised and quickly changed, with animation which, I assume, is much more complicated and time-consuming to alter or adapt. How did this work when you all came together in the R&D?*

I think that's why improvization was so helpful to the process. Paul would watch our improvizations (the short story and music) and we'd try some sections of film out and then he would take it back and remake. In our early work, on both *Between the Devil and the Deep Blue Sea* and *The Animals and Children Took to the Streets*, there was only Paul and Derek Andrade working with him as Animation Associate, so the pace at which they were able to update and develop the animation dictated the pace of development of the show. This was all handmade animation.

These beautifully hand-drawn images and paper puppets that he would move and manipulate using a stop-frame approach. But the improvization in the room meant that we could work around, or with, the animation. So, with my musical improvization, I could cut bits and respond live. We were good at not being precious about cutting bits that weren't working and reshaping what we'd drafted. Later on in our work, the technology moved on and Paul was creating it on different software. But for *Between the Devil and the Deep Blue Sea* it was recorded and then rendered on a DVD! I have a memory of us being on this amazing tour after our run in Edinburgh and we took the show to South Korea. People couldn't believe, when we turned up at theatres, that we had the show on a DVD. We didn't have a budget for anything more sophisticated than that. But of course the technology got better and we were able to apply for funding to get the technology that the company needed. The improved software allowed us a bit more freedom in how Paul created the films. But in the early work we created, due to the nature of the animations, there was a rigidness in performance as the films couldn't change: this was set in performance.

This changed for our next production, *Golem*. Again, we had a long period of R&D for the show. The Young Vic was involved and supported it from the start as we knew that we would be presenting it as their Christmas show, but there were also a lot of international partners, including the Salzburg Festival. We didn't work in the Young Vic's building until quite late on. With *Golem* we worked in a warehouse for six months. On *Golem*, though, the rigidness in performance had gone, thanks to the new technology that we used. There were about 500 very short sections of film which would be cued live by the technician. It meant that the technician, Helen Mugridge, had to be really on board with the timing of the show. The live musicians, performers and the cueing of the film and the lights all worked together. There was a real sense of cohesion. In the R&D and rehearsal process for *Golem*, it was all about bringing in the technicians so that everyone was living and breathing the show and understood its rhythms. So a lot of our R&D process is about problem solving with the technology as much as it is creatively telling the story. I love the notion that constraint breeds creativity, but as the technology improved, it allowed us to relax on certain elements and sculpt the performance live, responding to the audience.

I remember in the performances of *Golem* and *The Animals and Children Took to the Streets*, when we took the plays on tour and we'd perform night after night, even though the score had been set and written down, there were still moments of ad-libbing, and also your tempo, mood, the energy of the show, varied hugely. I'm almost always composing. At first glance it might seem like a pretty rigid show, but once you understand the rules of how a 1927 show works, if you're someone who enjoys that sort of freedom, it feels like a game. I think that's what kept me touring for so long!

*Could you say a bit more about the 'rules' of a 1927 show?*

One of the things that we discussed a lot was training our new actors, in the R&D, to speak to music: the rhythm and musicality of the spoken voice. Speaking on rhythm.

We'd have a loop of music and animation to provide a rhythm for movement in our workshops with new actors, so that it appears that the projected world and the live actors are one: they belong in the same world. There were other rules: if the actor looks at the screen then the whole world dies. The actors had to live inside the animation. This sort of R&D with new members was an important part of the experimentation. The spoken rhythms were just as important: to respond to the music in the moment in the same way in which I responded to the performer. This is why I needed to create a bed of music – this soundtrack – where the music doesn't pull focus but is malleable enough to respond to the performer. It was like an intricate dance.

*Looking back, do you see a difference between R&D and rehearsals?*

In the very early stages of R&D, we'd have informal conversations and our intimate work, with just myself, Suzanne and a piano; that very early stage of thinking what it could be. This was the most experimental phase. When I think of R&D in terms of a funding model, I see it as valuable space that has been provided through some form of support. A key part of R&D is coming together with other people to dream and hope about what the show could be. That's one of the most exciting feelings when I've been invited to other R&D periods. You are invited to come to a place to talk about this idea and when we are there we will dedicate our focus to the project. When we are outside this space, we have all of our life admin and juggling to do, but R&D gives you the space for everyone to focus together. R&D can probably mean lots of different things to different people, but for me, it allows you to see, with the focus of other people, whether an idea will work. It might work theoretically, but practically, in the room with collaborators, does it work?

*Were the long periods of R&D funded?*

In the very early days, no, I don't think these periods were funded. I wasn't involved in the fundraising for the show, but from what I understand, it was quite hard to fundraise to create theatre in this non-traditional way. It wasn't just a rehearsal period – it was more like the development period of a film. I think we were all working other jobs as well. Developing in as low-cost a way as possible, but at least knowing that we would be paid once the show was being performed, when there would be ticket sales generated.

How you get work made is a really important question. It feels a big question as buildings are facing challenges after the pandemic: how do they support artists? I feel really passionate about this. Looking back, without the support that we had to take risks and try new things, being offered space, we wouldn't have been able to develop as artists and make this work. The question of how you get buildings and artists to talk to each other is really important.

Something that I'm discovering now as an artist and musician is that I have to offer an idea that relies on my time and my expertise in order for the idea to be pitched. So, while it is important to be paid for the time you put into a project, you've also put a great deal of time and thought into the project before it is commissioned. There are so many unpaid hours! I don't know how this can be recognized, but clearly the time taken to develop an idea into a proposal is central to developing new forms of theatre and storytelling, and yet somewhere in the timeline of generating an idea, we put no fee value on it. Perhaps it's hard to quantify this on a funding bid. The question of how to make art sustainably is being asked more and more between artists post-pandemic. If buildings provide paid time as well as space for artists just starting out and at mid-career, that would make a big difference to artists making work today.

*Alongside your work with 1927, you have performed as a silent film pianist. How did this come about, and what links this work?*

I rather fell into being a silent film pianist, partly as a result of the style of music I was creating with 1927. Though our 1927 shows included spoken dialogue, the music was strongly inspired by silent film live accompaniments. In our first show, *Between the Devil and the Deep Blue Sea*, we had a silent film, and I found it a really fun way to tap into my creative storytelling as a performer. I remember meeting the broadcaster and silent film pianist Neil Brand at Edinburgh. I was very inspired by his show *The Silent Film Pianist Speaks*. In the show, he spoke about how a silent film pianist will make judgements and guesses about the film they are accompanying. I love that. It reminded me how much I enjoy musical improvisation on the piano as a way to lead the audience, and the power of music and how I can use it carefully and knowingly. Surprising the audience, being the antithesis to what they are watching.

I love the experience of live music performance in theatre: you are there in the moment together. That's why silent film with a live audience is a perfect form for me: you have this film recording which is set – whether it is perfect or not, that is what has been made – and you get to play and respond to it. When I've accompanied a Buster Keaton film, I find him so melancholic and witty. I love the deadpan nature of his expressions. You can play so much or so little onto what he is doing. Even with a film that you've scored before, you respond differently each time. This all draws on my work with 1927. You are so present and in the moment and the form is so ephemeral: once the moment has gone, it's gone.

*You've recently worked at the National Theatre and developed your work as a dramaturg.*

Yes, I received a Developing Your Creative Practice grant from the Arts Council and it is only recently that I've started to reflect on my work with 1927 and outside it. You could describe it as musical dramaturgy: making judgements with the music, thinking about your function, which might be commenting on a character, capturing the atmosphere of a room, moving the story on.

After the end of the run of *Golem*, I was invited to take part in some musical theatre workshops at the National Theatre Studio. There were two amazing people running the sessions, Victoria Saxton and Joel Fram. They invited a wide range of practitioners, playwrights, musicians. We each had different experiences and skills and we were just exploring what collaborations might happen. Chris Bush and Tom Wells were there; I worked with Suhayla El-Bushra and from our discussions we developed a project on sleep for schools, *The Magical Land of Sleep: A Musical for 5–7 year olds*, which children could perform in their primary schools. The National Theatre Studio provided a space to play, to discuss and explore ways of collaborating. I think the reason that we were invited there was to see what sort of musicals might develop, or what relationships. This was over the period of a year and a half or two years, from 2015 to 2017. We had one week together at the beginning and then we'd meet each month: we'd meet for a day to discuss, explore, play with a collaborator, then we'd go away and write it and then have actor-musicians sing it. Alecky Blythe and Adam Cork came to give a talk to the group and spoke about their process. I also found it very useful in terms of developing my work as a musical dramaturg. I'm interested in how I can use my skills to support other practitioners to develop their work and find new ways of working. How to support musicians working on a show. How does their work contribute to the story? The dramaturgy of music. Why are some moments scripted and some moments sung? Who sings it and why?

3 February 2023
Interviewed by Tom Cantrell

## Questions and Prompts #3

- Think carefully about who owns the project: Is this the R&D group, a director or a theatre? How can you ensure that the group has a sense of ownership of the project?
- Who should be involved and when? Do you want musicians or actors immediately? Who is in the room throughout and who do you invite (and when)?
- Be clear about the difference between R&D and the 'machinery of production'. Have clear aims for the R&D that are distinct from those of staging a production.
- How do you protect the process, care for those involved and together look after the best interests of the project? Can you be clear about the expectations (or the lack of expectations) for the end of the R&D?
- How can you build flexibility into your process? How flexible can the R&D be, session by session and day by day? Can this flexibility allow you to pursue possibilities which arise in the R&D but which might not have been predicted beforehand?
- What, for your R&D team, constitute the 'best conditions' to develop the work? Perhaps discuss this at the start. How can you create these within the time and financial constraints in which you are working?
- How do you build an environment in which you can take risks and which embraces failure? Where experimentation is valued above progress towards an end result?
- Might you bring together new collaborators in your R&D, including people with a range of skill sets and those who wouldn't ordinarily meet?
- What are the needs/working processes of the different members of the team? How might you structure the R&D to allow maximum potential for collaboration between them? This might inform the space you use, the preparation you do outside the room, the equipment you bring into it.
- Think about useful structures within the flexibility. Would daily reflections or debriefs help identify the group's shared interests? Would it be useful to share work with someone outside the group? Would a sharing at the end of the R&D period be useful – or not?

# Percolating and plummeting

## Artist perspectives on R&D

Deborah Pearson

## Introduction

It's some time in 2015 or was it 2014? I'm on a stage at the Norwich and Norfolk Festival that feels *very much* like a stage, in the worst way. In my memory it was 3 feet higher than where the audience were sitting, though memories aren't measuring sticks. I remember it being tall primarily because of how very far away I felt from the baffled faces watching me perform. This was a show that a year from then would become my best piece and at that point was likely my worst.

*History History History* was a solo performance I toured internationally between 2016 and 2019. The tour was a major highlight in my career. It was translated into Spanish, Portuguese, Greek, Czech and Mandarin and performed at prestigious venues, galleries and festivals in fourteen countries and four continents including Australia and China. When we were at Baltoscandal in 2018 sharing a bill with Jérôme Bel and Forced Entertainment I remember my production manager Greg Akehurst commenting that the tour for the show had gone 'next level'.

But back in 2015, on that stage at a live art night at Norwich and Norfolk, if there was a next level, the elevator was headed down. At that point the show was called *The Wonder Striker*, and it very much sucked. In its aftermath, as members of the audience filed out, half-heartedly congratulating me or politely trying to acknowledge what had just passed between us, I repeated a mantra out loud like a broken record, hoping it would protect me from how embarrassed I felt: 'It's a work-in-progress. If you have any thoughts, ideas or feedback, let me know.' That request hung in the air, a question that nobody that night seemed able to answer given what they'd just seen. Although I knew the potential, what they knew was the finite imperfect thing I'd tried and failed to express. I'd communicated poorly and they were confused. Their expressions said that they didn't believe I wanted feedback, that they didn't know how to fix the show, that they sort of pitied me and that even if it was a work-in-progress, they didn't really care. The term 'work-in-progress' couldn't undo that what they'd just seen was bad.

This chapter attempts to take on both the abstract and concrete concerns brought about by the research and development process from the perspective of an artist. These concerns have been organized into three sections – one on exploration and trying things out, one on money/funding and one on how and when to decide that a piece that is being developed is finished. I interviewed several colleagues for this chapter, to gather opinions and experiences past my own. I primarily spoke with artists who I've worked with in some capacity, either as a curator with Forest Fringe, as a dramaturg, or both. These artists came to mind because I've had a window (even a small one) into the unfinished stages of their process. Unsurprisingly, I heard many similar strategies and concerns crop up repeatedly. These were strategies and concerns that often reflected my own artistic experiences in 'R&D'. Nearly every artist I spoke with described R&D as a period of exploration and 'trying things out', and every artist had an unresolved and ambivalent feeling around how to fund these periods. Many artists I spoke with mentioned a blurring or uncertainty around when the project moves out of research and development to completion, if ever.

Throughout this chapter, in an attempt to articulate an artist's relationship to research and development, I will reflect primarily on my own experience developing the show *History History History*, which I refer to as *HHH*. *HHH* was researched and developed for four years before its purported 'premiere' in Bergen at BIT Teatergarasjen in January of 2016. I use *HHH* as a point of comparison with the experiences of other UK-based artists I interviewed for this chapter who I have worked with as a curator and dramaturg over the years, including Jemima Yong, Richard Gregory from Quarantine, Chloé Déchery, Gemma Paintin of Action Hero, Brian Lobel, Paula Varjack, Jess Latowicki of Made in China and Xavier De Sousa.

## Exploring and trying everything

In September 2012 the Bristol-based theatre company Action Hero asked me to dramaturg their newest work-in-progress, *Hoke's Bluff*. I curated and produced their work several times in Edinburgh and in our national and international microfestivals as a co-director of Forest Fringe. Forest Fringe, which I co-direct with Andy Field and Ira Brand, ran a free experimental performance venue at the Edinburgh Festival which was collaboratively staffed by the same artists who curated and performed there. Because of the nature of our cooperative staffing model, I'd ushered many of the shows, seeing some pieces over a dozen times. The email inviting me to join the creative process for the team comprehensively outlined a proposed working relationship together, complete with a devising schedule specifying when I would be needed and in what capacity. The subject line of the email was 'dramaturd'. This was apt preparation for Action Hero's devising process. These periods are irreverent, playful and unerringly professional.

*Hoke's Bluff* was about the manipulative yet undeniably moving narrative of American sports films. Although the text had not been completely set before I joined them, the piece had already been through a devising process for the script, where Gemma Paintin and James Stenhouse worked collaboratively with playwright Nick

Walker on the text. When I joined the team, staging, design and text were beginning to take shape together. As is the case for many devised contemporary performances, there was no director for the piece. Staging ideas were offered up by anyone in the room with the rule that every idea, no matter how visibly distasteful to lead artists Gemma Paintin and Jim Stenhouse, was somehow tried before being discarded. Although this approach suggests the expansive and permissive environment one may associate with early research and development, I joined the project quite far into the script's development, as we were moving towards a 'sharing' at the end of a two-week residency at Warwick Arts Centre. The piece underwent several more residencies focused on design and staging with text changes often happening as a result, occasionally culminating in performances that were open to the public, occasionally not. It was 'premiered' in 2013 at our venue in Edinburgh, Forest Fringe, as part of the British Council Showcase.

*Hoke's Bluff*'s text began almost by accident at a residency hosted by China Plate called 'The Dark Room'. This residency invited several experimental performance makers and playwrights to pair up and share space and practice over the course of a week without any expectation to produce anything shareable. It was the project development equivalent of inviting two compatible single friends to sit next to each other at a dinner party as opposed to explicitly 'setting them up'. Gemma Paintin from Action Hero cites this hands-off approach to outcome as a key element that enabled them to make work:

> They paired us with a writer, Nick Walker, for two weeks and they said don't make anything, just explore practice. Explore what you want to do, explore anything that's interesting. It's open ended. You don't have to show anything. You don't even have to share anything. You can keep it completely private. For us it completely changed and revolutionised our whole practice, and of course because we didn't have to do anything, we did loads. Two pieces of work, *Hoke's Bluff* and *Slap Talk*, came out of that process. [. . .] It changed our whole practice and process in regards to writing. We started calling ourselves writers after that. (Paintin 2023)

Although Action Hero spent years developing a 'try everything' process in their rehearsal room since beginning their work together in 2006, this same permissiveness did not apply to their approach to writing text before the Dark Room residency in 2012. They weren't comfortable identifying as writers, even though writing was a big part of their process. This residency with Nick Walker at the Dark Room expanded their 'try everything' approach into a kind of permission the company were able to give not only to their work but to their practice itself – particularly in terms of how they thought of themselves as artists. The writing process on that residency also engendered an unusually collaborative text from three writers. Like my most recent collaboration with Action Hero, *The Talent* (2023), *Hoke's Bluff* was composed of material written by three people – in that case Nick Walker, Gemma Paintin, and Jim Stenhouse – in a text equivalent of their staging process.

Defining the chronology of how text and staging develop for an Action Hero process in a chapter like this one is surprisingly nebulous and difficult to do, even though in the room the making of one of their shows often feels very controlled and has its own momentum. In my experience, contemporary performance pieces often emerge from porous processes that are difficult to place borders around. As an artist, the expansive element of the research and development stage of a project can be both tremendously exciting and very daunting. Many artists I interviewed for this chapter made some reference to the uncertainty and malleability of research and development. I put out the question, 'What does R&D mean to you?', to colleagues, and the below comments give some sense of the ubiquity of approaching this stage of development as permeable and permissive:

> I test things. I test hypotheses. I try out intuitions without knowing where it might lead us. (Chloé Déchery)

> A period of time – sometimes individual/sometimes collective – where we're (attempting to) openly explore something – usually starting (in my case) with a set of questions or a provocation that sounds more concrete than it will become. (Richard Gregory)

> R&D is the time when you have had an idea but you don't know much about it yet other than some loose imagery and concepts you want to investigate further before you get to create a performance with it. I always find that the R&D is one of the most gratifying parts of making work because you are learning new information, acquiring new skills that activate your mind and creativity. (Xavier De Sousa)

> It's a period in the early stages of a project where I am researching the idea, and using that research as stimulus to develop the beginnings of the work based on those themes/source material. (Paula Varjack)

> Collating a list of things to read, watch, listen to and experience that casts a broad net in the direction of travel – and then (hopefully) engaging with these in a thorough way, but also being open to deviating and making sublists should new directions emerge whilst the research is taking place. [. . .] It's also very much a lens through which I view the world and make connections at any given moment. [. . .] Testing questions out in a physical space and 'on our feet'. (Jemima Yong)

A willingness to 'test hypotheses,' as Déchery puts it, is a common desire among very different artists who also describe employing very different approaches to research and development depending on the project (Déchery 2023). Perhaps this seems obvious to creatives – research and development needs to be an open period when almost anything related to the initial inkling could be on the table. Even in corporate environments, new projects tend to begin with a kind of 'brainstorm'. But as mentioned below in the section of this chapter on funding, this unformed element of the creative process can also be seen as risky or 'undeveloped' by those who hold the purse strings. This often forces artists who are seeking funding for research and development work to create a plausible disguise for the project as much more defined than it is in reality. Although ideas change and develop over the course of a research and development process, sometimes resulting in an abandoned project, or in more than one eventual output (Action Hero describe two new pieces resulting from the Dark Room residency, for example), there is almost always some kind of starting point which, as Richard Gregory puts it, 'sounds more concrete than it will become' (Gregory 2023).

## When simplicity slips away . . .

In my case, the starting point for *History History History* was my desire to collaborate with a film from 1956 – a Hungarian football comedy starring my mother's father which had been slated to premiere (coincidentally) on the same day the uprising began in Budapest. The Corvin, the cinema where the film was meant to premiere, was taken over as the headquarters for student protesters. The film was later released in a censored form and that version of the film was as much a feature of my upbringing as an old framed photograph of a relative on the mantelpiece. Every now and again my mother would put it in the VHS player and we would watch scenes featuring her dad. He was speaking a language I didn't understand, immersed in a time, plot and country I didn't understand, but the effect of his celluloid presence on me was undeniable. This tall reedy man in his early thirties was recorded proof of the family stories I was told and the vague but potent childhood memories my mother sometimes did her best to share.

My mother moved to Canada when she was seven years old as a child refugee. Her parents told her they were going on vacation and then she never saw the apartment where she'd grown up again. She also didn't see her grandmother again, a major fixture in her life and upbringing, until she was a teenager. Before they'd left, her father had been a movie star in Soviet Hungary, where she lived in what she described as near-perfect privilege, surrounded by family and caregivers. After 1956, her life became infinitely more precarious, isolated and difficult in ways that she felt deeply as a child but lacked the language (either in English or in Hungarian) to express. A shadow of my mother's trauma was in that VHS we watched when I was little – and I knew that, even if I was also too young to tell her so.

When the idea came to me to use the film as material for a performance, it was 2012. Funnily enough, I'd initially conceived of it as quite a small piece – perhaps an interactive installation for one audience member at a time that could be tucked away in a corner at our Edinburgh venue Forest Fringe while I continued my work hosting and producing other artists at the festival. Once I began thinking through the execution of a small piece, it became clear that the story was much bigger, and my intervention with it would need to be more significant and time-consuming than this initial concept.

As I thought through the project, it began to feel like this was the one story from my life and my family that had objective value and interest to an audience, but the more I explored the material, the further simplicity of the form began to slip away from me, making way for something much more daunting and difficult, revealing a series of threads and questions without answers. This is not unusual for artists who are beginning a project or indeed for anyone trying to execute any kind of idea. In the execution, the idea reveals itself to be more complicated than you had initially thought it would be. This is often where a formal or informal R&D period needs to begin.

The R&D process in my case began with a series of questions. The first question that arose was how could I make someone else's artwork, a pre-existing film that was also a comedy, tell a story about an uprising it had no idea was coming? How could I tell a story that was both mine to tell and also really not mine to tell, particularly when telling it could hurt family members if handled clumsily? And most worryingly, as someone who was not a filmmaker, how could I work with film in a way that was efficient and professional-looking enough that it would not detract from the story I was trying to tell?

There were two known quantities that I held onto like life rafts – there was a story about my family and there was a real film featuring my grandfather, and somehow those two things needed to be working in tandem live. That life raft had me convinced that the show was a good idea, and the story was worth telling. But I had absolutely no idea how to tell it. R&D began to feel like an endless process. The dramaturgy took four years, many collaborators and countless baffling 'work-in-progress' performances in front of audiences to crack. This is what my 'R&D' looked like.

## To share or not to share? That is the question.

When acting as lead artist in a process, 'trying everything' is a process that nearly always involves audience members watching the experiment. Because of this, work-in-progress performances or 'sharings' for small or large audiences have been a marked element of nearly every show I've ever made. As co-director of Forest Fringe I have also facilitated countless work-in-progress performances for other artists, both in Edinburgh at the festival and in other contexts, usually through microfestivals and artist development residencies which we ran internationally and nationally. Through this work, however, I learned that a willingness to 'test drive' and try work in front of an audience is by no means a common desire among performance makers.

My own relationship to work-in-progress performances as an essential part of the R&D process came about as a result of being supported early in my career by Battersea Arts Centre under the artistic directorship of David Jubb and David Micklem. Jubb and Micklem were great believers in what they termed the 'scratch' process, a particularly good way for emerging artists to get their work seen and produced by the venue. Jubb explained the thinking behind this approach to research and development in a round table event at Central School of Speech and Drama in 2009 with what he calls 'Scratch: The Ladder of Development':

> At the heart are three basic principles: to take risks and experiment; to gain feedback from audiences and listen and respond to that feedback; and to take time to develop an idea. So you can see at the bottom of this there's various different first ways of scratching a piece of work, starting with a Scratch Night, where an artist will show maybe five, or ten minutes of work at its very earliest stage of development in front of an audience. Then the audience and the artist decamp into the bar, and hopefully the audience buys the artist some drinks, and gives them

feedback, and responds, and tells them what they think about the work; or simply just says what they saw, which is sometimes the most useful feedback you can give. (Central School of Speech and Drama 2009: 4)

By referring to 'the ladder of development', Jubb alludes to the fact that 'scratch' was employed by Battersea Arts Centre as an iterative form of development, both creatively and financially for the venue and the artist. Most 'Scratch Night' performances would begin with little to no financial compensation for the artist, particularly if an artist was working with Battersea Arts Centre for the first time, and then if the performance showed promise in front of an audience, there might be seed commissioning money available, with a full commission as a potential (though never guaranteed) end point, sometimes provided by 'match funding' from an Arts Council grant applied for by the artist.

Returning to scratch, stand-up comedians often trial their material this way, and for some artists working in other performance-led mediums, it can be the best way to 'crack' a performance. Equally, in my experience of directing and writing at more conventional new writing theatres like the Royal Court and the Yard, the previews process is also an institutional trial by fire. After weeks of carefully considered performances and invited sharings, the first week of a performance can be subject to extreme and sudden daily changes to direction, staging and text depending on that night's performance. The changes are often given as directives from producers and need to be assimilated into the show instantaneously. It is a final sleep-deprived show development on steroids, which can leave cast and crew discombobulated and overworked. That said, in UK new writing, it is the common practice.

'Scratch' is related to but distinct from a work-in-progress performance. It was a model that was embedded in Battersea Arts Centre's working relationship with artists. The term 'scratch' is a work-in-progress showing that may or may not lead to further development of the piece. Scratch is an unfinished but still shareable form of performance shown at a venue that does not necessarily have any financial commitment to support the artist. This technique was the most accessible way of showing work for me as an emerging artist and a common way of working for makers throughout the UK when I was forming as an artist. As mentioned, our Edinburgh venue at Forest Fringe staged work-in-progress performances for audiences that we often called 'scratch performances', and one of my first professional performance engagements was at a 'Scratch Night' at The Arches in Glasgow in 2006. As an artist, I internalized this semi-committed approach to piloting work into my process.

It seems that scratch as a term and technique is less commonly employed in 2024, perhaps because it is very much audience and programmer focused. It arguably functions as a public 'audition' piece for an artist. If the scratch is successful with audiences, the venue may commit more time and money to it. This public audition also provides low-cost programming for venues to stage and audiences to watch, as artists are usually unpaid or paid very little to scratch. It is not a gentle way to support the artist's R&D as it arguably places pressure on the artist to 'perform' at an early stage of development when the piece may not be ready to show an audience. That said, for better or worse, 'scratch' was the way I learned to develop my work.

Even once I was no longer working with Battersea Arts Centre, I found myself requesting work-in-progress performance slots and programming myself at Forest Fringe with this kind of work. Occasionally, excruciating performances in front of perplexed but generous audience members, like the live art night at Norwich and Norfolk Festival with *History History History*, marked key dramaturgical stages for me to *really* test the material I'd already been gently experimenting with in a rehearsal room. It was only through the eyes of the audience that I ever felt I could know whether or not a show was actually working.

At our artist-led curation collective Forest Fringe, one of our defining characteristics early on at our annual Edinburgh Fringe venue was that the work presented could be at any stage in its development. This resulted in several new work-in-progress pieces from artists. Occasionally, they went on to have a life by being further developed with a paid commissioner, and occasionally they were never performed again. As our venue and our artists became more established, the slots became more competitive and 'scratching' less fashionable. As a result, showing works-in-progress at our venue was more of a rarity in our Edinburgh context. There were some exceptions to this rule – notably, Bryony Kimmings showed a work-in-progress of *Fake It til You Make It* in 2015, and I showed works-in-progress of what later became *History History History* in 2014 and 2015, premiering the final finished product as a one-off performance at the Cameo Cinema in 2016, followed by a short run at Cameo Live, my curatorial initiative with Corin Christopher, in 2017.

In later years, as works-in-progress at the venue became less frequent, we decided to create a space and residency to explicitly host an artist for a week or more to conduct research and development. There was a small room hidden in the corner of our venue (the Drill Hall in Leith) that was ideally suited to performance installations or to being used as a temporary studio for artists who wished to do R&D in the context of the Edinburgh Fringe Festival. Selina Thompson undertook a notable research residency with us in 2015 when we hosted her for a week and she created the work-in-progress *Race Cards* – an installation of hundreds of index cards each posing a different question about race. Canadian artist Adam Kinner used this space to explore choreographic ideas around putting the discourse of a festival into the body, and Brian Lobel used this space with us in 2014, creating the autobiographical installation *Letters from Lehman Brothers*.

In the installation Brian carefully recreates emails between himself and his best friend and ex-partner Grant, who had tragically died in an accident two years beforehand. Grant was a lawyer. He painstakingly cuts out and glues characters from Grant's section of the investigation into the Lehman Brothers' many financial crimes to carefully recreate loving correspondence with Grant. It was an incredibly beautiful and moving installation reflecting on grief, politics, love and the economy – and it was much more polished than any of us had been expecting in our initial conversations with Brian. In these exchanges we both described him 'workshopping' the idea. While the installation hinged on Brian researching a task that was emotionally and physically difficult, the moment Brian began working, it was a complete offer to an audience. Given discussions I've had with Brian, this blur between a work-in-progress and a finished piece is not surprising. As he says, 'in the making, in the producing, is when

I'll R&D it' (Lobel 2023) The piece is being researched and developed at the same time as it is also being staged and performed.

Brian further reflected on his tendency to mix staging and development in the making process for another work, *Purge* (2011).

> I just kind of jumped and did it and I always thought instead of R&D, well let's find a small gig that I can do a middling job at and then do a bigger gig when I should accept more money for it, and now it's done. Now it has a fee attached to it and I can just kind of rely on that. [...] I'm also comfortable waiting, waiting, thinking, thinking, thinking, thinking and then just doing it. (Lobel 2023)

Although Brian Lobel and I share the process of developing work in front of audiences, my work with Action Hero made me realize that sharing works-in-progress is not ubiquitous among all other performance makers. For our most recent collaboration, *The Talent*, made by myself and Action Hero, a constant point of contention with the group was whether or not to stage work-in-progress performances. Jim and Gemma often characterized it as unnecessarily exposing, opening the process up to unhelpful feedback when the piece was still not finished. Although Action Hero came of age as artists in the same era of scratch as I did and as Brian did, they did not internalize it as a key element of their artistic DNA in the same way as me. They knew how to move out of R&D without witnesses, perhaps suggesting they also have a different understanding of R&D itself – it does not always need to lead to a product.

## Money and funding

Sometimes when attending Improbable's 'Devoted and Disgruntled' meetings (gatherings where the industry meets voluntarily to discuss contemporary issues and problems with theatre and performance) a participant will suggest a kind of embargo on complaining about Arts Council funding, as though it is an unhelpful cliché. This suggestion often comes from a programmer, artistic director or other salaried individual in attendance, but for a freelance artist, there is no way to avoid the cliché that funding is almost everything.

Although this section is exclusively dedicated to discussing funding, funding is an undercurrent in every other element of an artist's experience with researching and developing their work. Professional artists living under late capitalism are not exempt from the necessity to pay bills, rent, mortgages (if they're very lucky) and any number of other living costs including caring for dependents and access needs. To pretend that this does not deeply impact the creative process and those most able to practice creatively is a fallacy. Very few shows appear like Moses in a basket: they are not fully formed gifts that arrive immediately ready to be rehearsed and staged. They are inklings – hunches – passions and curiosities that need testing, sometimes testing in front of an audience, sometimes embarrassing testing, to become fully formed, and for an artist to engage with this testing period, they need time, which means they need financial resources.

Arts Council England (ACE) seems to be aware of this, but its relationship to funding this precarious stage of development is increasingly fraught. While ACE once regularly funded project grants dedicated to 'Research and Development', since 2016 ACE has directed this type of request into its 'Developing Your Creative Practice' (DYCP) scheme. This is a scheme inviting artists to apply with something akin to a self-directed programme of study which theoretically allows them to expand their network and/or skill set into previously unexplored territory. Unlike project grants, which can be applied for at any time of year, DYCP is run in rounds – several times a year they invite applications for the fund, but an artist is not permitted to apply if they have already made two unsuccessful applications in the past year and a half. Whereas project grants allow artists who are unsuccessful with their applications to consider the feedback, redraft the application and reapply, artists applying for a DYCP grant cannot reapply until the next round, which will be months in the future. If they are unsuccessful a second time, they are not eligible to reapply at all for at least six months.

The vast majority of artists are unsuccessful. As ACE advertise on its website, in the last three years it has received 18,000 applications for the DYCP programme and funded 4,000 of those – meaning that nearly eight out of ten artists who apply for DYCP are rejected from the scheme. The availability of grants so drastically outweighs the number of applicants that Arts Council England recently clarified eligibility criteria to discourage artists from applying if the bid is likely to be unsuccessful. This overwhelming demand for DYCP grants is largely due to the fact that, as mentioned, research and development periods previously applied for as project grants before 2016 simply aren't eligible through any route other than the very limited competitive DYCP scheme.

I have applied for DYCP for my personal practice twice and been rejected twice. Both times were in the aim of expanding my practice into new and more ambitious areas, both times I had set up extensive mentoring relationships with respected artists and both times the feedback was 'other applications preferred'. Neither project moved forward after being rejected, as the programme of enquiry I'd applied with was dependent on paying collaborators and very much tailored to the specifics of the DYCP scheme. Jess Latowicki from the theatre company Made in China had a similar experience:

> I applied twice during the pandemic and at least one other time after. [. . .] I have always had great mentors, I've always had a really strong budget and I've always had a really strong offer which was about my individual practice growing into telling stories that are presented in a video format, which I don't really know how to do. [. . .] So I applied for all these things and because I've been rejected so many times I go back to the drawing board and rethink how to do it. Like do I need more mentors? Do I need a specific project that I'm working on? I've never been able to get it but it's something that I really really want to do [. . .] And by not getting DYCP I've not been able to do it because I don't have the resources [. . .] Oh also, they were all rejected, all of them, as 'Other applications preferred'. I think that's what all the rejections say, unless there's a glaring error, because they are oversubscribed. (Latowicki 2023)

Given the obstacles to successfully applying for a DYCP grant (it is oversubscribed, the rounds system is challenging, the criteria are constantly changing), many artists might choose to apply to fund their research and development through a project grant instead. However, though Arts Council England is not explicit about research and development periods being ineligible for a project grant, the likelihood of getting this period funded is low as a result of recent changes to funding policy through the 'Let's Create' scheme, particularly the emphasis on funding artistic projects that are clearly beneficial to communities. The most recent material on funded project grants cites 'Insufficient benefit to people and communities' as a reason that a project may be ineligible for funding, elaborating:

> We want the projects we fund to support our strategy Let's Create, by engaging people in England with creativity and culture. Engaging people and communities can be achieved by enabling other people to experience your activity as creative practitioners, participants, contributors and/or audience members. [. . .] Tell us about the steps you will take to make sure your project is open and accessible to people within communities you plan to work with. (ACE n.d. b)

This recent approach to funding puts pressure on artists to immediately identify the benefits to 'communities' for a project that is still germinating, which can be counterproductive to artistic development. It's a bit like asking a writer to livestream themselves writing, proving that there is a community who will want to watch that livestream and will benefit from watching it. As Gemma Paintin puts it, 'It absolutely kills it and we can't do it anymore' (Paintin 2023). Jemima Yong mentioned this blurring between social work and artistic development when I asked whether she applied for funding for R&D. She said, 'I think it has become very clear to me that unless the audiences and communities I'm working directly with are considered "minoritised" or "marginalized" from the vantage point of ACE, I won't be getting funding' (Yong 2023). Equally off-putting to those seeking funding for the early stages of a project, is the recent guidance from Arts Council England, which cites 'Underdeveloped' as a reason to deny funding to artists (ACE n.d. c). They provide a tool on the website which is an online quiz called 'Is my project ready?' One of the questions in the quiz is 'Do you have a clear idea of what your project is about and what you want it to achieve? [. . .] Can you describe it in one sentence?' (ACE n.d. a)

Gemma Paintin elaborated on the frustration to be outwardly facing with a project while in the research and development phase if a funding body is involved:

> The problem with R&D funding is that you have to say what you're going to do. You have to try and predict what your outcomes are going to be to try and get the funding in the first place. But the natural process of R&D is that it changes and it shifts and it becomes something completely different. So sometimes when an R&D process goes well, it's bad for funding. You end up in this position where you've had good R&D but you can't report very well against the funding, or you want to report well against the funding and it kills the R&D. (Paintin 2023)

The fraught relationship between funding and creation is keenly felt by many artists, often 'killing' a project before it begins. This can happen because the piece received funding but, as Paintin mentions, the pressure to prematurely report on it or to bring other people in too early extinguishes the creative possibilities of it. There is a connection here to the pressure to share work-in-progress material in front of an audience, as there is a section in an Arts Council project grant application called 'Engagement' (ACE 2022). This is a section where artists predict the number of audience members, freelancers and other individuals who are likely to benefit from the activity. Including a public sharing in a funding bid increases the number of people engaging with the work, which may make a bid more likely to be successful, which arguably provides motivation for artists to commit to publicly sharing work before it is ready. If an artist does not want to expose their R&D period to an audience, they may be motivated to apply for a Developing Your Creative Practice grant, but given the large number of artists denied funding for DYCP, this makes it likely that their project receives an early rejection from a funding body, which could mean the artist is disheartened and decides to stop working without remuneration. I would argue that this amplifies the industry's relationship to privilege as it requires privilege – systemic, professional and monetary – for an artist to either self-fund their research and development or to have the confidence and resilience to keep moving ahead with a nascent project after rejection.

There are a huge number of projects that never make it off the ground because of the funding gap for research and development within Arts Council England. The projects least likely to be accepted will be nascent projects of emerging artists – artists who "struggle to emerge" are often artists from working-class backgrounds, artists with caring responsibilities, artists who are differently abled and artists from marginalized groups. This is ironic, given 'Let's Create' – the current policy behind Arts Council England's approach to project funding – purports to prioritize vulnerable members of society.

The established artist Paula Varjack describes her reasons for always seeking funding for research and development as follows:

> The main reason is a boring one, that if the time isn't paid time I find it hard to justify taking it, particularly as a freelancer constantly in the cycle of juggling work and searching for it to survive. And in order for me to take the time it requires to begin to get stuck into an idea, it needs me blocking it off, even if it's just the odd day here and there. And I find it hard to do that if it's not paid. Also I know once I deep dive into it I won't want to do anything else, so by making sure it's paid time it creates a restriction on the time I spend on the first steps. (Varjack 2023)

Varjack makes an important point about money and funding not simply as a way of ensuring an artist's survival (although it is absolutely that) but also as a way of usefully delineating time. This reflects my experience with research and development in the past and is one reason I often find myself abandoning ideas that take too long to attract a commissioner or that are rejected by ACE. I must admit that this is exacerbated since having a child, given new demands on my time.

It is a cliché but a true one to say that 'time is money' or, as Paula Varjack describes, for an artist, 'money creates time' (Varjack 2023). For a freelance worker, the best way to ensure the time to create is to be able to block off that time through funding. Psychologically, the funding can validate and motivate the artist to make work during the time they are being paid. Practically, the artist can take time off from their other jobs, to ensure that creating their work does not mean that they can't pay their bills. In my experience, a financial commitment from a funding body or commissioner, however small, does make the time spent on R&D for a creative project feel real, urgent and accountable – all very useful motivating feelings for a creator in the early stages of a project.

## Time for R&D on *History History History*

One reason that *History History History* was in development for four years was due to funding. The piece was funded piecemeal.

Early on in the process, I was invited to do a two-week residency at an arts centre in Budapest, unpaid, and rejected for funding to complete this residency by the British Council, as it wasn't a priority group. I did go to Budapest for two weeks, but the residency space was unheated and too cold to work in, so I ended up self-funding a residency at an Airbnb for the duration of my stay. There was a week-long residency at the National Theatre Studio in 2012 where I was paid £80 a day and able to bring in Tania El Khoury and Daniel Kitson to do some dramaturgy on the piece. Norwich and Norfolk paid me £1,000 to perform a work-in-progress at their festival, as mentioned earlier in this chapter. I performed several unpaid works-in-progress through Forest Fringe and a work-in-progress where I was paid £200 to present something at a festival called DICE run by graduates of Central School of Speech and Drama. The Progress Festival invited me to Toronto to present a paid work-in-progress with no technical support but which enabled me to keep working. All of these work-in-progress performances were helpful in the sense that it kept the piece alive, even through limited support, but the show's concept was technically complicated because it worked closely with a film. None of these works-in-progress could offer me more than a couple of hours with someone with any technical or video skill and without more funding I could not yet afford to employ someone to fully execute the conceit.

Finally, through an invitation from London International Festival of Theatre (LIFT), I was able to pitch the piece to the House on Fire scheme, a Culture Europe fund where two European commissioning houses could partner to fund a new work with match funding from the EU. This funding route took two years and many meetings and aggressive emails on my part to programmers in Europe to pin down. Théâtre Garonne in France eventually secured BIT Teatergarasjen in Norway as a partner, and this was the reason the show was made with a production manager who had the skill set to run the piece, and with more extensive dramaturgy.

I found myself pitching this show over and over for small amounts of money and support for years. That pitching process was demoralizing and exhausting. Nevertheless, it was likely also a key element of the creative development of the work. It forced me to crystalize the idea, and made the writing and making more fruitful and efficient once I could actually pay for it. I am aware of how lucky I am that the project eventually made it to 'completion' and how close we came to that never happening. It is no coincidence that I had PhD funding during those years of aggressively pursuing funders and achieving piecemeal research and development. Without that regular income, I would have almost certainly abandoned the project or settled on a less ambitious and complete version. It very easily could have ended with the baffled faces looking up at me at the Norwich and Norfolk Festival in 2015. In my case, external funding was what allowed me to be resilient enough and to buy the time to 'hustle' to get the project over the line in terms of securing funding and commissioners – moving the idea from an idea to a possible reality.

## Moving out of R&D

An active question for any artist or company that is engaging in research and development lies in deciding when the research and development stage is finished. Sometimes this is because the research and development resulted in a product that is ready to tour or to be performed publicly. Sometimes this is because the artist has learned whatever skill or answered whatever question they were hoping to answer with the research and development. Often, it's because funding and time have run out. Whatever the reason, ending research and development periods is a point in the process that an artist or company needs to make peace with.

Richard Gregory from Quarantine creates conceptual work for performance. His process is very much about starting with a 'hunch' which moves towards the concept, but when the concept is found or discovered, then the finished piece has begun:

> That's what the process is and has been about – discovering what is the task. I guess mining something conceptually so that there is a sense where we try to arrive at a version of the concept that is rigorously tested. Then that finds its form in a task or set of tasks that we play in rehearsals so that we know what they're likely to produce. (Gregory 2023)

Many of my projects have followed a similar trajectory in that works-in-progress are about discovering the clearest and simplest version of the concept that communicates most elegantly to the audience. Unfortunately, this does not always align with the premiere.

If you are lucky enough to get a commission or funding for a piece, who gets 'the premiere' is an important contractual point. Although *History History History* was 'premiered' at BIT Teatergarasjen in Bergen, the premiere was something of a disaster. My production manager was working on the enormous task of programming the piece into QLab until hours before the show went on its feet. My final conceptual decision was that the show would last the length of the film, and that the film would play in its entirety alongside the performance on a small picture frame, occasionally moving onto the big screen. Although this idea was relatively easy to execute with a little projector in a small space when I first arrived at it by using a mini projector at a work-in-progress in a warehouse at the DICE Festival, it proved a mammoth task once we were in a cinema. Unlike in the warehouse, the image would not map neatly onto the screen behind me without major programming assistance in QLab. My production manager began working around the clock in Norway to make this happen, and his task was not quite done by the time we premiered the show. There was a technical hiccup in the premiere meaning that the show ground to a halt twenty minutes before it was meant to. The computer had a meltdown and the performance could not be completed. The second night was better, but the show had also not quite been completed from a dramaturgical perspective. I would go on to have several more extensive dramaturgical sessions with Daniel Kitson and Laura Dannequin who worked on the premiere of the French version of the piece. The 'final product' was shown at the UK premiere in Bristol at Mayfest in May of 2016. Mayfest paid me the standard touring fee for the piece and were not listed as commissioners, but they presented the first 'finished' version of the work.

To put it simply, for me, a show is 'finished' when I finally know I've done justice to the idea. Sometimes that takes years. Sometimes, for a huge variety of reasons, it never happens at all. In that sense, seeing R&D as an end product for an artist can be a painful thing which takes a lot of perspective and time. Off the record, I asked several artists whether or not they had ever developed work that didn't go anywhere, and they all had, but they spoke about it in a wistful way, as you might describe an old relationship. Yes, it had changed them, often for the better, but there's a bit of heartbreak in walking away from something early. In my experience, R&D periods, no matter how separate from a 'product', nearly always contain a glimmer of hope that something brilliant and shareable may emerge or result. I think it runs contrary to human nature to truly work without working towards anything concrete.

## Concluding thoughts

The R&D process is about exploring, testing, learning and inviting in collaborators. These are all elements of a process that needs to leave some room for failure. Then there are those instances where it's happened accidentally, where it seems to come easily, because in fact you've done the R&D through living.

When I asked Brian Lobel about his show *An Appreciation* (2009), in which he invites the audience to touch and describe his single testicle, a result of testicular cancer as a teenager, he told me this about his relationship to research and development:

> I thought about it for about five years, this idea of wanting to acknowledge the difference between my body and other people's bodies, but I hadn't quite thought

of the concept. Then I thought of the concept in the middle of the first half of an Akram Khan show, and then wrote the entirety of it in the interval of the Akram Khan show, and then it was done. It was a ten minute process. But that also came from years of thinking in the back of my brain about wanting to do something on this subject. So maybe that's how I R&D. [. . .] I tend to think about my works when I'm swimming, when I'm cycling, when I'm watching TV, which is my brain at rest. (Lobel 2023)

This is not unique to Brian, and in fact, his description of *An Appreciation* aligns with an ancient Chinese story that Italo Calvino describes at the end of his essay on 'Quickness' in *Six Memos for the New Millennium* (2016). He tells the Chinese story of Chuang-tzu drawing a crab:

Among Chuang-tzu's many skills, he was an expert draftsman. The king asked him to draw a crab. Chuang-tzu replied that he needed five years, a country house, and twelve servants. Five years later the drawing was still not begun. 'I need another five years', said Chuang-tzu. The king granted them. At the end of these ten years, Chuang-tzu took up his brush and, in an instant, with a single stroke, he drew a crab, the most perfect crab ever seen. (Calvino 2016: 54)

Calvino's tale demonstrates the slow process of percolation, similar to Brian's process for *An Appreciation*, that can result in the illusion of a perfect first draft. His story also teaches us about the importance of a supportive and pressure-free environment for an artist to germinate or gestate their ideas in. It may seem overly convenient from an artist's standpoint to conclude with the thought that artists need paid and relaxing time in which to do nothing, but this approach has borne fruit in the past. As Lin-Manuel Miranda writes of famously coming up with the concept for *Hamilton* while on holiday, 'It's no accident that the best idea I've ever had in my life, perhaps maybe the only one I'll ever have in my life, came to me on vacation [. . .] The moment my brain got a moment's rest, *Hamilton* walked into it' (Miranda quoted in Price 2021: 64). As Devon Price mentions in his book *Laziness Does Not Exist*, 'idleness can help us to be insightful creators and problem solvers [. . .] When we give our lives space for slowness, relaxation and "doing nothing," we can begin to heal some of our greatest wounds and to create lives for ourselves that are nourishing rather than exhausting' (2021: 64).

As Gemma Paintin remarked of the lack of pressure to create a finished product while doing R&D on the China Plate residency, 'because we didn't have to do anything, we did loads.' The product-oriented approach to creating work can be helpful to some artists, but it kills creativity for others. What seems to work well for most artists however is time, space and financial resources being contributed to their practice. Artists like me will probably do a few embarrassing work-in-progress sharings by choice when given this kind of space and freedom (and that process being optional is key to its success), while other artists might quietly work behind closed doors before delivering or not delivering a finished concept. In either case, like the artist who after years of feeling supported was able to draw the perfect crab, what artists really need to successfully R&D their work are practical conditions that help them to keep going and keep the faith.

# References

ACE (n.d. a), 'Is My Project Ready?'. https://www.artscouncil.org.uk/ProjectGrants/my-project-ready (accessed 23 Feb 2024).

ACE (n.d. b), 'Let's Create'. https://www.artscouncil.org.uk/lets-create (accessed 23 Feb 2024).

ACE (n.d. c), 'Unsuccessful Applications: How We Make Decisions'. https://www.artscouncil.org.uk/dycp/developing-your-creative-practice-faqs/dycp-unsuccessful-applicants#t-in-page-nav-3 (accessed 23 Feb 2024).

ACE (2022), 'Engagement'. https://www.artscouncil.org.uk/blog/engagement (accessed 23 Feb 2024).

Calvino, I. (2016), *Six Memos for the New Millennium*, London: Penguin.

Central School of Speech and Drama (2009), 'New Theatre Roundtable'. https://crco.cssd.ac.uk/id/eprint/27/1/CEN_new_theatre_edit.pdf (accessed 23 Feb 2024).

Déchery, C. (2023), Unpublished interview with the author.

Gregory, R. (2023), Unpublished interview with the author.

Latowicki, J. (2023), Unpublished interview with the author.

Lobel, B. (2023), Unpublished interview with the author.

Paintin, G. (2023), Unpublished interview with the author.

Price, D. (2021), *Laziness Does Not Exist*, New York: Atria Books.

Varjack, P. (2023), Unpublished interview with the author.

Yong, J. (2023), Unpublished interview with the author.

# 8

# Interview with Rosemary Jenkinson

**Rosemary Jenkinson** is a playwright and short story writer from Belfast. Her play *The Bonefire* (2006) won the Stewart Parker BBC Radio Award in 2006. Her plays have been produced in Dublin, London, Edinburgh, New York and Washington DC. She was the 2017 Artist-in-Residence at the Lyric Theatre and in 2018 she received a Major Artist Award from the Arts Council of Northern Ireland. She has also written four collections of short stories and was shortlisted for the Edge Hill Short Story Award in 2023.

In this conversation, we discuss Rosemary's research process, which frequently involves either immersing herself in particular communities or working via long-form interviews with key collaborators over extended periods of time. She shares how these research periods inform the plays she writes and how her plays have then developed in various different contexts. We also talk about funding for R&D in Northern Ireland and how the majority of her own research takes place unpaid, through lived experience and away from funding mechanisms, reflecting on how the challenging financial landscape affects the extent to which playwrights have access to these kinds of processes.

*In this book, we think of R&D as a practice that encompasses many different ways of thinking about rehearsal room practices, devising practices, research practices and script development practices. Thinking generally across your work as a playwright, how do these terms or processes resonate with you?*

The whole thing about my research and development approach is to give readers and audiences something that no one else will have, something that's totally unique. That's really what I do. But there's very little development nowadays. I find there are a lot fewer processes now because of the lack of money here in Northern Ireland. So I think there's more onus on the writer to be fully formed, to give [early readers and funders] a great piece right from the start.

The very first play I wrote, *The Bonefire*, was totally immersive research. I actually lived the research. How it happened was, one night I passed by the bonfire in Annadale Embankment in Belfast [a Loyalist community who, like many other similar communities, build huge bonfires in their local areas in the weeks leading up to the night of 11 July, when the bonfires are lit ahead of widespread Ulster Protestant celebrations on 12 July]. I knew I was going to be doing a commission for Rough Magic [a leading Irish theatre company, based in Dublin], but I didn't know what I was going to do with it. I saw these youths up on a hill and they looked like they were having a fantastic time, a party. I could see them, and I thought, wow, imagine what would it be like to be with them? The bonfire is a real Loyalist icon, but a very dangerous place because it's so localized, and because the bonfires are often under attack by either the Catholic community, Republican community or by their own communities who want to burn it down [in advance of 11 July] out of revenge motives. So it's a dangerous place to be. And I just wanted to be there. I suppose I'm a Protestant, that's my culture. But even so, Annadale Embankment was a place that I had been to maybe a couple of times as a child, but there's so much you don't know about the bonfire. Who builds it? Who guards it? Who's in charge of it? So I wanted to know all of that. And I came up with a kind of crazy plot, kind of inspired by the bonfire. And I thought, I'm going to go in, in order for this to be authentic. I could write the play without it, but I knew I needed to know the inside information. What I wanted from them was the kind of language of the bonfire. And so it was the dialect and everything that I wanted to be authentic because they have real rhyming slang, you can't make it up. So verbally, it was very interesting. And the actual burning is truly exciting.

*Following that research experience, can you talk to me about the writing process for* The Bonefire, *and using what you had gathered in order to write the play?*

I didn't write that summer at all, apart from notes. I wrote the play once the 11 July bonfire was over. I gave the draft to Rough Magic and developed it with Declan Hughes [playwright and co-founder of Rough Magic] as my mentor. After another few drafts, we had public rehearsed readings, which I think was the next summer, so I may have had more bonfire experiences by then, because obviously the next summer I went back and gathered more material and pushed it in, crammed it into the play, whatever I could. And the feedback was good after that, and Rough Magic said they would produce the play. I would have done a draft with Lynne [Parker, co-founder and Artistic Director of Rough Magic] after that, because she was going to direct, and then we went into rehearsal.

In rehearsal, I had to explain that world quite a lot to people. In particular, some of the cast members were from a Republican background and it was hard for them to actually identify with the characters and sympathize with them. So you're trying to explain all this excitement. It was a difficult process. They would suggest things that they thought they knew about, and they weren't right. I remember, actually, in the final draft there's some line about something being made out of matchsticks, something you do in prison, and one of the actors said, no, no, they're made out of lollipop sticks. And I changed it just to make her happy, but it wasn't true. I mean, it's matchsticks. Why would it be lollipop sticks? Maybe in the Republican jails, perhaps. But I knew what I'd been told by the Loyalist community. Then there was another issue with an actor. In Annadale, Catholics are [derogatorily] called Taigs. The actor insisted on calling them Fenians [another derogatory term for Catholics], and it wasn't true. Different areas use different words, and it wasn't quite the authenticity I wanted. If I wanted to use something, I expected that they'd believe me a bit more, or at least believe that I know what I'm talking about. I wish I'd taken more control of the play, but it was my very first. Now, I would know to say, look, I did my research, this is how it is.

*You've mentioned the idea of trying to gain access to interviewees and to gather and hear people's stories. How do you work with interviewees in interviews and then with actors once you've gone through that research process?*

*Stella Morgan* (2010), I wrote about a fortune teller. I had met her at what was basically a drunken night with a group of girls, and we got the fortune teller round. Do you know what, I think I'm actually a stalker, I think my research is stalking! Anyway, after that night, I knew I wanted to write about her so I found out where she worked. I wanted to see her face and say, can I interview you? Can you trust me? I'm going to write about your whole life story and I mean, it's a big deal. I think I'm asking a lot for people to trust me. And I think that's what's really interesting about my own research and development process, because it gives more value to the work. I will never do research via the internet or Google because it's just not authentic. If anyone can look up something, I'm not interested, I want everything I write to be personal and unique.

When I work with actors and directors, I'm listening for the rhythm, for errors and inconsistencies, the ways in which they preserve the emotional through-journeys of the people I interviewed. Also, I'm trying to cut out words constantly, which directors help with. I have all sorts of my own verbal signifiers. I do a lot of 'well's and 'so's and they cut them. And the main point is, does the ending pack a punch? And that's actually very hard to see even at a rehearsed reading. But I can usually guess if it's working or not. We actually changed the ending of *Lives in Translation* (2017) after the rehearsed reading, because I didn't feel that it had the desired impact, it wasn't dramatically tight.

In fact, for *Lives in Translation*, the only reading we had, not a public one, was about three months before the actual production. I kept interviewing my main character for over a year. I had gone through various people to finally work with her, and I found the gatekeepers of the asylum seeking groups were really, really difficult to talk to because they protect their people, of course they do. But then once I started working with her, it was brilliant, she shared so many stories, which is different to the immersion process that I did at the bonfire, because I was coming up with the stories for that. The most important thing about *Lives in Translation*, it's not just that I wanted to know about the asylum system or what happened to her in Somalia, I wanted the whole local culture here [in Belfast] to see it through her eyes. We invited her to the reading and the stress we were under was absolute hell. There were a few other Somali people invited who had been involved in the process as well. It was very, very important that the Somali community would see themselves represented. I've never had that experience before. The play was so close to her and she was going to be there to judge it. And I looked at her face a lot and it looked angry, so I was really worried at the end. But I realized it was her being angry about what had happened to her. She was going through the intensity of the whole story, and it meant that we were doing justice to that story.

*How does funding operate in Northern Ireland for these research and development processes?*

I had funding from Kabosh Theatre Company for *Lives in Translation* and *Silent Trade* (2023). I was also given funding [from EastSide Arts, an east Belfast arts organization principally funded by Arts Council NI and Belfast City Council] to develop the play *Billy Boy* (2021) [another play, like *The Bonefire*, about Belfast bonfire builders], because that was actually made with a Loyalist community. It was a bit of a disaster because we had to do the interviews over Zoom, which is hard because you can't see the people properly or get a sense of them, you can't make ad-lib jokes or crosstalk over people. Also, for *Billy Boy*, the Zoom interviews took place with the community leaders present, so I felt I only got half the truth – important truths but not everything. In the same way, with *Silent Trade*, the Nigerian community in Belfast is very worried about the whole issue of trafficking, so no one wanted to be named or identified when I interviewed them, nor did they come to the final production, because there's so much awkwardness and embarrassment about trafficking. The thing about funding for this kind of research, though, is that you have to say, I talked to this person, I talked to that person, and you have to provide proof and a list, which is, you know, kind of also putting a bit more pressure on the interviewee, because sometimes they don't really want to be named. But I did get paid for those three projects! Those are the only three times when that's happened. All the other research I've done is my own.

*Are there other departure points for you or other ways of exploring the pre-writing process?*

Sometimes it's like being a journalist. You're basically almost doorstepping people to get their answers. But it doesn't always work that way. With *May the Road Rise Up* (2018), which was about homelessness, I thought I could do it from the outside, doing it with someone who worked with homeless people instead of interviewing people. But I found that I also needed to go to a homeless centre. So it's sometimes about visualizing things as well as talking to people, and it's very important to go to a place to understand that, I think.

With *Planet Belfast* (2013), I had an idea about the environment and that the planet could potentially be destroyed. I thought of two characters, one who was a historian writing books about the Troubles, and the other an environmentalist MLA [Member of the Legislative Assembly], so a politician. The historian gets a job in a trauma centre [a cross community support service for people bereaved, injured or traumatized as a result of the Troubles conflicts in Northern Ireland] trying to help people with the Troubles instead. And I went to the Belfast trauma centre one day to see what it was like, and it was empty. I could see for myself that there were millions of pounds being pumped into this, and I looked at their entrance list and there was hardly anyone visiting, and that was a fascinating thing for me. Sometimes you only need to do one day of research and it blows your mind, because one day can give you everything that you want to know.

For that play, Tinderbox had the budget to do proper development, and [their dramaturg] Hanna Slättne would have given me advice. I think actually she got me to do writing exercises. I don't do writing exercises, I don't list any characters, I don't do any of these things, I just write through voice. I prefer to find my way and feel my way blindly, that's how I like to approach writing, because I think it's more surprising, and I want to be surprised when I write. So Hanna would have given me proper exercises, what is this person like, or what the person likes and hates, or what is the goal of this scene. I had to do a bit of work, write some things for the next day, change the script a little based on the exercises and see what happened. For me, that's a little more experimental. I did quite like it, and it really helped me in general, because the script was tighter earlier in the process, rehearsals were so much easier and less fraught, and there was the chance of more development money in the future.

30 November 2023
Interviewed by Karen Quigley

## Questions and Prompts #4

- How do you know when a piece of work is finished? Is it ever finished?
- Might your process benefit from working with a dramaturg? How could you fold a dramaturg into your R&D practice or into a devising process?
- If you are working without a director, how can you make sure that staging offers and ideas in R&D are made thoughtfully and generously to those performing?
- How might you draw on your own life as inspiration in your theatre-making work? Who in your life might be affected by this, and how might you navigate it with them?
- When you get to the stage of sharing 'work in progress', how can you elicit feedback from your audiences in a way that is most useful to the ongoing development of your work?
- Remember that you're working on R&D even when you're not in a specific R&D session – ideas or breakthroughs may come to you at other moments as they percolate while you're doing other things or while your brain is at rest.
- If a particular project seems to be taking a number of years to find its form, or find its feet, how can you think about a long life cycle? Are there small pots of funding you can apply to, in order to access a day or a week of time for R&D? How can you and your collaborators continue to connect?
- If immersive research in/with a particular community is appropriate for your project, how can you conduct this in a way that is safe, considerate and generative for everyone involved? Who can support you in this?
- If you're a writer working as part of an R&D process, what are the parameters of your role? How might you agree ways of working in advance?

9

# Questions, materiality and negotiation

## The role of the designer in R&D

### Katherine Graham

Recent years have seen a significant expansion of research about performance design, with the 'scenographic turn' ensuring that design is 'formally instated as a significant contributor to the production of knowledge' (Collins and Aronson, 2015: 2). This chapter, then, enters a context in which ideas relating to the agency of scenography and scenographic materials have been firmly established in subject literature. Scenography is an unfolding temporal phenomenon entangled with all other elements of performance, generating both meaning-making and sensory experience. While current scholarship secures the dynamism of scenography as a phenomenon of performance,[1] the kinds of research conducted *by designers themselves* have to date received limited critical and professional attention. Design is widely understood as a process, both in live performance, where it emerges in conversation with all other elements, and in the creative processes of theatre-making. Drawing from Elin Diamond's articulation of performance as 'both a doing and a thing done' (1996: 1), for example, Hannah and Harsløf explore what design can 'effectively *do* as a practice (a doing) and as a production (a thing done)?' (2008: 13, emphasis in original). This chapter aims to sit with the 'doing', unpicking the role of designers in collaborative settings from the initial stages of a project. I explore the work of designers, drawing on interviews with professionals and reflections on my own practice, to recognize that scenography is, as Irwin argues, 'part of a complex network of creative actions and things within both a theatrical apparatus and a fluctuating and interdependent social context where meaning is anything but fixed and stable' (2017: 111). In this way, this chapter aims to draw from research about design, to illuminate the detailed and impactful research – and development – conducted by designers.

As Stephen Di Benedetto observes, designers 'seem mysterious to actors and audience because their work takes place out of sight. Where do their ideas come from? Why do they make the choices they do?' (2012: 8). This appears to be a tension felt in both directions, with designer Grace Smart writing that 'endless discussion with

---

[1] Examples of this scholarship include: McKinney and Palmer (2017); Aronson (2017); Hann (2019); Graham, Palmer and Zezulka (2023).

designers [has] led me to one overwhelming thought: set and costume designers feel as though no one knows what we do' (2018). The role and remit of designers in performance-making is demonstrably less studied than the practices of their directing, writing or performing counterparts. Analyses of performance design often linger with the ways in which the work is or might be encountered in performance (McKinney 2015) and where scholarship has focused on more processual aspects of design practice (Zezulka 2023; Hunt 2013; Palmer and Popat 2007), this has rarely been through a lens of research and development (R&D).

The work of performance designers is accounted for, broadly, in two camps across existing research. Handbooks and manuals addressing designers and directors tend to position design development as a relatively linear process, often preceding rehearsals, where script analysis yields key concepts, augmented by collaboration with a director and later, potentially, nuanced by observation of rehearsals (DiBenedetto 2012; Porter 2015; Pavelka 2015; Palmer 1994). This model remains relatively commonplace in mainstream theatre practices, where funding models often dictate that a stage design be developed long in advance of rehearsals, through an established process that moves from conversation, to exploratory 'white card' stage models, through to full models and final construction. Elsewhere, contemporary research in scenography is replete with examples of scholar-practitioners leading development of performances or performance-experiments through (and as) practice research (Shearing 2023, 2019; Shyldkrot 2023; Penna 2017; McKinney 2015; Palmer and Popat 2007). These examples illuminate scenography's capacity to become performance (Shearing 2019; Palmer and Popat 2007), to foster relational encounters among audience members (Shyldkrot 2023), to model modes of cognition (Penna 2017) and to generate relational encounters between scenographic materials and audience (McKinney 2015; Shearing 2023). The range of this research speaks to a sophistication of design thinking and practice that warrants further examination of the creative labour undertaken by designers.

This chapter explores the material practices of design research and development in work that falls between these two frameworks – that of R&D in collaborative theatre practice. For designers working in this context R&D can be quite fluid, sometimes clearly defined (and funded) as an exploratory period, sometimes embedded more amorphously across the life of a project. Equally, designers may work in or beyond their own disciplines in R&D as hierarchies and boundaries between creative departments may be productively dismantled. To explore design R&D, then, is to distinguish the practice itself from any potential or actual resulting design on stage and hence to observe the work of designers in terms of creation, dramaturgy and company culture. In this way, thinking through the creative labour of R&D, or what it is to work away from rehearsals, can provide, as Gay McAuley puts it, 'vivid insights into the dynamically shifting and contingent nature of theatrical meaning-making' (2008: 277). Design R&D occupies a creatively rich position in collaborative theatre-making, where its meaning-making practices involve generating new possibilities in conversation with developments from other departments. As is made clear throughout this book, R&D is a fecund site for exploring the relationships and practices of theatre-making more widely. In this context, I am especially interested in Daniel Johnston's idea of theatre and performance as being a kind of 'manual philosophy', that the kinds of questions theatre-making invites – about the nature of a world, about the rules of behaviour in a given context – inherently involve a kind of philosophy in action, exposing 'how the world reveals itself to consciousness in different ways and how these are uncovered through some acting processes' (2017: 23). This chapter argues that such questioning about the ways in which being and representation might operate is as pertinent to design as to acting processes, and that design practice is, accordingly, as creatively consequential as the more studied areas of acting, writing and directing.

In thinking through R&D in this context I reflect on my own practice as an embedded lighting designer with the visual theatre company, Theatre Re, and place reflections on my own practice in conversation with interviews with others, mainly stage and costume designers, and published accounts from designers and design practitioners. Though I do not mean to present or enforce disciplinary boundaries across fields of design, there are productive points of resistance and slippage between the ways in which R&D manifests across material (broadly, stage and costume) and immaterial forms (in this case, light), and these tensions gesture towards larger thinking about materiality, certainty and metaphor in performance-making. By interweaving some reflections on my work with light with accounts from other designers, this chapter presents a plurality of voices as a means of illuminating the breadth of design R&D in contemporary British theatre-making and brings to the fore the hidden creative and dramaturgical labour of design.

## Research, development and R&D

Research is integral to performance design practice, manifesting in a range of forms and structures depending on the designer and the production context. As Alison Oddey writes, the 'collaborative, cooperative working relationship' between director and designer builds from 'a successful prior-rehearsal understanding' (2009: 89). This 'prior-rehearsal' work may or may not be officially designated as R&D and is often subsumed under preparatory work that directors and designers undertake in line with production and construction timescales. In this way, designers' processes of R&D are often rendered invisible despite revealing what director Phyllida Lloyd calls 'the architecture of the piece' (in Oddey 2009: 89), that is, determining not only physical structures but also the relationships between story, space and body. This model of prior-rehearsal work aligns with the majority of handbooks written as guides for both directors and designers and tends to imply a need for designers to conduct their own R&D behind closed doors, with exploration absorbed into the initial work of script interpretation, historical research or conceptual propositions. This can push design practice into the margins, and force early fixing of ideas without scope for play, negotiation or risk-taking.

Forms of research for designers often include spatial and visual provocations. Shizuka Hariu's design work is informed by her practice-led PhD research in which she used architectural methods to develop scenography. In this process, she tells me, research comes first, describing a methodical process that begins before an initial meeting with a director or choreographer and continues through rehearsals. Careful consideration of the physical performance environment is integral to Hariu's practice, and she will examine the qualities of a space alongside its background and history. From that point, her research shifts to sketching and 3D modelling of the space, embedding precise physical details such as height, depth and obstacles into her earliest sketches for a potential design (Hariu 2024).

Sketching is also a key feature of research for Eleanor Field, who tends to 'bring into the space a lot of visual offerings' and 'do a lot of drawing during research and development' (Field 2024). In addition to bringing material into the space of R&D, Field has also 'occasionally taken actors and directors to particular art exhibitions and prompted them to see different things or watch a particular film to get a glimpse of something I'm thinking'. Across both of these practices, then, R&D often manifests as a kind of visual thinking. Designers may work in a way that is alert to the dynamics of an individual space or the ways in which other reference points might seep into a creative practice and develop and share these insights through tangible images.

Design R&D may also extend beyond such visual practice. 'One of the hardest things about live theatre', writes Grace Smart, is 'that it continues to grow and change and evolve' (Smart 2022). Design is a process in constant flux, evolving in relation to developments in the action, changes in a script and/or shifting performance dynamics. Talking me through her process for a recent production, *Dark with Excessive Bright* (2024), Shizuka Hariu shares that 'in between white card and the final design I made, I don't know how many versions, maybe 19 or 20'. The piece, part of the Festival of New Choreography for the Royal Ballet, was performed on the floor of the auditorium of the Royal Opera House's Linbury Theatre, with seats removed so that the audience could move around the dancers freely. Hariu had to compose a stage that would sit within the expanded architectural space, invite freedom of movement for the audience and simultaneously demarcate zones for the dancers to move in safely. This reflects a wider trend in Hariu's work; often her research dwells in questions of bodies and sites, especially in dance where the 'choreographer and I are going to speak in numbers: "so what do you think here, there are going to be like two or three dancers, then this part is going to have five different dancers coming together"'. As we speak about *Dark with Excessive Bright* Hariu shows me some of the computer renderings for the versions accumulated through R&D, each one articulating the space differently, with sweeping gestural structures of hanging steel cords. The process, as she describes it, is both artistic and technical, simultaneously exploring how the audience might experience these structures and working closely with production and technical managers to work through numerous permutations of their construction. The significant number of reimaginings and revisions is indicative of the labour involved in design work and the high degree of skill with which Hariu has shaped this performance. Through a protracted and detailed development process, Hariu's design work offered a series of visions of possibility towards what would define the experience of the resulting performance.

Nor does development necessarily cease when a production officially opens. Eleanor Field recounts an experience of working on *A Family Business* by Chris Thorpe (2022–4) in which the premiere performances sparked further R&D on the piece before it was remounted. The first performances revealed opportunities and possibilities: 'we knew there was loads more that the set could do and actually watching the cast on it gave me so many ideas of how the design could have been pushed even further'. Invited to remount the production in the same venue the following year, the company in fact insisted on completing a new phase of R&D before going back into rehearsals, 'so we were able to really push design aspects in a way I hadn't before because you never get to have a trial run on the actual stage'. This incident of R&D continuing even after the first run resulted in both changes to the physical structure of the set – an extraordinary, and somehow beautiful, mass of tangled cables – and the ways in which the performers interacted with it, demonstrating an ongoing conversation between a production's materiality and its dramaturgy. For Field, returning to a process of R&D on a production that had already been staged was immensely generative – 'we can make *this* even more exciting, and *this* can do more' – and evinces ways in which integrative collaborative R&D sustains momentum and discovery and underlines how scenographic and directorial decisions are entwined.

In my own lighting design practice, similarly iterative phases of development on and offstage have been fundamental to the work. As an immaterial material, light occupies a peculiarly liminal space in the development of performance in general and Theatre Re's work in particular, because the company's approach to R&D emphasizes material specificity. This is research through action; there is very little discussion in a Theatre Re R&D, but rather work is discovered via movement. While it is conceptually important to the company that everybody starts together in an act of collective imagining and experimentation, there is a clear discrepancy between how performers and musicians are able to work and my design practice in this context. For performers and musicians, the link between exploration and action is immediate and tangible. Musician, Alex Judd, for instance, will have his instruments and will compose and play original music in the room, both responding to what the actors are doing and providing triggers for new ways in which their work might develop. Likewise, director Guillaume Pigé will use particular props or pieces of furniture as prompts from the earliest point in the devising process, and this material engagement will shape the discovery of character, action and story. Light, however, comes into actuality only in the performance space, often under intense time pressure and after other materials have been finalized. It is often, as lighting designer Peter Mumford describes it, 'the last creative act' of making theatre (in Moran 2017: 49). In the early stages of R&D, therefore, I tend to occupy a kind of dual position, present in the room as a kind of dramaturg while imaginatively holding potential provocations of light. In this context, moving from the R&D studio to the stage and back again facilitates a cycle of thinking about and with the materiality of performance that generates the detail of the work.

To give a particular example, in late 2015 we began R&D on a piece that would become *The Nature of Forgetting*, which premiered at the London International Mime Festival in January 2017, then ran as part of the British Council Edinburgh Showcase that August and has since toured extensively. The question from which that performance grew was 'what is left when memory is gone?' and early R&D was informed by our collaboration with the neuroscientist Professor Kate Jeffery who shared ideas about memory and the brain. She explained that the hippocampus is a region of the brain that drives memory, and that it functions like a workshop, in which the components of a memory are reassembled each time it is recalled. That idea unlocked the central metaphor of our production – a mini stage on the stage that could function in precisely this way. Another insight from Jeffery (in my understanding) was that when something is forgotten it does not disappear from the brain, but rather the connection to it breaks. I found that concept both incredibly moving and inspiring. The ideas of something being present but inaccessible, and of the repeated construction of memory yielding a sense of instability or impermanence, correlate so immediately with light's capacity to transform and manipulate the presence of things onstage that it suggested a clear intervention that I might make with light.

This research inflected how I thought about light in the ensuing R&D, providing a lens through which to shape interventions with light around the action. When, much later in the process, a story and a set of characters emerged, it became clear that the piece was about a man grasping onto scenes from his earlier life in the face of memory loss. The emergence of this narrative and emotional material suggested a particular orientation of light, one that could slip between clarity and transformation. But it was not until work-in-progress sharings at Lincoln Drill Hall (June 2016) and Bracknell's South Hill Park Arts Centre (July 2016) that I was able to develop these ideas on stage, with material light. Individually, these periods of technical development were subject to the intensities of pressure common to all creative processes; there is never quite enough time to fulfil the detail, the process is always being torn between diverting new discoveries and the drive to ready something for a public sharing. Cumulatively, however, they create pockets of expansion in which the work can develop. Another lighting designer, Chris Swain, describes an analogous process of extended periods of R&D in his work with Gecko, through which his lighting and the show become 'more nuanced', developing 'aspects which you just wouldn't be able [to] in a week's tech' (Swain 2024: 17). In developing *Kin*, Swain reports having weeks of R&D in a 'resourced warehouse' (2024: 16) enabling the light to move apace with other elements, but this is unfortunately not a standard model. Like Field's experience with *A Family Business*, *The Nature of Forgetting* has enjoyed a long creative afterlife, and the work, and especially the light, has been revised, developed and nuanced through subsequent tours and performances. In this vein, early performances in particular extended R&D into the auditorium, with the resources of production and audience responses feeding back into ongoing development and discovery that manifestly changed and refined the work itself. During the month-long run at the Edinburgh Festival Fringe, for instance, and unusually for a lighting designer, I operated the light at every performance and made substantial changes to cue composition and timing throughout. In this way these public performances became a kind of extended R&D for me in which I discovered new rhythms and possibilities that, in turn, shaped and supported new discoveries for the performers.

This expansion of R&D throughout the creative lifespan of a project is also advocated by Simon Donger who argues that 'the entire creative process from beginning to end can be a form of research if we allow ourselves to keep discovering and developing from these discoveries until the work is completed' (2018: 129). Unusually in the field of design, Donger explicitly traces his R&D work on a project, *Wearable Shadows* (2011), moving from an initial interest, through cycles of laboratory experimentation and historical research, towards a public performance. In this particular case, Donger began from an initial interest in peripheral, concealed or negative spaces, thinking about how the darkness of a black box theatre space provides a 'radical exposure' to negative space as a 'presence' (2018: 129). From here, he traced his initial interest backwards – finding a historical precedent in Loïe Fuller, whose performances in the early 1900s merged dance, light and fabric through specially patented costume and projection technology – and forward, through producing drawings and then embodied experiments with light, the body and space (2018: 136). While Donger's project was wholly led by material exploration with and through design, there are clear parallels with the intricacy of design R&D in collaborative theatrical contexts. The process Donger describes moves both outward – through historical and contextual research – and inward – through direct experimentation that shapes the work materially. This outward (towards external references, associations and contexts) and inward (following the felt and affective possibilities of the stuff of design itself) duality is evident in different ways at all stages of the scenographic process. For designers working in theatre companies, outward and inward R&D involves the kind of contextual and material work described by Donger but may also encompass broader dramaturgical and collaborative questions such as storytelling and the relationship(s) between design and all other elements of production. Crucially, the interrelationship and entanglements between design and other areas of performance may continue to shift across the life cycle of a project and may manifest very differently during R&D and on stage.

## Collaboration: Directors, designers and ensembles of practice

Processes of R&D in theatre frequently rely on collaborative overlaps and intersections with creative partners. 'Designers are supreme collaborators' who can 'blend and unify the various ideas in the room', writes Grace Smart (2020). In practical terms, individual designers most often work alongside directors (generally considered the creative leaders of a given project) but also have significant working relationships with other designers, associates, assistants, production managers, technicians and performers. Frequently designers will work across a number of productions simultaneously, because design fees, often calculated at a flat rate across a project regardless of the hours worked, are rarely sufficient to enable exclusive focus.[2]

Funded periods of R&D can open up a different model with designers and design teams receiving weekly attendance fees in line with directors and performers. As Selina Thompson argues elsewhere in this book, integrating designers into initial periods of R&D means that their work can be 'a part of the *thought*. I want what my designers are doing to also shape the writing and everything else' (p. 35). Or, as designer Es Devlin puts it, 'the visual world that tells the story, and the relationship between director,

---

[2] In a guest blog post for the Society of British Theatre Designers, for instance, Daniel Bye advocates for better pay and conditions for designers, noting 'Divide your designer's fee by the time they've actually spent on the work and you'll terrifyingly often find they're barely making minimum wage' (2020).

designer, writer and the work itself, is the crucible where the work is made' (Devlin 2023).

In this way, formal, collaborative phases of R&D enable direct exchange between designers and an entire ensemble, opening up productive points of cross-fertilization unavailable in the more linear models discussed earlier. The actor Gary Sloan, for instance, writes that designers 'always seemed more a part of the director's world than mine until they themselves broke through my ignorance with an interest in my own process or ideas about the play' (2012: 112). Wales-based designer, Ruth Stringer, recounts a particularly cogent example of R&D opening up meaningful interplay between performers and design as part of R&D for the dance piece, *Fabulous Animals* (Joon Dance 2023). For that project, emerging from accidental and practical discoveries about what the performance needed from costume, Stringer became interested in ideas of 'abstracting recognisable clothes' so that the dancers might wear pieces 'the wrong way', such as a 'dancer wearing high heels on their hands and their feet' (2024). To explore this idea, the company played with clothes extensively in R&D, using pieces donated by those in the room or bought from charity shops, experimenting with 'fashion show'-type exercises in which the performers would extract things to wear from a pile of clothes and try them on in unusual ways. Stringer reflects that, through the playfulness of this exercise, the dancers 'came with really brilliant things that I never would have thought about if I had just been in my studio with the mannequin, so it was really, really vital to have that time'. Moreover, having that time to play together and to experiment directly with material options for the clothing meant that the dancers 'were able to trust in the idea' and interacting with costume in this way meant that 'everybody was really on board with it'. Here, R&D enabled not only shared creative exploration across design and performance but also a deeper sense of agency and ownership for the dancers about what and how they would wear costume. For Stringer, this 'space for conversation' between the material and the performer is both conceptual and practical, attending to both how a performer feels about their costume in terms of character and atmosphere and also how a costume facilitates the movement required for dancers.

This structure extends into wider design networks, too. Ruth Hall is an accomplished associate designer, who reflects on the process of being 'the next person along' (Hall 2024). As an associate, working closely with a designer on a production, Hall's work often occurs 'alongside a process that's already happening and [some aspect of it] needs a bit more specialised attention. Where a designer might be doing the overall, I can be delegated to look specifically at a certain prop or problem and figure out the best way to make it work'. Like some of the other examples discussed here, this work flows in and out of the R&D studio as associate designers straddle creative and technical teams, working with designers, actors, technicians and carpenters. Hall notes that the tendency in industry to bring those working in associate roles on board at a much later stage can be 'like tying their arms behind their backs', whereas being involved from the very beginning expands possibilities in terms of sustainability, feasibility, and 'if you've got a stronger, better thought-through overview, it allows more creativity [when the work reaches] the rehearsal room'. The relationship between designers and associates, Hall says, is like a 'cottage industry' where 'you're not employed formally and there's no safety net'. This precarity was brought into sharp relief by the Covid pandemic when 'all of a sudden we all lost all of our work and it was quite a shock'. During the pandemic, Hall was instrumental as part of *Scene Change*, a community of theatre designers that began via an informal network of emails in April 2020. Within weeks of forming, inspired by the hazard tape erected at the National Theatre to keep people away, and 'making it look like a toxic site' (Fleischle 2020), the group staged a scenographic intervention, *#MissingLiveTheatre*, wrapping 110 closed theatre venues in specially designed hot pink hazard tape in a visual gesture that 'reaffirmed just how powerful art can be' (ibid.). As part of a network of action and events, Hall led a consultation with a group of design associates to share experiences and develop a set of guidelines of best practice for the role. This document, originally published on the *Scene Change* website, argues that the role of design associates 'should be recognised and valued as a profession in its own right' (Hall 2022: 2). It also provides clear definitions for the previously nebulously used terms 'associate' and 'assistant' and lays out minimum expectations about the terms of the labour involved, including pay, contracts, crediting, scheduling and working environment. While not all of the recommendations have yet been formalized in industry, Hall reflects that 'the sense of being part of a bigger community has helped people to be a bit bolder in asking for better'. In a period of hiatus for the theatre industry, the wider *Scene Change* movement (and allied organizations like *Freelancers Make Theatre Work*) took space to agitate for change in the theatre industry. Though Hall does not discuss *Scene Change* in these terms, I think that the movement itself can be thought of as a kind of R&D in which designers gathered to reflect on working practices, to translate tacit professional knowledge into political activism and to make the case for the value of the labour that underpins the creative industries.

This sense of interplay between designers and other artists is a recurring idea in all of the interviews conducted and collated for this chapter, highlighting the ways in which R&D fosters generative networks of ideas and practices in collaborative theatre-making. Stressing the importance of 'storytelling' and 'deeper expression', for instance, designer Katrina Lindsay argues that theatre 'is collaborative and at its best it's about all the disciplines being able to knit together' (in Hoggard 2021). This kind of knitting together is a core tenet of R&D for Eleanor Field, who tells me that collaboration in R&D demonstrates 'that designers aren't just about providing the aesthetic' but rather aim to find ways to 'offer something that's more of a playground', enabling a more dramaturgical sense of design and 'how it can feed into the story too'. For Shizuka Hariu this responsiveness involves direct conversation between her own early ideas and those of the directors she works with: 'in the theatre, I think the directors who choose me to work with are often a little bit more flexible, I think, because my design is a bit more abstract. So they often give me no restriction at the white card stage and then see how I imagine the space, and then they respond'. Here, design ideas might cascade into directorial possibilities, rather than design responding to a fixed brief.

Moreover, this shared dramaturgical endeavour of collaborative R&D does not always mean straightforward, additive exchanges. As discussed in the introduction to this book, and many other chapters in it, the moments of failure, disjuncture and slippage that are opened up in R&D create departure points that can generate new ways of thinking. Field reflects that, though 'as designers we're taught that we have to be able to visually communicate perfectly', 'misinterpretation is a gift in R&D'. In the context of R&D, insulated somewhat from the pressures of public performance, 'there's amazing opportunities in putting something in front of someone and them misinterpreting it and seeing something completely different in your work'. For Donger, 'uncertainty is critical because it opens up the doors to creative exploration and development' (2018: 11). Yet, while he clearly advocates for exploratory work of this nature in one's own design practice, he also cautions designers to collate visual material in a way that will avoid 'misunderstandings' (2018: 110) in collaborative contexts. There is a tension here that speaks to conflicts in a designer's position within theatrical hierarchies. As Christin Essin notes, 'the complexity and significance' of backstage labour have been 'mostly overlooked, misunderstood, or deemed unworthy of examination' (2021: 9). Examining the work of lighting designers and programmers as a particular subsection of this backstage labour, Kelli Zezulka observes that 'the lighting profession's historic and continued marginalization' (2023: 107) impacts on the degree of agency designers are understood to have in their work. In this context, Field's observation of the power of misinterpretation is especially significant. While design in R&D might sit anywhere in the continuum 'from the more traditional role of designer as the visual interpreter of a director or writer's idea at the start, to the designer contributing a significant input from the beginning to a devising process that explores and develops visual ideas' (Oddey 1994: 60), designers themselves may occupy a more fluid role in the development of performance. This fluidity is facilitated by the kinds of collaborative R&D processes, discussed above, where designers develop their work alongside other creative partners, perhaps 'allowing something to be a first domino' (Field 2024) rather than presenting a fixed or final design for a company of actors to work around in rehearsal.

## Metaphor, meaning-making and negotiation

Offered as an example rather than an exemplar, my own practice with Theatre Re provides a productive lens through which to unpick some of the complexities of R&D in design practice, offering a view of the ways in which the detail of a design score emerges alongside and around other elements of storytelling. All of the company's work to date has been devised collaboratively, through iterative cycles of R&D. For Oddey, the devising process begins with a stimulus of some kind, where the group of collaborators 'absorbs the source material, responds to it, and then generates a method of working appropriate to the initial aims of the company and project' (1994: 24). This aligns with the processes described by a number of prominent devising companies, which often talk about starting from a shared reference point, an image or an atmosphere – for example in the work of Gecko (Mermikides and Smart 2010: 171) and Frantic Assembly (Evans and Smith 2021: 34). However, every Theatre Re process begins with a question rather than defined source material. This sense of questioning mobilizes a particular approach to R&D, as each of us engages in distinct but overlapping processes of research in response to a shared starting point.

Starting from a question, or a pair of questions, rather than a distinct stimulus, image or idea, yields both an openness to early R&D work and a vertiginous sense of vulnerability. The kinds of questions with which we start a process are often rather open: 'why do we do what we do?' (*Moments*, 2024); 'why live theatre?' and 'how do we care for those born after us?' (*Bluebelle*, 2021); 'when does memory begin?' and 'what is passed down from one generation to the next?' (*BIRTH*, 2019). That these questions are broad can be both daunting and freeing. As a designer, my interest in light lies in its transformative and temporal qualities – its ability to shift and flow through stage action and to respond to moment-by-moment changes in story, space and feeling. My interest in these transformative qualities of light means that I am more driven by its affective qualities than by visual or pictorial uses. In this context, starting from a question liberates me from loyalty to an image, or visual reference, and invites a more oblique approach to research. This approach tends to involve shifting between amassing tangential and associative research material to later attempt to translate into light and responding to developments that emerge among performers, music and props.

The development of *BIRTH* through a series of phases of R&D between 2017 and 2019 provides a good example of the creative dualities that characterize the liminal position of light in this context. From very early in the process, the actors were working with a piece of fabric that was large enough to almost cover the full stage. This yielded many visual possibilities and became a cornerstone of the stagecraft of the eventual production; we later added a second piece of fabric to develop this gesture further. The opportunities and possibilities of the fabric were explored by the cast in R&D, and they grew into a visual language where the fabric would sweep or billow across the stage, while setting or characters would change around it. Most of this work happened in bright, airy rehearsal rooms, and so the visual language developed around the actors' manipulation of the fabric in the absence of stage light. Had there been more time to work together in the early stages, we would have found more integrative opportunities for light and fabric to work together. But this work was already so specific by the time we had the chance to play with light for an early work-in-progress sharing in July 2017 that light mainly served to manipulate the appearance of the work already established, missing, I think, opportunities for more substantive exchange between light and action.

Conversely, that same work-in-progress sharing afforded a more productive example of failure in R&D. A narrative that had emerged at this point centred around pregnancy and loss, and one of the performers had discovered a potential image, curling up with the fabric covering him in such a way that it looked like the screen of an ultrasound. Seduced by the potential of this image, we had placed it as the final moment in the performance, hoping that light would solidify the reference. The way that I had planned to do this simply did not work in the space. With more time to play together we would certainly have found a way to draw body, fabric and light together to complete this image. However, the failure of light in this instance in fact revealed that the image was tonally wrong for the story that we had found. As a visual metaphor, the image of a foetal ultrasound equated a happy ending with the idea of a new pregnancy. Abandoning that image enabled us to end the story with the couple reconnecting after loss, rather than associating 'success' with a subsequent pregnancy. Here, a failure in design and technical terms led to a more fitting kind of positivity and hope for the story – one which allowed us to take better care of our audience in the context of the subject matter.

The practice of lighting design is by necessity one that straddles technical and dramaturgical facets of theatre-making, alongside substantive and ephemeral scenographic elements. This positions the task of R&D for the lighting designer, in my experience and more broadly, as a kind of negotiation. It involves negotiation between the space of the rehearsal room and the stage, between the rhythms of work in development and potential interjections of lighting cues, between light-based responses to research and the unfolding of other material. This interstitial creative practice means that lighting designers often operate in what we might think of as a doubly contingent space: working with a material that is itself contingent and unstable and developing that work in contexts where that material is often (usually) unavailable. In airy rehearsal rooms, filled with daylight, lighting designers negotiate between the material performance work unfolding and an imagined response through an already slippery and ephemeral medium.

This negotiation between imagination and materiality is acute in the case of light but is also applicable in other disciplines of design. As Rosie Elnile makes clear in the interview that follows this chapter, the challenge of developing a production without opportunity for performers to engage with set materials until technical rehearsals creates profound challenges for stage designers, often to the detriment of a design's dramaturgical framing (p. 144). These tensions emerge as a result of funding limitations, in spite of wider scholarly understandings of expanded and increasingly scenographic ways of understanding dramaturgy. Trencsényi and Cochrane position dramaturgy as 'the inner flow of a dynamic system' (2014: xi), pointing to an expanded understanding of dramaturgy that sits in a 'wider paradigm' of ideas that are, among other things, post-mimetic and process-conscious (ibid.). This paradigm of dramaturgical thinking and practice flattens hierarchies of meaning-making across all elements of performance-making and is especially applicable to scenography as a practice that entwines aesthetics, ethics and dramaturgy. There is, therefore, dramaturgical potential to be mined in resourcing design materials in R&D. Reflecting on the relationship between director Simon McBurney and designer Tom Pye, for instance, Oddey observes a 'radical use of technology' (2009: 95) in which the 'excitement for Pye as the designer' lies in material exploration, 'to not have stipulated every idea but to see what happens with the tools made available' (96). This sense of a creative exchange in which design materials become tools for an ensemble to play and experiment with articulates a generative process in which shared thinking can lead in unexpected and often fruitful directions.

The potential of material exploration also lies in the particularity and untranslatability of design materials. Director Phyllida Lloyd talks about a process with design as one that invites 'that un-definable thing to emerge', that can't be found in discussion but rather '[y]ou have got to get in there, and put something in there and look at it' (in Oddey 2009: 99). This also chimes with observations from the designers I spoke with for this chapter. Eleanor Field reflects that design thinking offers 'something that's really malleable and less pin-downable' and that, in practice, she has accordingly 'learned to not over-explain, or overprescribe but just to sort of bring something in and then step back and watch and let other people have at it, and take different things from it'. Ruth Stringer talks about trying 'to think more in shapes and colours and tones' as a designer in R&D, particularly towards the development of new work, where she aims 'to give suggestions of shapes and colours and textures rather than a historical context or something like a social context, it just helps with not boxing the process in, visually, too soon'. This kind of associative framing of design is echoed by Rosie Elnile in this volume, who says that design 'is closer to the language of poetry, or of association or suggestion, rather than literal description' (p. 144). R&D can enable richer and more textured, and 'just cleverer' (Hall 2024) associations to emerge in a company's material language and stronger dramaturgical connections between designers and performers.

## Conclusion

Addressing a context where the creative labour of designers is often obscured, or where designers are assumed to do their thinking at a remove from the work of other members of a theatre ensemble, this chapter has illustrated the multiple ways in which design R&D can generatively intersect with wider collaborative practices. In doing this, I have interwoven reflections on my own practice with the voices and views of a range of other designers through both original and collated interview material. The insights from practitioners here serve to reveal the networks of labour involved in work of this nature. As Ruth Hall so succinctly puts it, 'theatre is a gang, like, it's much better if it's about collaboration and you've got different people in the room with different skills that all come together'. Through the reflections included here, what emerges is a sense of the interconnectedness of creative endeavour in theatre-making. Grace Smart's sense that designers are underestimated or misunderstood – 'that nobody knows we run large teams. That we do dramaturgy, we come up with concepts, we know how much a show costs and manage the budget, or that we line up whole personal seasons of work' (Smart 2018) – starts to be offset here by these collected voices, though there remains more to be explored about this area. Implicit in the argument of this chapter, then, is a call for the wider recognition of the collaborative and dramaturgical potential of design labour and for funding structures to recognize the value of resourced time for all company members.

In exploring design R&D in collaborative theatre contexts, this chapter has illustrated a number of points of slippage and resistance. Open-ended exploratory phases of design can be complicated for designers in under-resourced settings. The materiality of scenographic practice can be rendered immaterial when designers are expected to work without the stuff of their designs. Equally the tendency in mainstream theatre to seek to finalize designs before rehearsals begin can also elide R&D possibilities for designers, placing individual research and development practices at a remove from other artists in a theatre company. However, these points of slippage and resistance might also be generative. Moments of failure, misinterpretation and the unexpected can yield new discoveries and demonstrate a direct relationship between scenographic offers and dramaturgical insights. The budgetary constraints placed on design practice can also open up opportunities for designers to extend their R&D work into performance, when this is appropriate to the company model in question. For R&D to blur into the entire life cycle of a project enables designers to continue to reimagine the spatial, dramaturgical and ethical dimensions of their work in performance – using the resources of production to negotiate across previously imagined potential and felt, affective performance in real time. In so doing, designers can harness the ethos of R&D throughout every stage of a project to meaningfully co-construct experience with actors, directors and audiences.

In this context, light is an especially contingent material but its contingency also makes plain that all design is contingent on its material conditions and relies on a precise interplay of qualities and associations that emerge across the confluence of materials in performance. In this vein, the role of design in theatre R&D is at least partially one of negotiation – of navigating potential between the real and the imagined. In the slippage between the material and the potential, space opens up for mistakes, misinterpretation and failures. All of these can be productive discoveries in R&D, making it possible to see things in new and unexpected ways. Away from the pressure of public performances these surprises and frustrations can create space for discovery and innovation. In this way, design is a fundamentally transformative performance language operating alongside and overlapping the work of performers, composers and directors, both responding to and prompting developments in other areas of creative practice.

Theatre-making is an artform of space and time, therefore it matters how objects and bodies are held in space and in relation to each other. How objects, bodies, spaces and ideas show up on stage is not a question of decoration but of dramaturgy. This is as true in R&D as it is in performance. Design is a significant contributor to the emergence of meaning and offers from designers in R&D can yield new avenues of thinking and provide framing metaphors that shape work in development. Design makes space in every possible sense of the phrase; it is a practice that shapes and produces the spaces in which performances unfold, it is an art of manipulating environments to allow for particular readings or associations to come to the fore, and in the process of R&D design and designers can make space for new ideas, connections and possibilities across a company.

## References

Aronson, A., ed. (2017), *The Routledge Companion to Scenography Aronson*, London: Routledge.

Bye, D. (2020), 'In Solidarity with Designers', *Society of British Theatre Designers Blog*, 24 November. https://www.theatredesign.org.uk/in-solidarity-with-designers/ (accessed 10 April 2024).

Collins, J. and A. Aronson (2015), 'Editors' Introduction', *Theatre and Performance Design*, 1 (1–2): 1–6.

Devlin, E. (2023), 'Interview with Liz Hoggard', *The Stage*, 2 November. https://www.thestage.co.uk/big-interviews/es-devlin-its-hard-to-imagine-another-garment-that-would-have-fitted-me-as-well-as-theatre-beyonce-superbowl-leham-triology (accessed 29 February 2024).

Diamond, E. (1996), *Performance and Cultural Politics*, London: Routledge.
Di Benedetto, S. (2012), *An Introduction to Theatre Design*, Oxford: Routledge.
Donger, S. (2018), *Scenography*, Marlborough: Crowood Press.
Essin, C. (2021), *Working Backstage: A Cultural History and Ethnography of Technical Theater Labor*, University of Michigan Press.
Evans, M. and M. Smith (2021), *Frantic Assembly*, London: Routledge.
Field, E. (2024), Unpublished interview with the author, 26 April.
Fleischle, A. (2020), 'How a Group of Designers Disrupted the UK's Dormant Theatre Industry with Endless Rolls of Pink Tape', *Independent*, 10 July. https://www.independent.co.uk/voices/theatre-arts-funding-designers-missing-live-theatre-scenechange-a9610996.html (accessed 31 July 2024).
Graham, K., S. Palmer and K. Zezulka, eds (2023), *Contemporary Performance Lighting: Experience, Creativity and Meaning*, London: Bloomsbury.
Hall, R. (2022), 'Scene/Change Guidelines for Employing Design Assistants and Associates', *Scene-Change.com*. https://web.archive.org/web/20230607103040/https://www.scene-change.com/post/team-talk (accessed 31 July 2024).
Hall, R. (2024), Unpublished interview with the author, 7 May.
Hann, R. (2019), *Beyond Scenography*, London: Routledge.
Hannah, D. and O. Harsløf (2008), *Performance Design,* Copenhagen: Museum Tusculanum Press.
Hariu, S. (2024), Unpublished interview with the author, 30 May.
Hoggard, L. (2021), 'Designer Katrina Lindsay: 'I Like the Aesthetic World But How the Story Unfolds is What Interests Me', *The Stage*, 7 December. https://www.thestage.co.uk/features/designer-katrina-lindsay-i-like-the-aesthetic-world-but-how-the-story-unfolds-is-what-interests-me (accessed 10 April 2024).
Hunt, N. (2013), 'Exosomatic (light) Organ: Creating and Using an "Expressive Instrument" for Theatre Lighting Control', *International Journal of Performance Arts and Digital Media*, 9 (2): 295–313.
Irwin, K. (2017), 'Scenographic Agency: A Showing-Doing and a Responsibility for Showing- Doing', in J. McKinney and S. Palmer (eds), *Scenography Expanded*, 111–24, London: Bloomsbury.
Johnston, D. (2017), *Theatre and Phenomenology: Manual Philosophy*, London: Bloomsbury.
McAuley, G. (2008), 'Not Magic but Work: Rehearsal and the Production of Meaning', *Theatre Research International*, 33 (3): 276–288.
McKinney, J. (2015), 'Vibrant Materials: The Agency of Things in the Context of Scenography', in M. Bleeker et al. (eds), *Performance and Phenomenology - Traditions and Transformations*, 121–39, London: Routledge.
McKinney, J. and S. Palmer, eds (2017), *Scenography Expanded*, London: Bloomsbury.
Mermikides, A. and J. Smart, eds (2010), *Devising in Process*, Basingstoke: Palgrave Macmillan.
Moran, N. (2017), *The Right Light: Interviews with Contemporary Lighting Designers*, London: Bloomsbury.
Oddey, A. (1994), *Devising Theatre: A Practical and Theoretical Handbook*, London: Routledge.
Oddey, A. (2009), 'The Organics of the Rehearsal Room: Contemporary Directing Practice and the Director-Designer Relationship', in C. A. White (ed.), *Directors and Designers*, 87–100, Bristol: Intellect Books.
Palmer, R. H. (1994), *The Lighting Art: The Aesthetics of Stage Lighting Design*, 2nd edn, Englewood Cliffs, N.J.: Prentice-Hall.

Palmer, S. (2013), *Light: Readings in Theatre Practice*, Basingstoke: Palgrave Macmillan.
Palmer, S. and S. Popat (2007), 'Dancing in the Streets: The Sensuous Manifold as a Concept for Designing Experience', *International Journal of Performance Arts and Digital Media*, 2 (3): 297–314.
Pavelka, M. (2015), *So You Want to Be a Theatre Designer?* London: Nick Hern Books.
Penna, X. (2017), *Towards a CogScenography: Cognitive Science, Scenographic Reception and Processes*, PhD Thesis, University of Leeds.
Porter, L. (2015), *Unmasking Theatre Design: A Designer's Guide to Finding Inspiration and Cultivating Creativity*, Oxon: Focal Press.
Shearing, D. (2019), 'Black Rock: Routes Through Scenographic Translation, From Mountain Climbing to Performance', *Performance Research*, 24 (2): 36–44.
Shearing, D. (2023), 'Felt Dramaturgies of Light', in K. Graham, S. Palmer and K. Zezulka (eds), *Contemporary Performance Lighting*, 46–63. London: Bloomsbury.
Shyldkrot, T. (2023), 'The Unbearable Brightness of Beams: Light, Darkness and Obscure Images', in K. Graham, S. Palmer and K. Zezulka (eds), *Contemporary Performance Lighting*, 82–99. London: Bloomsbury.
Sloan, G. (2012), *In Rehearsal: In the World, in the Room and On Your Own*, London: Routledge.
Smart, G. (2018), 'It's Time to Let Theatre Designers Do the Talking', *The Stage*, 4 December. https://www.thestage.co.uk/opinion/grace-smart-its-time-to-let-theatre-designers-do-the-talking (accessed 2 May 2024).
Smart, G. (2020), 'Theatre's Return is an Opportunity to Show What Designers Really Do', *The Stage*, 26 August. https://www.thestage.co.uk/opinion/grace-smart-theatres-return-is-an-opportunity-to-show-what-designers-really-do (accessed 2 May 2024).
Smart, G. (2022), 'The Ferocious Pursuit of the Better – Just Annoying, Or Worth It?', *The Stage*, 4 October. https://www.thestage.co.uk/opinion/the-ferocious-pursuit-of-the-better--just-annoying-or-worth-it (accessed 2 May 2024).
Stringer, R. (2024), Unpublished interview with the author, 7 May.
Swain, C. (2024), 'Chris Swain: Lighting a Devised and Constantly Changing Show', *Focus* (December 2023-January 2024), 14–21.
Trencsényi, K. and B. Cochrane (2014), 'New Dramaturgy: A Post-Mimetic, Intercultural, Process-Conscious Paradigm', in K. Trencsényi and B. Cochrane (eds), *New Dramaturgy: International Perspectives on Theory and Practice*, xi–xx, London: Bloomsbury.
Zezulka, K. (2023), 'Language, Creativity and Collaboration', in K. Graham, S. Palmer and K. Zezulka (eds), *Contemporary Performance Lighting: Experience, Creativity and Meaning*, 103–118, London: Bloomsbury.

10

# Interview with Rosie Elnile

**Rosie Elnile** is a performance designer whose practice explores the political, cultural and narrative capacities of scenography. She has worked extensively as a designer with credits including *Unknown Island* (2017); *The Convert* (2017); *The Wolves* (2018); *Three Sisters* (2018); *Abandon* (2018); *Returning to Haifa* (2018); *The Ridiculous Darkness* (2018); *The American Clock* (2019); *Our Town* (2019); *A Fight Against* (2021); *[Blank]* (2019); *Run Sister Run* (2021); *Violet –* (2022); *Thirst Trap* (2022); *An Unfinished Man* (2022); *Beautiful Thing* (2023); *The Odyssey* (2024); and *Peaceaphobia* (2021–4).

Rosie's first solo work, *Prayer* at the Gate Theatre (2020), explored questions of labour and care, offering a dismantling of colonial spatial and narrative structures. She is an associate artist of the Gate Theatre, London, was a recipient of the 2020 Jerwood Live Art Fund and won best designer at the Stage Debut Awards in 2017.

In this conversation, we talk about R&D processes in Rosie's work, the creative power of research and structural issues facing the role and recognition of design practice in UK theatre more widely. Rosie shares examples from a number of particular productions including *Jason Medea Medley* (2023), performed at Dresden Staatschauspiel, which offered an insight into material-led research processes facilitated by the German state-funded model. She also discusses a new solo piece, in progress at the time of the interview, and reflects on the rich journey through R&D for that project.

*How does R&D appear in your practice as a performance designer?*

There's two versions of the way that I engage with R&D or have done. The first is maybe more common, that's when I might have already been contracted to make a play and within that contract, there's a period of R&D before rehearsals. Or it might just be that somebody is thinking about an idea and wants to have me in the room to think about that idea. That's quite complicated, I think, for a designer, because the tools and materials that I use to think through my work are very different from that of a writer or a performer where you don't actually need extra materials. To be honest, what I can achieve in that time, that's useful to me, is often quite limited. I think that that is also connected to a very text-based culture of theatre-making. A lot of R&D is often about investigation into the text. I do also think of myself as a dramaturg, especially in those situations where we don't have materials to play with, it's being a dramaturgical brain in the room, asking questions about the text. Sometimes those are design specific questions, and sometimes they might be political questions about the piece. That's probably the most common form of R&D that I've undertaken.

The more interesting form of R&D for me is where I have some support to play with and think through ideas spatially. I'm making a project in Dresden at the moment. In Germany there isn't really a culture of R&D in the same way that there is here. For me, it would be pretty unusual to go into a project in the UK without having done any time thinking about the thing before rehearsals. But in Germany, they don't tend to do that because the German theatre system is much better at providing tools and materials. Well, the theatre that I'm working in anyway, which is a state theatre, is much better organized, has a much bigger prop store, has much more efficient mechanisms for storing and delivering material to rehearsal rooms. So I was able to give a list of a hundred objects that arrived the next day that we were able to work with. Also, their rehearsal rooms have lighting and sound rigs in the space so I was able to test out ideas in R&D.

Maybe more exciting and transformative was their *Bauprobe* system, where they build a one-to-one scale model of the set. They have an incredibly efficient system for doing that, which is they have these metal frames that they cover in paper. The *Staatsschauspiel* in Dresden has a massive technical team that are able to construct a space really fast. We've got a revolving object in our show and things that fly in – we were able to have one-to-one scale replicas of those to work with. And that to me seems, to be honest, like the only way to truly R&D a design. And I think one of the reasons why that's not a common practice in the UK is that to an extent, I think there's still an idea that the majority of the information or the majority of the experience is coming from the words, from the text and from the actions of the performers, less of an understanding of how material, scale, et cetera, all co-create meaning. The *Bauprobe* was one of the most transformative days of my working life, really, in being able to understand a space that I designed; to imaginatively and materially test it before it's sent to production.

[Before that experience] I had done most of my work in the UK, and had in my imagination that what I wanted was incredibly radical and impossible. And then working in Germany, going to a culture where it's incredibly normal made me think, 'yeah, should one theatre not try and model this version of working?!' Even in terms of sustainability practice – which sometimes feels like the only area in which people are interested in re-imagining design – it feels like a system where research and development of design is more embedded into a process would absolutely create less waste and absolutely create more reuse and absolutely create more intelligent ways of working with the materials that we have. As well as creating greater creative opportunities. It can feel to me like there's a lot of conversation about reinvention when actually I think there are all sorts of very intelligent, interesting models that we could literally copy.

One of my frustrations with my practice is that often the design and the action have a slight disconnect because the time at which we're placing them together is in the technical rehearsal which is the most stressful and, I think, least creative time. And so you're unable to actually work in a way that is conducive to producing new forms or new effects because when there's a lot of time pressure and external pressure on the director, you double down on things you already know. There isn't much space for [something] expansive or unknown to occur in that space.

My other experience of R&D is on my own pieces of design-led work, which are new forms for me in the sense that I don't have an exact blueprint to copy. The first was called *Prayer* (2020), which was really about process and what extended investigation without product meant in all sorts of contexts. I think the context that people took away from it was within the context of the climate crisis. That's, in a way, slightly incidental. I was looking at organic materials, but it was more about design as a tool to think through rather than design as a finished presentational tool: design as a mechanism to *think* rather than as a mechanism to *describe*.

The second piece, which I've been working on for quite a long time, is about architectural modelling; about scenographic modelling. I started thinking about a very specific building – a job centre in the town I grew up in, which was a very clear architectural example of the way that the benefit system is a kind of oppressive, obviously classist system, which tries to discourage organising of the unemployed. Through R&D I have been looking at the ways in which that architecture was set up, what kind of politics was embedded into it. One of the magical things about set designers is we're very used to looking at space as incredibly malleable. So [the project is] using the brain of a set designer to think, 'OK, what if we used that kind of practice to reimagine spatial politics in a real space?'

I came up against a lot of problems in the development of that work because of a lack of space to physically experiment. I also placed parameters upon myself imaginatively because of a culture within the UK of not seeing design as a material, not seeing design as a mechanism to create story and create narrative and create politics, but as a third stage in a process. So I became very stuck within my own personal research and development project and actually going to Dresden allowed me to say: 'what do I actually need?' and 'what do I actually want from a design-led investigation?'

*It seems very interesting that that process has now been interspliced with this project in Dresden that opens up ways it might transform in its next phase of R&D. Could I ask you to give a pocket history of the R&D work that you have done on that project thus far and what you might be imagining or hoping for the next phase?*

So far, it's been quite a long investigation. This is also the way that I work, which I think is quite sprawling. It's been a lot of research into the history of job centres, and tangentially the history of my family in the area that they live, which led me to an investigation into my great grandfather, who was the first member of my family to come to this area. He was from Cornwall, his family worked in the tin mines, but he was born with only one leg, so he was unable to work in the tin mines so he moved further up Britain, to Cheltenham. He was a communist, a very dedicated communist. And so, I started drawing this imaginative lineage between myself and him, and started thinking about this idea of inherited hope and the desire to remodel. [That] led to a lot of thinking about the Paris Commune. I did a lot of research into that and read an amazing book called *Communal Luxury*, which is all about thinking through action. So that was more like a written research part of the project. Then the material investigation started by me modelling spaces on my computer with some of these ideas embedded into them, and then working to get them 3D printed.

Actually that was the part of the project which stopped making sense to me, because I was interested in an idea of communally modelling or co-making something, but I was actually just taking ideas, [and] illustrating them with models. I wanted to use action, or needed to use action, to investigate these ideas. So then it developed into writing a kind of narrative play; a durational performance with my great-grandfather as a character, set in a production line in a clay tile making factory. While I was making this work, my partner was sent to work in a clay tile making factory, and there's something very interesting to me about this mechanised repetitive labour that was born out of his enforced job hunting. So I started writing a narrative play, and then a proposal for an idea which would be live modelling within a narrative structure using tons and tons of clay, which obviously requires a very different kind of material, very different investigation to small-scale modelling. But I think I would have reached that much more ambitious idea sooner if there was a culture of physical R&D in Britain. It's taken me eighteen months to reach that conclusion, it's a very long, tangential thing. In a way, that R&D process for me has also been about a lot of space and time to tangentially follow, research, led by desire, and intrigue and interest, which is also an important part of R&D. I think what I found is I got quite stuck in something that was incredibly academic and small, and I found that my imagination was limited by the parameters that are placed on design research and development.

*Do you think that's tied to questions of funding or producing models? Do you find that you're trying to shape a project towards those parameters?*

Of course, because part of the stipulations of a funding application is that the idea is achievable. It's very difficult to imagine how to produce an R&D in that way, without space, without dedicated spaces for design R&D.

One of the things that I do, as well as being a designer, is I run study groups. One is a reading group for designers, where I curate the text, another is a group for early career designers, the group's mission is to keep imaginatively expanding in a period of austerity, and to investigate design as a tool in and of itself. Within that second group, a lot of what I'm doing is trying to help early career designers keep imaginatively stretching, because so much of what we're being told as artists is that things aren't possible. There are groups, like the Royal Court Young Writers Group, where writers and directors are given space to imagine what kind of practice they might want to have, to experiment with form or whatever, but not really for designers in my experience. So, leading those groups, which are courses of eight months, is as much a part of my practice as my design work. But there's a palpable feeling of hopelessness, I would say, amongst young designers, because cuts to arts funding mean that the incredibly low fees that designers are already receiving are not changing. And it also means a lack of resource, both for the development of ideas and for the implication of ideas. I think they really feel like spectacle and the ability to think through design is really limited. In its best version, research and development is where you are allowed to fail, and are allowed to try out ideas that might seem stupid, or ideas that you don't understand yet. In the current conditions, all of those things feel less possible.

*What would an ideal R&D process look like in your approach to design?*

I think it's quite straightforward, to be honest. It would be a fully resourced theatre space for an extended period of time. It would be technicians to physically build structures, [and funding] to purchase materials or spend the time sourcing second-hand materials. And it would be producers, and I suppose artistic directors, who understood that a designer's set of things to investigate might look incredibly different from a page-long synopsis of a play. And so somehow creating a literacy within producing houses of design as a separate and different art form from writing.

One of the things that I'm trying to think through at the moment is this idea of 'design-led work' may be quite unhelpful as an idea, because most performance is design-led in some way or another, or is at least co-led by design. And so I don't think this desire of giving time and space to design is an abstract proposition like 'how can we develop design into this new thing?' It's just acknowledging that theatre is a visual art form. There's a real lack of resource given to the development of the visual side of it. We would make these thicker, richer, more fertile performances if design was basically recognized rather than trying to create a new field, which is sometimes what it feels like.

*That comes back to what you are doing in a lot of your work, which is using design as a mechanism to think through wider questions.*

Our material world shapes our political imagination. And one of the things that I feel at the moment is that our political imagination is very small because we're stuck in this very unimaginative centre and the gains or the things that we imagine for our lives, it feels like they're becoming smaller and smaller as conditions become harder and harder. Understanding and demonstrating that our material world is malleable, that power structures are malleable, that you can really change the power in a space by moving walls and building walls out of different materials and creating spaces to rest and by co-making a structure together, is an incredible tool but I don't think that is seen in those terms. Scenography is quite unique in that it's not architecture. We're not building things which need to last. It's like a very restless imagining and re-imagining, in real scale. That's incredibly unique and incredibly underused. Often I go and see installations by artists and they're thinking through these things in a much less advanced way than scenography is, but the work is given time and a space to ask much deeper questions. Scenography is incredibly advanced in creating these alternative spaces, but not given the breadth of investigative space that visual art is.

Most of the time the texts that we're working from are play texts and I'm very interested in what it means to make from or with texts, but what if the texts that we're making from or with are different sorts of texts? So, oral histories or the book about the Paris Commune? We can still build from ideas and thinking, but maybe the rigidity of a play text, which is often saying 'it's set here, this needs to happen, this needs to happen, this needs to happen', can be a bit suffocating. But I don't know how design could grow into this or create this ancillary project without deep time for development. I mean, wages for designers (which is also connected to R&D, because obviously that's often within your overall fee) are incredibly, shockingly, low. That shows what people think design is capable of imaginatively and what respect, I suppose, is placed upon the role of a designer. Part of the reason that those fees are so low is because it's often thought design is a kind of illustration of a story or something.

*This comes back to the example from the* Bauprobe, *of being able to imagine materially. I suppose I'm interested in hearing about the kinds of discoveries that become possible when you can do your developing or do your imagining with the material itself, or a proxy of it.*

Yes, absolutely. There's a quote from the book about the Paris Commune which says that actions precede dreams and ideas and not the reverse. I've often found that to be true, but what was being asked of us was to do that in reverse; to have an idea and then to create a set of actions out of it, rather than understanding that ideas are produced through material and action.

Often the language of design, I think, is closer to the language of poetry, or of association or suggestion, rather than literal description. You find poetry through practice and associative ideas often come in the middle of action. If there isn't space for that action, I don't always have the space to find the associative or poetic ideas because you're asked to justify it with language before you've even done it.

*Could you talk us through an example where perhaps R&D hasn't quite worked or has asked you to jump through stages before the work was ready?*

I made a project recently where it had a very specific dramaturgy embedded into the design that we started in an incredibly naturalistic space that was dismantled and then a new space arrived. It had a very particular rhythm to it. And we did two weeks of R&D on this piece, but the theatre wasn't available. It was just all verbal discussion and then in rehearsals, the resources weren't there to rehearse these particular mechanisms. So, because these design ideas were quite complicated, requiring live use of power tools and very particular rhythmic flying, and because the only justification we had for them was verbal there was a real lack of will from the production department, I think, and a real lack of belief in the ideas. That created a lack of preparation from the technical department, which meant that the ideas were massively reduced, and in one case cut, which completely destroyed the dramaturgy of the design. It became something totally different. I think if we were in a kind of German system, potentially, and we had had time to workshop these things, time to work out the exact rhythm of them, time to understand what wasn't working about them to work out what needed to happen, then I think we would have been able to make the work. In this case I wasn't able to make the work, but I know for a fact that if a writer had a very strong intuition that a piece of the text needed to stay, it wouldn't have been cut, it would have been pursued because I think you can read the text on the page. It can do an approximation of what it's going to do in the space, whereas tiny card model or 3D renders can't really. So many times in new writing I think the design, when it's complicated, is seen as a luxury. And if that in any way interferes with the text, or, you know, the ability of the actors to be confident in what they're doing, it's cut. But it's definitely not directors that I hold accountable for that. It's the system of not being given space to R&D design ideas, actually.

One of the questions I've been asking myself recently is, 'where does my work belong?' I think because of certain aesthetics within it, I often get asked to make new writing, which is already a kind of R&D within itself. And in actual fact I think my work would actually be much better sitting with a classic text or something that was already finished and could be taken apart or could have a conversation with design but I think there isn't such a culture of reimagining pre-existing texts in the UK at the moment. It feels like a lot of the capacity for development is absorbed within text-based investigation. And it's very dependent on having a writer who is interested in design as a language, which is often not the case.

*I'm keen to ask you about the role of research in your work as an artist. You've mentioned here about researching things laterally and of course you've talked about the reading groups that you run as holding a space for research and expansion for other designers. Can you talk a little bit about how research manifests in your work?*

Yes. Research is incredibly important to my work, and it's something that I find incredibly pleasurable. And it takes lots of different forms. But I believe that somehow research is magical. I don't know how to explain it, like it has its own consciousness or something. What I mean is: so often I have a thought about something and then that echoes in some research I'm doing somewhere else. There's something about really being engaged and open in a period of research that I think creates almost metaphysical results, because it's a space of being incredibly, incredibly open. It's probably where my brain is most porous. It's not just a dry space for me, it's this incredibly fizzy space and I think it's about being incredibly open to both what falls into your lap but also where you find your brain being led. Because in my artistic and political imagination, there's a lot to do with resonances across time and space and history, and finding connections with your beliefs or your struggle with the past.

Somehow the more honest and open I am about my research, the more it gives me. So I guess an example is that I think there's a real culture, because of the pace at which designers are asked to work and the lack of money, there can be a culture of looking at the work of visual artists and just taking that work and re-appropriating it as a stage design. I think there's a secrecy around that work and it creates this very rigid form of research which is just like a line. But when I allow my research to be very open and I think of it as more of a conversation, and I'm also very open with my collaborators about what I'm researching, where I'm taking ideas from and what those conversations are, that's when these magical occurrences happen, I think.

Part of my piece *Prayer* was about acknowledging that I am in an ecosystem of art(ists) and makers and by researching their work I am having a conversation with them about their work. I often use visual research – which is sometimes my own photographs and occurrences I see in the world which I have a big store of, the work of visual artists – but also a big chunk of my research is reading. And the reading group. I believe that collective study, of your own choice, if you're choosing to come to a space and collectively study or think through a text together, produces incredible communality within the group but also creates new thinking in a way that I don't experience when I'm reading a text on my own. It's not like there's the 'research' part of my practice and then there's the 'doing' part of my practice, they're like a soup. I think I'm less advanced in my material research because of all of the things that we're talking about but that is what my dream is, to have greater opportunity to research with material, and with action. So the piece that I am I in the process of making, is a lot about what language might develop through when you're working and modelling large amounts of clay. I'm interested in how the material research produces language rather than the other way around.

*I think you're articulating here that a deep engagement with the world around us and our own positionality becomes a kind of bedrock from which a design practice emerges or flows.*

Yeah, and I think expanding what we think research is. There's obviously one version of research, which is very specific for me, which is reading texts and then reading more texts from the texts. But conversations are research and walking around a theatre that you're making work in is research. I think there can be this feeling that, you need to sit and research and it's this really static practice, that you need to give it a specific amount of time and then it needs to produce a set of stimuli which can then make a design. Really, it's like the whole process is research. And if you're working on a project that you feel really embedded in, then I feel like the whole of your daily life becomes research for that project.

One of the things that I'm thinking about in this piece that I'm making is this idea where workers use the materials and time of their employers to make something for themselves. I was researching this in this big, stately home which was totally by coincidence where my mum used to work as a cook. I just got offered a residency and then discovered it and was reading through all of their old brochures and found one from the time when my mum would have worked there in 2003 and people that was incredibly trippy, like transcendental meditation. I phoned her just to tell her that I'd found this thing, and she was telling me that when she worked there, she used to cook extra food to take home. In the site that I was researching this concept, my mum had been doing this action of creating her own meals out of the food that she had been given. So I was involved in this kind of work and that I was being fed by that as a child. I feel like when you're porous in that way, it allows for a different system of thinking, which is often a lot deeper than when we try and produce a really specific effect from the act of research.

4 April 2023
Interviewed by Katherine Graham

## Questions and Prompts #5

- What are the tools and materials that you need to think through for your R&D? How might this material thinking happen in the space? For example, if appropriate for the project, could you ask for a distinct budget for R&D?
- Can you find space to allow materials to trigger new ideas? In lieu of working towards a specific production goal, what might happen if you bring unexpected or playful materials (maybe: 400 tea spoons; grass cuttings from someone's garden; telephone books otherwise bound for recycling) into the process as departure points for play?
- If the precise materials you are interested in are not available, or if you are not yet sure of the exact materials you might want to explore, what kinds of proxy materials might you deploy?
- What are the creative and collaborative relationships that are important to this particular process? How do you want to work on this project, and what kind of expectations do others have of you?
- Think about the things you want to share with your collaborators; are there images, inspirations or reference points you want to bring to the process?
- What research, or preparation, or development, will you do independently? And what research might you do in the context of collective exploration? In other words, how much research and thinking will you arrive into the process with, and how much will you discover in context?
- Can you be open to research and to letting connections emerge through your engagement with questions? What lenses might you use to accumulate further research through the process?
- What kinds of political and ethical ideas are you interested in? How might you use design to explore (or rebuild) the politics of space? How can you use design thinking to shape encounters and relationships, in the room, and in the work?
- Take note of the parameters within which you are working. Do these feel right to you? Is there space to push against these boundaries? Or can you make them useful to you? What does it mean to you to 'keep imaginatively expanding' your practice beyond the expectations of others?
- For R&D to be a space for genuine discovery, it can be helpful to be open to mistakes, misinterpretation and failure. How do you make space for this in your process? Can you, for example, invite your collaborators to forge their own connections to your ideas, even if this involves abandoning what you originally planned?

11

# Developing a dramaturgical praxis through repetitive R&D

Rebecca Benzie, Harry Kingscott and Nora J. Williams

Via a roundtable discussion between key members of the creative team, this chapter reflects on over seven years of work on a project called *Measure (Still) for Measure*. The project combines physical theatre techniques, feminist dramaturgies and Shakespeare's play *Measure for Measure* (Shakespeare 2020) to help young people grapple with issues around rape and consent cultures.[1] The project originated with an accidental moment of juxtaposition: Cheek by Jowl's 2015 livestream of their production of *Measure for Measure* with Pushkin Theatre and the media storm around Emma Sulkowicz, at the time an undergraduate student at Columbia University in New York. Echoing Isabella's plea – 'To whom should I complain? Did I tell this, / Who would believe me?' (2.4.171-2) – Sulkowicz became (in)famous for their final-year performance art project, *Mattress Project (Carry That Weight)*, in which they brought a mattress everywhere they went on campus in protest against the institution's handling of their sexual violence complaint against a fellow student. Witnessing these events in parallel, the project asks: What might these two young people say to each other, if they could reach across the 400-year gap that separated them?

From this question grew the *Measure (Still) for Measure* project, which has seen numerous iterations over its life so far. The project resists a straightforward description because it shape-shifts significantly to accommodate the needs and priorities of each new group that encounters it. But, at its core, the project aims to help young people navigate the constant and treacherous waters of rape and consent cultures through creative expressions of agency. As a play that dramatizes gendered violence and abuses of institutional power, *Measure for Measure* provides an apt beginning point. At the same time, the use of physical theatre techniques that focus on collaboration and ensemble responsibility offer a platform for experimentation that empowers participants to resist Shakespeare's dramaturgies – which are themselves misogynist (see Williams 2022). As a result, participants feel able to ask and answer the question, 'how would we tell this story differently?'

---

[1] For readers not familiar with *Measure for Measure*, a brief plot summary is available at this link: https://shorturl.at/mHT59.

What follows is a roundtable discussion between Nora J. Williams (Project Lead) and Harry Kingscott and Rebecca Benzie (referred to in conversation as Bec) who have been company members across different phases of the project, including in the roles of Movement Director and Dramaturg, respectively. The discussion reflects on their experiences of returning to the R&D process over several years on this project, including R&D periods at the Bike Shed Theatre, Exeter (2016); Nichols School, Buffalo (2016–17); Dalhousie University, Nova Scotia (2018); and Essex University, Colchester (2022). From this longitudinal perspective, Williams, Kingscott and Benzie resituate the work as fundamentally about the R&D process, rather than a final performance, and consider how this has shaped their practice as an ensemble, along with their relationship with the audience. The chapter explores how training on intimacy coordination shaped the R&D process at Essex University in 2022 and the questions concerning rape and consent culture outlined above. A focus on dramaturgical practices runs through the discussion as the project team examines their evolving relationship with the source text of *Measure for Measure*.

## The foundations of the project

**Nora Williams (NW):** In a way – and this will sort of be the thesis of this conversation – our whole process has felt like an extended R&D. But we started initially with just some workshops in the department at the University of Exeter. We had a few exploratory, see what happens, kind of sessions.

**Rebecca Benzie (RB):** I remember meeting in your flat, Nora, and looking at the shape of the text around that time.

**NW:** Yeah, you and I and Sharanya Murali – another friend and colleague who was a student with us at Exeter and has come in and out of the project – spent a day pulling the whole thing apart.

**RB:** What's going on here? What is happening dramaturgically, and what's the structure of this play?

**NW:** I don't know that we used this language at the time, but the project has evolved into a project about dramaturgy – that is, about the structure of this thing. And both how we understand the structure that Shakespeare put there, but also what we can do to intervene and make it different. That's where a lot of the R&D begins. How do we break this play apart so that we can make something different with it?

**RB:** Those structural questions have run alongside contemporary socio-political questions about patriarchy: things like Trump, #MeToo, Sarah Everard, the revolution in Iran, Black Lives Matter, questions around the police, questions around safety in public. And it feels like it's often been paralleling the cultural structures when we ask: how do we push against these things? How do we pull these things apart?

**NW**: There's been a lot of helpful scholarship[2] in that direction, too, in the last seven years – I keep thinking about Kate Manne's *Down Girl* (2018), for example – where people are working hard to move away from that neoliberal, hyper-individualistic way of thinking about problems and towards a more holistic, structural view of things.

We initially did a handful of one off evenings in the Drama department at Exeter with whoever was around. Harry, you and Bec (RB) were involved from the start. Sharanya was involved from the start. We had Sally Naylor. We had Sam Theobald-Roe. It was a group of fellow students, because I was finishing my PhD. There were a whole bunch of undergraduates and postgraduates, who I had worked with throughout my time in Exeter, for four or five years.

We were kind of just playing with the text initially and seeing what would come out. And then, the Bike Shed Theatre in Exeter – which, sadly, is no more – had a scheme where they partnered with the Council to make use of vacant shop fronts. We didn't get any money from it, but we could use this vacant space for a period of five days for R&D work, and the only stipulation was that you had to do some kind of sharing at the end to show them what you'd been working on.

We had that R&D week in late January, early February of 2016. It was six or seven of us who were there every day, and then there were a few people sort of floating in and out. We had a core group of performers, and then we had people who were playwrights or dramaturgs, or outside eyes.

The starting point for that week was, 'Is there anything longer term in this idea? Is this something that is going to run out of steam very quickly? Or could we think about a whole show that looks like this? Could we think about a bigger piece of work?'

**Harry Kingscott (HK)**: With R&Ds, it's always really ephemeral; we've got this vague idea, and we're going to see if it's got legs. I remember everyone getting involved in that project – people coming in and out – and we all agreed that there was something there, and there was something to be said, and that we didn't really know how to do it.

It says something about the subject matter that we're looking at with this project, because sometimes you go into an R&D for theatre, and after about three days, there's just nothing exciting there. This project has had so many iterations because it's trying to answer an unanswerable question. Because if we answer it in the R&D, there isn't much point making any more art out of it. It's like trying to grab at smoke, especially in those early days. I think with where we've come to now, there's something a little bit more substantial that we're working with. But there is still that sense that there's a thing that we're trying to say, and we don't really know what we're trying to say with it.

**RB**: Now I'm just getting really reminiscent, but it's all coming back. I remember that suddenly being in a new space in 2016, outside of the university, made it feel really

---

[2] Scholarship includes: *Fix the System Not the Women* by Laura Bates (2022), *Lean Out* by Dawn Foster (2015), *Feminism, Interrupted* by Lola Olufemi (2020), *Complaint!* by Sara Ahmed (2021), *Tomorrow Sex Will Be Good Again* by Katerine Angel (2021), *Imperfect Victims* by Leigh Goodmark (2023) and *A Feminist Theory of Violence* by Françoise Vergès (trans. Melissa Thackway, 2022).

different. We weren't being examined anymore, this was away from our studies, and this was actually, like, rolling our sleeves up. And suddenly the process felt really important. There's an itch that needs scratching and exploring and interrogating. And I remember that feeling really exciting.

## R&D techniques and approaches

**NW**: In Exeter, in 2016, we had five days and nobody was doing it full time. Everyone had other jobs and other commitments. So just as a totally practical solution, to make it easier, we said, 'alright, no one needs to memorise any script'. We had disembodied voices, with the performers who were not in the movement work at any given time voicing the lines.

We learned a lot from that, but it's not something that I repeated very often in future iterations.

**HK**: There was something quite weird about going in and out of choreography. We'd do the movement and then we played the disembodied voices. So you'd do your choreography, and then you'd go to the wall – like you'd return to Shakespeare, and you'd sort of weirdly be standing facing the wall, whilst trying to time it to the movement. Then you'd move away from the words. Then you'd come back to the text and then move away from it again.

**RB**: It repositions it: it feels like there's been a wonderful snowballing of adding in other elements, other movement languages. I'm particularly thinking about Viewpoints (Bogart and Landau 2005) and intimacy training, and all these other things coming into the mix. I wonder if that's meant that we've held the text a little bit differently? Is there something in how the text has become repositioned? This returning to it and coming away from it has that meant that the text didn't become too elevated.

**NW**: I'm probably less precious about the text now even than I was in that first stage, because I think I still felt that it had to be recognizably *Measure for Measure* in some way. Now I'm much less worried about that. I'm more interested in the text becoming a stimulus for storytelling – from the performers, from the participants that are involved in any phase – which I think is reflected in how far from the text we got in the most recent phase at Essex University, in 2022. We really went left field on the adaptation there, whereas that first time, in Exeter, we were pretty much still just doing scenes from the play, with some choreography.

**HK**: Although, even in that iteration, we were starting to play with character and multi-roling. That's a big thing that we always come back to: taking Isabella and making her multiple, played by multiple people. That comes back in quite a few of the different versions.

**NW**: That's also where we started playing the game of physical numbers representing power in various different circumstances. We had this idea that maybe if there were two, or three, or four actors playing Isabella at the same time, that would change the balance of power against Angelo and the Duke. Or, if that power balance didn't change, that there was something worth exploring in that, too.

**RB**: The chorus has often felt really crucial when we've thought about Isabella and when we have those multiple voices.

**NW**: In Buffalo, New York, in 2017, we worked with Nichols School on a 'Pilot Project', which ended in a short run of public performances, and the students were assessed on the work, but throughout their teacher and I really wanted to emphasize process and experimentation. Bec and Sharanya were Skype guests. We had five months to develop it, which was such a luxury. Kristen Tripp Kelley, their theatre teacher, worked with us to think about how the project could be a vehicle for this group of seventeen- and eighteen-year-olds to grapple with the looming world of university and adulthood. The aim was to empower them to change the narrative of *Measure for Measure*. We were working within a class structure at the school, so we had short daily workshops – I think forty-seven minutes each! – and then a longer, double block once a week. We added some evening rehearsals as we got closer to their performance dates.

One of the scenes in this iteration that I really loved appropriated text from – well, we now know her name is Chanel Miller – but at the time she was the anonymous victim-survivor of the Stanford rape. That was very much in the news at that time, and she gave a statement in court about the process of being interviewed by police (Buncombe 2016). It's a whole series of these really banal questions: what were you wearing; how much did you have to drink; what time did you eat dinner? Did you come with your boyfriend? Was your cell phone charged? All these questions trying to victim-blame her, essentially. And the Nichols students took Isabella's speech at the end of Act 2, scene 4 – 'To whom should I complain? Did I tell this, / Who would believe me?' (2.4.171-2) – and mixed it with that court statement from Miller. They had the actor playing Isabella, Kelah Winfield, standing in the centre of the school's big proscenium stage. As she started that speech, the other actors crossed the space at speed and bumped into her with these questions – so literally, physically hitting her as they asked those really intrusive questions, and getting faster and faster, and overlapping, and she finally cuts them off. She says, 'stop!' really loud, and then just says, 'Who will believe me?'

I loved how they were again thinking about the chorus, and thinking about how we use the other actors to represent what is going on at a deeper level. That is actually really hard to represent, especially with a small group of people.

**RB**: How do we do that and not outweigh the presence of Isabella? You don't want a bigger chorus, you don't want it to be a battle of choruses, because it feels like the important thing is to give her story that space. But how do you represent the systemic side?

**NW**: It's definitely difficult to balance the weight of that individual story against all of these big questions, systemic stuff, social stuff. It takes a really skilled actor, and a really skilled ensemble to make it feel like she matters as a person, but she also is emblematic of this larger, structural problem. This was the iteration where they cut the Duke and cut Mariana.

**RB**: The students had become bolder with cuts, which felt like real ownership.

**NW**: For context, the 'rules' that we gave these students were that they could cut anything they wanted from *Measure for Measure*. They had complete freedom to mess around with the text, as long as they could justify their choices somehow. So the choice to cut Mariana was all their idea. They were like, 'Yep, she's a plot device. She's not a 3-D character. We don't need her.' And then, of course, they had to grapple with the dramaturgical ramifications of that, because now they had no way to save Claudio's life. She's only a plot device, but she's still serving a purpose! They were so confident that they could just trash this whole character, and there wouldn't be any consequences for the rest of the story. So they did grapple with that one.

As a group, we were also having trouble with Act 5, and Bec, Sharanya, Kristen and I were asking, 'what do we do?' Because Isabella is here, but she doesn't talk very much. The Duke is so over-represented, and so much the puppet master of that scene. I had lunch with one of my former teachers, Kevin Costa, and he asked, 'what would happen if you just cut the Duke out of it?' It's one of those things you can only answer by trying it, right? It's a practical question. So I put that to this group of students, and I said, 'here is a suggestion. Should we see what happens?' And in the end they cut pretty much everything in that scene apart from Isabella. Her text became a monologue that the Duke and Angelo kept trying to interrupt, and ultimately they couldn't.

But that group also rewrote the Duke as an ally to Isabella, which he really is not in the text. So because he'd been absent, because he wasn't there, the Friar disguise thing was just gone. They were able to sort of remediate him in the end, as someone who ultimately stops trying to interrupt them, and actually listens and has Angelo arrested at the end. With hindsight, that ending is something we wouldn't have come to without the processual emphasis of the project, this sense that it's almost *always* in R&D mode.

**RB**: That's a really clear, dramaturgical question: what if the Duke's not there? In that case the demographics of the group made a difference, too, because we were working on it in the first half of 2017, Trump had just been inaugurated. There was this huge spike in hate crimes, and the women's march, and all this stuff going on.

**NW**: There was a lot happening, socially, politically, that I think felt very big and present to them because, again, they were seventeen or eighteen years old, about to launch into this scary world. And the student who played the Duke was the only Black man in the cast – Myles Hervey is his name. I think they all felt quite uncomfortable with casting him in a role where he represented the force of the State. They felt like some sort of positive representation was needed for that particular character. In this group, actually half the performers were students of colour – three out of four women and one of the three men. And just because of the nature of the story they were telling, the women in the cast had a lot more opportunity for positive, redemptive, empowered embodiment in their performances because they were all playing Isabella – sometimes all at once, sometimes one at a time, but they all rotated through the part at different points. But for the men I think it was more challenging to find those reparative moments. So looking across these interconnected issues of race and gender, as a group they came to this idea that the Duke – who, again, in their version really only showed up at the very end – would actually listen to Isabella and take her concerns seriously.

## R&D for devising ensembles

**HK**: This all says a lot about the effect of who's in the room for an R&D. And because I know it can be a bit of a debate – particularly at mid- to large-scale, particularly in the UK – that companies will do an R&D, and they'll do many stages, but they'll change artists every time. There's a bit of a thing about credit, and where that goes. But I think, just talking about that iteration at Nichols, and thinking of all the other versions, it shows how much sway a person in the room has on where the piece ends up going – not even necessarily just performers, say you've got a designer in the room, or a movement director, or whatever it might be, a dramaturg. It's that strange thing, isn't it? We can't give Shakespeare the credit, because we've come up with the ideas. But then, where does that credit go? Even in the most recent version at Essex University (2022), we almost flipped the Nichols approach on its head and said, 'No, the Duke is actually the most present person'. Literally, he became the framing for the play. And that's because of who we had in the room, and what they saw. That's something that we've been keen to avoid. We have not gone into the process thinking, 'Well, I've actually done five versions of this now, and these are my ideas of how it should work'. It's still very open. So every human in that room has an influence on where that ends up going.

**NW**: I think that might be why the whole project feels like R&D, because every time we are genuinely going into a new group saying, here are some skills, here are some exercises, here's a text. And here are some people in the room who have done this before, but, otherwise, tell us what you think is interesting. I think I will keep doing it that way until I run into a group that isn't very interesting, and doesn't come up with something.

But every time, I'm just really amazed by how, when you hand the agency over to a group of young people – people who generally now are younger than us, which was not the case at the beginning! – they will run with it, and the way that they will take it somewhere that I could never have imagined on my own. Never, in my wildest imaginings, could I have come up with the version we did at Essex, alone. I just would never have gotten there, and I think there's such value in listening to the people you're in the room with and putting people in that room who really bring something special to the project and look at it with fresh eyes.

**HK**: And who are game to try stuff out, too.

**RB**: I've never felt that the stages of the process have been of different value. I always feel like it's been about who we are in the room, when we're doing it, and who is invited.

You are welcome. You are valued, you are here, and I never felt, Nora, that you were pushing for a final one, or this is the ultimate one, or this has got to be the best one. It never felt like I was joining a project that was trying to tie everything in a bow. And especially when we were in Essex, it didn't feel like this is the ultimate one, just because we've done lots before. It felt like, this is the next one.

**NW**: It's been a luxury in a lot of ways to get to do something that is all about the process, because the industry is so outcome-focused. Both academia and the theatre industry want you to produce the thing in the shortest amount of time, for the least money. And make sure you sell tickets, because the funding is so outcome-focused. I remember filling in the funding application for the project we did at Essex, which was funded internally. So the Pro-Vice Chancellor for Research's Strategic Fund paid for that, and I had such trouble with the application because I thought, 'how do you fit, into 200 characters, a process that is now seven years long and something that is really about process?' It is really about getting people in a room to see what happens, where I genuinely am going in with very little idea of what the thing that comes out the other side will look like. And what's valuable is that I don't know what it will end up being, research-wise. Harry and I always, every iteration of the project, hit a point where he's like, 'but what are we *making*, Nora?' And I say, 'I don't know yet, Harry!'

**HK**: That's just a little voice in my head that goes all the time, probably from growing up in this industry that, as you're saying, is so product-driven. Even now I'm like, what is the point of this? Where is this going? But, yeah, it's absolutely true. But because we're always doing it in a new context, it is always going to be fresh. There's a value in that, you could argue, product-wise, because the audiences that see any sharing that we do aren't seeing something that we were thinking about seven years ago. They're seeing something that a group of people that we have only just come to are thinking about and are making. So it is always going to stay fresh, as long as the question keeps being juicy and unanswerable. But there's always going to be something of value to see, and/or to experience, in terms of a piece of art at the end of it.

**RB**: It's about what the people in the room get, particularly thinking about some of the discussions we held. In 2022, we did a reading from *Tomorrow Sex Will Be Good Again* (Angel 2021), and from that reading, we had some really tough discussions, and we sat in some really hard stuff, and it didn't feel like we were thinking about our audience at all; we were thinking about who was in the room, and the conversations we were having. I feel like it being an R&D process has helped us reposition the weight of the audience, and that actually, we've been fed as well.

**NW**: We never think about the audience until we do, right? There's always this period at the start where it is just juicy and fun, and we're trying stuff out, and we're learning. We're getting to know each other and reading some stuff, and we're just gonna see what happens. We're throwing spaghetti at the wall until it sticks, and then once it starts sticking, then we start thinking about an audience. I have ADHD, so it's useful for me to have a deadline, because I could happily play with spaghetti forever – but we know the funding ends on this day, or we have to do a sharing on this day, or we've booked the theatre for this day, and that quite usefully forces some of those discussions to a conclusion. But what's also nice is that I don't feel like any version of the project we've done, either the facilitators or participants have felt at all that we nailed it or we've come to *the* conclusion.

Especially for students, so much of their lives are result-driven – it's exams, and it's assessments, and it's get your degree. And then, even when you get out into the industry, it's get funding, put on that show, fill those seats, produce or perish. So there's something existentially valuable in participating in something that is, from the outset, saying, 'We're not going to solve this problem'.

## R&Ding Shakespeare for the twenty-first century

**NW**: When I think about stepping away from this work – this is a slightly different point, but what I think about most often is that I'm sort of stuck with Shakespeare. Why is Shakespeare the vehicle for this? I still don't think I have a great answer other than just that's what I happened to be working on.

**HK**: Is that the original thing you were saying though? The fact that you have this play, which was written 400 years ago, and then you had the story in the news, and they were the same thing, and so it makes sense to use that text that he'd written in order to explore that. Thinking about the audience again, that's what they are familiar with, as well.

**NW**: It's also about how you get funding to do this kind of work. How do you get people in the door to that kind of show? Shakespeare is very powerful that way. It's very handy.

One of the things that I really hope participants walk away with, though, is the sense that they have a toolkit for breaking these plays to pieces, if they want to. And I hope they do want to.

**RB**: But 'why Shakespeare?' feels like a good question to return to. Do you think that's something you return to through the project?

**NW**: Sharanya asks me that question frequently. 'Why are you still bothering with Shakespeare?' She is my wisest friend. It's one of those questions that is worth continuing to reflect on, even if the answer continues to be that I think there *is* value in doing it this way. Just as the project is different every time we approach it, we grow and change as well, and our interests move and shift, and the world changes around us. If the project is going to continue in any form, I want it to continue feeling fresh and urgent and part of an ongoing conversation.

**HK**: If you had a company that was doing R&D over a long period of time, but they were very stuck in their ways, you'd miss a few major things there. And I guess that's where intimacy training felt like it took us into a whole new realm when we brought that in as part of the process at Essex in 2022. But that's now stuck in the project as well. There are a couple of things that stick, and the intimacy work is probably a really sticky bit of spaghetti that, wherever the project goes next, that's always going to be there.

**NW**: We had the advantage that a lot of the people who stuck with the project were also getting lots of new and exciting additional training in the early years. So, Harry, for example, you went to Lecoq, and there were people in and out of the project who were themselves in training outside of the project at various points. Now that we've all settled into our careers, it was really valuable to bring in a skill set like intimacy coordination that none of us had trained in, to update our toolboxes.

**RB**: Elle McAlpine (Hardman and McAlpine n.d.), the intimacy coordinator who worked with us, gave us another shared language. She encouraged us to ask, 'if there's intimacy, why is it there, how is it functioning?' You can't just say, 'they kiss'; you have to know why. One of the key things I've taken away from that day is that there's always another way of doing it. If two performers don't want to kiss, okay, what happens in the absence of it? What happens if you do it on opposite sides of the stage, but they physicalize it in a different way? She brought us new tools for questioning that.

**HK**: It definitely got into our heads. Practically, we could then start to ask the question: do they need to touch? Do they need to kiss? What are we trying to say here? But then also zooming out: do we need to talk about the real reason that we're interested in this scene where he touches her? And how do we create that effect, without just playing it literally? There was a really powerful moment in the last iteration, where Angelo just did a gesture, and Isabella felt it, but they never touched. Bringing that coaching into the R&D process gave us a shared language and also put us all on the same level with it. I think it's fascinating, that idea of training and R&D coming together.

**RB**: I remember the first time we did consent to touch after Elle had been with us, in a like, 'okay, let's all try this' way. I remember writing the notes in my notebook and saying, 'okay, well, I learnt this the same time you did, and now I'm going to try and facilitate it!' It felt like that was a leveller in the room. Since that work with Elle – and I guess again this is a development of the industry – I think so much more now about how a room is held, how it operates.

**NW**: That training really prompted me to take a step back and think about my unexamined assumptions about how particular people might respond to this training, or who would be the most vulnerable in the room.

**RB**: It's so much about who's in the room and about how that shaped each phase. But also that the joy of R&D is getting to focus on the room rather than, like, 'okay, day one scripts up, please, positions, we're blocking the scene'. It felt so far from that. It really affords the time to go, 'how do we want this room to run as a company?'

**NW**: You brought in the exercise to create the community guidelines, a collective agreement about how we would work together, on the first day of the Essex process. It was a classic think-pair-share setup, but it gave everyone space to think individually about their needs, and then to slowly widen the lens (Lyman 1981). You structured it so that we could each think about to what extent our needs were in alignment with others' needs in the room, or whether there were any conflicts or places where maybe we needed to negotiate.

Our community guidelines from Essex included embracing messiness and failure. And we really did need that space for failure! I remember when we had that call to say, 'We've forgotten Isabella!' We had done this thing where the Duke was the puppet master, and he was structuring the world, and I think I jolted out of sleep one morning thinking, 'wait a minute!'

**RB**: Yeah, we did have an emergency meeting to think about how to approach the next weekend.

**HK**: Again, the advantage of an R&D is that we've got time to work on that, whereas if the show has already gone up, and you're two weeks in, and then you go and check on it, you can't necessarily make those changes

**NW**: That realization hit us at a point where actually we had started thinking about the end product. We'd started to shape the sharing. And so we then had to think, 'how do we not trash everything we already have in an effort to add this new angle in?'

**RB**: That felt like a moment where we had to think about how we were approaching the room. We could not go in and tell them, 'everything you've done, we're throwing away'. Even with our limited time frame, because it was an R&D, we had the space to make those mistakes. In a traditional rehearsal process there's no time for that. Learn your lines, walk on, walk off, get your blocking right, hit the emotional notes you need to hit and go home. There is real skill and real artistry in that. But the other end of the spectrum is important, too, to have space to fail.

**HK**: Is there something in that about devising generally? Because if you've got a three-week rehearsal process, it's all very rushed usually. You've got a script, and that script has gone through that lengthier process of making all the mistakes and having rewrites. Whereas I guess, in this sort of process, even though we're still working with a text, we are pretty much devising, and so we do need time to make those mistakes. I think that's something actually, the theatre industry doesn't realise: with scripted work, all of that messiness has already happened over many, many years of development, but sometimes companies don't give the same amount of rehearsal time for a devising process. I think that R&D in that sense is really, really important if you're devising.

**RB**: I think this is about how the script was positioned in the room. I feel like we've held the script in its rightful place. Shakespeare hasn't had all the power in the room because the text doesn't have all the power in the room.

One of the things I found really helpful was to know who I've been asked to be in this room: that my role in the room was as a dramaturg.

**HK**: I was having a really interesting chat recently with some other movement directors, and we were talking about the point of a movement director. So I'll be there to choreograph a scene or work on character movements or whatever. Why can't the director do that sort of thing? But in this process, and in R&Ds that (in my opinion) are run well, it's less, 'I need someone to come in and do this thing that I know nothing about' and more like, 'I'm just going to give you this hat so that I can wear this other hat'.

**NW**: And I then have permission to not worry about that. Because of the two of you, I can zoom out and look at how it all fits together, which is luxurious, honestly.

## Looking back

**NW**: I also think, when you write something up, or when you reflect on something, it can feel, suddenly, like this very linear, predetermined thing. But thinking of this project through the lens of R&D really foregrounds the extent to which we are sort of always figuring it out as we go. We come in with a toolbox, but there is that sense that anything could happen, and we could end up anywhere. Even though we started with the same toolkit, and we added some things like the intimacy training, or the Lecoq work, or the explicit interest in dramaturgy, actually, ultimately, we are just some DIYers who walked into a falling-apart house.

**RB**: Also, so much surrounded the R&D logistically and practically. I'm trying to remember when we did that lovely work outside – I can't remember why we ended up outside, but we discovered some really exciting things, and maybe that looks back to what you said about the messiness.

**NW**: Logistically, the Essex project was built around intensive weekends where we were just doing the project for two full days and then having a three-week gap before the next one. It was for purely practical reasons that we did that because everybody had day jobs. Our participants were all finishing their degrees. But I think it quite usefully gave us a good balance between having those really intensive, fully focused periods of time, and then lots of percolating space, lots of time for stuff to just be happening in the background.

**HK**: I remember talking about it at the time as well; those creative chats you have in the break or on the walk home and stuff. You need that distance. Some of our best ideas came from, you know, just having dinner.

**NW**: And talking with people external to the project. James, my husband, was in the house when we got home. He'd ask a question, and we'd all start talking at once.

**RB**: There was joy in the intensity of doing solid weekends, rather than say, if we'd met once a week for an afternoon. I was really struck going through my notebook that every now and then I've obviously scribbled down the time of a taxi or the time of a train.

**HK**: I think generally that sense of being away from your normal life is quite useful for an R&D. You probably had less experience of this, Nora, because we were in your workplace, which was an advantage in itself. But you hear of companies that do spend a lot of time on R&D, like Cheek By Jowl and Complicité, and they insist on going away. I think Complicité always goes somewhere in the south of France. Being in Colchester still takes you out of your life so that you can totally focus on the subject matter, but also so that you can be in a separate place, and those chats will happen, that sharing of skills and experiences, and then all the stuff you then have to play with the R&D is so much richer. I do think you need that time on another planet.

**RB**: It always comes down to food, doesn't it? We were sharing dinner together. I think that it felt like the sense of community was then beneficial in the room because we were standing on that time together.

**HK**: It's a strange thing to talk about to people outside of theatre and academic land. Just because I don't think it really exists in a lot of other ways. Maybe in science and technology. But it's quite a unique way of creating something, I think.

**NW**: I don't want to give the impression that we've done this deliberately – that the whole concept is there's never a show. That also came out of a purely practical set of circumstances where in the beginning we were all physically together in Exeter and then we sort of scattered to different places, and the money has been in dribs and drabs. It's not a big AHRC project. It's not an Arts Council deal where we have long term funding that is supporting the process. It's been this kind of bits and pieces thing, which has the silver lining of not having to stress about producing something major at the end of it.

**RB**: It's the process again. I think this is a reminder of how much shared language and experience we have built together. In Essex, there were moments when we acknowledged that we'd all come from the same university and that we had some common ground from Exeter. And so it felt like, I'm particularly thinking of working at Essex, that there was both: we were standing on some shared language and shared experience, but there was also this moment in the project, and we recognized that this phase will be different. There was strength in the shared things we were standing on, that maybe enabled us to be more trusting of the present.

**NW**: So Harry can ask me that question of what we're making, and I'm pretty sure he's only ever half serious. And when I say I don't know, I'm only ever half serious, because we've done it enough times to know that we will figure it out. Sure maybe the very first time, in the vacant shop front in Exeter, Harry asked, 'what are we making?', I was like, 'I don't know', and I 100% meant that. But you know, there's something nice about being able to stand on seven years of a project and say, 'I don't know, but we'll figure it out'. And we have the trust that we'll figure it out rather than genuinely having no clue whether it will come together or not.

## References

Ahmed, S. (2021), *Complaint!*, Durham, NC: Duke University Press.
Angel, K. (2021), *Tomorrow Sex Will Be Good Again*, London: Verso.
Bates, L. (2022), *Fix the System, Not the Women*, London: Simon & Schuster.
Bogart, A. and T. Landau (2005), *The Viewpoints Book: A Practical Guide to Viewpoints and Composition*, New York: Theatre Communications Group.
Buncombe, A. (2016), 'Standford Rape Case: Read the Impact Statement of Brock Turner's Victim', 2 September. https://www.independent.co.uk/news/people/stanford-rape-case-read-the-impact-statement-of-brock-turner-s-victim-a7222371.html.
Foster, D. (2015), *Lean Out,* London: Watkins.
Goodmark, L. (2023), *Imperfect Victims: Criminalized Survivors and the Promise of Abolition Feminism*, Oakland, CA: University of California Press.
Hardman, K. and E. McAlpine (n.d.), 'About', *EK Intimacy,* https://www.ekintimacy.com/about.
Lyman, F. (1981), 'The Responsive Classroom Discussion: The Inclusion of All Students', in A. S. Anderson (ed.), *Mainstreaming Digest*, 109–14, College Park, MD: University of Maryland College of Education.
Manne, K. (2018), *Down Girl: The Logic of Misogyny*, London: Penguin.
Olufemi, L. (2020), *Feminism, Interrupted: Disrupting Power,* London: Pluto Press.
Shakespeare, W. (2020), *Measure for Measure*, Arden Third Series, ed. A. R. Braunmuller and R. M. Watson, London: The Arden Shakespeare, Bloomsbury.
Vergès, F. (2022), *A Feminist Theory of Violence,* trans. M. Thackway, London: Pluto Press.
Williams, N. J. (2022), 'Incomplete Dramaturgies', *Shakespeare Bulletin*, 40 (1): 1–22.

# 12

# Interview with Alex Kelly and Rachael Walton of Third Angel

**Alex Kelly** and **Rachael Walton** were the co-founders and co-artistic directors of the Sheffield-based theatre company Third Angel (1995–2023). They are theatre-makers, performers, storytellers, game makers and writers. With Third Angel, they created performances that connected the fields of theatre, live art, film and video, durational performance, conversation and digital media.

In this interview, Alex and Rachael discuss the development of their R&D practices across a range of productions, including *Shallow Water* (1997–2001), *The Desire Paths* (2016–22), *Presumption* (2006–9, 2015–16), *Class of '76* (2000–10), *Partus* (2016–17), *Pleasant Land* (2003–4) and *Cape Wrath* (2013–19), as well as exploring how such work is funded. They also provide a series of prompts and questions that they pose in their own R&D work as well as in the mentoring work they do, helping to shape explorations.

**Note**: In this conversation, Alex and Rachael move flexibly between talking to and about themselves and each other (using 'I' and 'you') and to Karen (using each other's names), and the edit honours this fluidity of speech.

*Thinking across the scope of your work, what is the function of R&D? Where does it sit? Where do you find that you encounter it?*

**Rachael Walton (RW)**: It's not one straight line. I wonder whether there are layers, lots of layers going on at the same time. There's a level of being artists in the world, and how that influences what you read, what you consume, what you take in, so that's a level that's happening all the time, that's constant. And then there'll be the run-up prior to thinking about starting work on something that will be specific reading, or watching, or going to see, which will be eighteen months, two years. It becomes more like being a cultural magpie, pecking at lots of different things. Some of that might be research in terms of making yourself more informed, or jumping off points from my own divergent thinking. Some of it might be not wanting to repeat what's already out there, to find a new way of thinking about something. And then as you get closer, R&D will be in a room trying out ideas.

**Alex Kelly (AK)**: Yes, it starts with looking outwards and then it becomes more focused on a particular project. And the research moves from thematic and subject matter research into what form might be best to explore. The research also involves finding someone who knows more about it and going and talking to them and telling them what we're thinking of doing and seeing how they respond to that. Or sometimes it starts with working out how you achieve an image. In one of our earlier shows, *Shallow Water* (1997–2001), we were trying to work out how to project onto water, and someone said something to us about powder lying on the surface of water, so we thought about talcum powder, and we discovered we could make it lie on the water and project onto that. So that was logistical research, but it was also about the environment the audience are in and what they can smell.

**RW**: There is even an element of our work where R&D is in the moment with a member of the public, because you can put everything in place, you can put the rules and the scaffolding required to do a show properly, but you don't know until that first encounter where it might lead you, and then it develops further. Our ethos is not doing theatre to people, it's doing it with them, and that exchange. You know, even with *The Desire Paths* (2016–22), each time it's gone out on tour, it's changed because of the learning that's happened before.

In terms of what we actually do, we've done R&D in several different ways. So we have had time when it's just me and Alex for a week and we're sitting and we're talking, like, what are you interested in? And what do we need to say? And where is that going to go? That will involve drawing and writing and reading and quite quiet kind of meditative things, not related to any kind of show, but about moving our ideas on really, in sync or in the same place. We've done R&D that's totally separate to a rehearsal making period with artists before (specifically Lucy Ellinson and Chris Thorpe, who we collaborated with quite a lot), shacked up in Tideswell village thinking about where things might go and future shows and how we could collaborate. Or there's just been the two of us up in Cove Park thinking about the evolution of the company and how we wanted to work with collaborators and how that might influence the work that we made. By the nature of the fact that you're devising, you're doing R&D side by side with that often. And what we've tried to do over the last few years is have as many people in the room as possible, so even though you might be designing the show or you might be doing the lighting, there's an invitation to everyone to take part in that devising process and add text or add ideas or whatever.

**AK**: Those weeks where we're in a cottage somewhere, just two of us or a specific group, that's sort of the base layer of R&D, where everything you read you're thinking 'is this relevant to a project we might want to do?' We might not even know yet whether it's a show or a short film or something else, but it's about identifying the angle you might take, which other people in the collective are interested, who you might make it with. So hopefully you'd come out of that with maybe four or five projects that are going to get pushed along a little bit more. So *Presumption* (2006–9, 2015–16) is sort of unusual in that sense in that it didn't come out of one of those processes.

**RW**: There's also a strand with the R&D of doing an experiment or doing some research and not knowing the form that it's going to take but investing in that. For *Class of '76* (2000–10) you knew that you wanted to go and find your classmates [from primary school], and for *Partus* (2016–17), we wanted to collect stories about birth, but we didn't know what form they were going to take or what the shows would be. With *Pleasant Land* (2003–4) it was just travelling around the country and turning up in a town and going to explore, then thinking about what we discovered, what's important, who we wanted to talk to. For *Cape Wrath* (2013–19) you wanted to follow in the footsteps of your grandad and that certainly didn't turn out in the form that you thought it might be. I think there's also an element of doing an action and seeing what comes out of that action, and then the material that you create then pushes forward a form, and then you start experimenting with the form, and then the two things come together.

**AK**: Yes, we've got these tools we think will help discover that show, we identify the process and we know it will generate material, through the stories we gather but then also through the process by which we gather those stories. So some of those processes produce storytelling shows on a stage, in a minibus, in a stage that's been made to look like a community hall, or an exhibition, and we try and hold off deciding what that form is for as long as funders and commissioners will allow us to, but there is a point where someone is saying, 'look if you want the gallery you need to tell us that you want the gallery and not the theatre', and you have to go, 'all right, we think it's a gallery show'.

**RW**: And there's an interesting point politically about how long that level of experimentation can continue as venues become more risk averse, but also about tying artists down to laying out exactly what the money is going to be spent on before you even start. How do you even know?

**AK**: We also think of getting a show ready to meet an audience, because material evolves organically just through presenting it to an audience. Sometimes the R&D process carries on. Once we'd made *The Desire Paths* and we knew how it worked with audiences, I heard about a book called *The Address Book* which is about how all around the world, addresses exist quite differently to how they do in Western Europe. Even though the show was 'made', I still went and got that and started reading it and talking to Gillian Lees (the co-lead artist on *The Desire Paths*) about the ideas in it, so it then feeds into the next time you do the show. The research is then about what you've made, and contextualizing what you've made in what other research is still going on, so if R&D is constant and different layers, you find yourself existing in one of the layers of research a bit more at any one time depending on where you are in various processes.

*Could you talk me through an example of a R&D process from your practice?*

**AK**: *Presumption* (2006–16) is the one that immediately comes into my mind. Because I can remember the moment you had the idea of it. In a budget meeting about a different project, Rachael suddenly said, 'Wouldn't it be great if a show started with a woman walking backwards onto the stage carrying a tray of glasses, and then she had to turn around to put the tray of glasses onto the table, but the table wasn't there, and the glasses all broke because she thought there'd be a set and there wasn't?' And I said that that sounded really good. And then we spent a week developing something we initially called *Best Laid Plans* [for a sharing at a Pyramid Festival in May 2005 at Sheffield Theatres], where the idea was there were two actors and they're doing a sort of a domestic drama, like a drawing room comedy or something, and they turn up and there isn't a set there, so they have to keep going into the wings to bring the furniture on. So you'd never get to see the actual play, you'd only get to see the setting up of it.

We went into an R&D and rehearsal process the following year, and Chris Thorpe joined us in that. And we commissioned the play that the audience would never see all of, which was trying to deal with the themes that we thought the *show* was about, which was about people who might find themselves in a relationship, and a few years down the line it's not as passionate as you see in the books and in the films, and people who can't afford to separate because they'd have to sell the house and neither of them would have enough money to actually live on.

**RW**: But we didn't get on with it.

**AK**: So instead, Rachael and Chris did a lot of improvization and quite traditional character work on this couple, and we had five or six quite long improvised conversations that we'd recorded and transcribed. And then we would all write audience-aware monologues that were either letters they were writing to each other or thought tracks or storytelling. We were making this process two or three days a week. And the rest of the week, I was driving around second-hand shops in Sheffield, buying furniture that looked interesting. So each R&D day we would also play the game of bringing furniture on until it looked like a room. We liked the moment after the performer has been bringing on random objects for a while, they're just a random set of objects, and then there's a moment where you add something and . . . oh, look, it's a room. This feels like an environment. And we were progressing both of those strands of the process at the same time.

**RW**: We were also trying to get so much furniture on that they were physically trapped on stage, so they couldn't get off to get the rest of the furniture.

**AK**: But then, whenever we tried the two people bringing the stuff on and then just doing a little fragment of the play, the two things that we got stuck on were, we weren't hearing enough of the drama to really get into the thematic idea of the show, and why aren't they helping each other? Quite often with these R&D processes, we'd do runs on Friday afternoons for the whole team. And we did a run through of this with a couple of weeks to go before we opened, and we couldn't make the two strands work together. I remember Chris Thorpe saying, 'Remind me that it's always this difficult. Have you ever been this close and this far away at the same time?' We all just kept saying 'We've just got to trust the process. We've got to trust the process.'

But then on the following Monday, I remember that you came in and you said, 'Well, what if it works the other way around? Instead of bringing the furniture on and that prompts them to do a little bit of material, what if they're trying to do the material and they keep discovering that the furniture they need isn't there?' So it was going back to that original moment of the table not being there for the glasses. They have to go off stage, get the bit of furniture they need, and then they start again. And I think you and Chris just put some furniture out, spiked it, took the furniture away. And so each time we get to a bit of furniture that isn't there, we have to go and get it and then we reset. And we carved up the text. And by lunchtime, we had the first half of *Presumption*.

There's a point where the room in practical R&D almost becomes like playing about in the space, just because you have licence to try stuff out. Like we realized that the performers needed to know where the furniture was going to go, and where you put the first thing dictated where the other things went. And because we didn't want to do almost hidden marks, like normal theatre, we just made it really obvious, like a square for every chair leg, rather than just a square where the whole chair went.

**RW**: But it was also the forensic nature of the furniture representing a relationship.

**AK**: An autopsy of a relationship. We liked the fact that it looked a bit like a crime scene. And then there was something that came in halfway through the show. The show changed tense and became . . . at one point, Chris went off and Rachael said to the audience, 'You've heard this, haven't you?', and you summarized the previous conversation in four sentences. And we really liked that energy, so we started using it. As the narrative moves forward into the following day and the next couple of weeks, we report to the audience as if they've heard the conversation already, even though they haven't (in that mode). And so other bits of text that we've got, we started with you paraphrasing it rather than learning it, which meant the show varied in length sometimes, because there were lists that got improvised. It all felt very organic, those processes.

**RW**: It was very, very far away from the first moment walking on with the glasses, but it was still pushing that idea of how long an audience would watch a bare stage, and how little you needed to do to be able to maintain a relationship that was fulfilling for both sides.

*How do you tend to fund your R&D processes?*

**RW**: Well, we have always funded them, we'd always make sure that we could fund the R&D even if we had to curtail our ambitions with the actual show. Then when we became an NPO, we would build R&D into our annual budget. But subsequently the money wasn't going as far, so over the years there's been more pressure on the amount of time and the amount of experimentation we've been able to put in place. And also because we moved from emerging to mid-career artists, the opportunities to apply for residencies or schemes became less and less available to us, but we'd always try to do our R&D with either a venue or a commissioner or someone that would give us space.

**AK**: From whatever point we became annually funded (via Arts Council England's Regularly Funded Organization and then National Portfolio Organization schemes) and had to start doing annual budgets, we always put in R&D weeks. If we needed to, we would usually look for other funding for them, like a venue commission, but otherwise we would fund it from our core money and do it more locally so we weren't having to pay residential costs. But when you do go away, to Cove Park or wherever, in a week like that, you're at work all of the time you're awake! We got paid a normal full-time week wage, but we'd be doing fourteen or fifteen hour days. So, whenever we are in a R&D phase we pay ourselves and our collaborators, but there's a layer of R&D that's longer and thinner that's not always paid. That's the sort of gardening level of R&D, feeding the plants, that's where any arts company gets ideas to make stuff. You know, the book you read on the bus because you think this could be a show, that's not paid.

**RW**: We've never got to that point of paying ourselves for doing the reading, the watching, the films, the going to the galleries, the going to see other people's work, that's all been on our own time. It would feel like such a luxury to just sit and watch something together.

Talking about funding is probably not the exciting bit of being an artist but it does need to be addressed. In some countries, they're trying to have a universal basic income for artists that allows you to exist as an artist and do that as your job, and then you might *happen* to make something rather than being project funded or company funded within the ACE NPO system. There has to be that switch, but it's about society valuing that way of thinking about art rather than it being an entertainment industry.

*As Third Angel, you've spent a lot of time mentoring other artists and supporting other R&D processes. Can you tell us a bit about that?*

**AK**: One of the things we say when we teach university students is to make the thing you really want to make. If you're interested in it, trust that; don't make the thing you think you ought to make on this module, pursue what you're interested in. We'd often be asked what our process is like, and we'd say it's different every show, it's never the same, and so when we came to mentoring I think we brought that philosophy with us. When we join an R&D process or set up a process for someone, we want to help them figure out how to make their show. We have a set of tools that we find useful, but we try really hard to not dictate how their process runs.

**RW**: When we first start working with someone we talk a lot about why. Why are we here, why us, what can we bring to the table, what's your notion of success, what do you want to achieve in the time that we're with you. We often encourage people to have a sketchbook, a work scrapbook, recording all your ideas in the same place. 'Beware the sofa' comes up a lot, there's often a fear of getting up and getting something into the space.

**AK**: And sharing stuff. If what you think you really need is a bit of text, and it needs to be quite crafted to do the job you want, that's fine, spend two hours writing, but after lunch you're going to stand up and read it to someone in the room.

**RW**: Always go back to the w's: the who, the where, the what.

**AK**: And some of the fundamental questions we always have. Who are we in front of the audience? Making sure you know that. Maybe you're going to be a character and you're not going to look at the audience, or you're going to be yourself and you're just going to tell the audience a story, and it's not an either/or, there can be a spectrum, but you need to ask those questions. We also discovered that, as mentors, we don't have to be in the room the whole time, and that sometimes giving someone the room was better than watching them while they're trying to write. Very early on, we ran our own scheme where we would pay people to be mentored, so for the week that they're in Sheffield with us, they just concentrate on their own project and don't have to leave early to go and earn some money.

**RW**: I think it's also about being open to developing our own practice by learning from the people we're mentoring. Action Hero was the first company that we ever mentored, through a particular scheme at Chelsea Theatre, so we started with that relationship, but over the years, it's moved on, and now we'd equally go to them and ask them about international touring or whatever.

**AK**: Mentoring is one of the most rewarding things we've done. I think of R&D and devising as getting yourself into trouble and getting out of it, so you find that each show has its own problems to be solved. Every process you learn something, and sometimes you only learn it for that process, but sometimes it's something that you can apply to other work, and that also happens when you're mentoring other artists.

**RW**: Another big thing is about what's the point of doing it if you already know the answers. You might be on a scary journey, you might not know which direction you can go in but it's part of the process and part of the serendipitous nature of R&D. And we like pens, and we like post-it notes and we tell people to have things on the walls and to make the space your own, make it a safe making space. Bring bananas. I hate bananas but Alex always has to bring in bananas if we're doing some R&D.

19 June 2023
Interviewed by Karen Quigley

## Questions and Prompts #6

- What pre-work, before the R&D itself, would it be useful to conduct? Who should conduct this?
- Might your research and/or practical questions be formulated through the R&D process itself? Who comes up with these and how?
- Can you formulate questions that can only be answered by practice – by doing it?
- Start with 'why?' and always return to the 'W's': 'the who, the where, the what'.
- How do the people in the room affect the project you are developing? How does the project inform who is involved?
- What are the roles of people in the R&D? Is it helpful to give people a role – 'who they are in the room'?
- Is your R&D designed to allow a core creative group to develop a project, or is it a way to allow several different groups (e.g. students, community groups) to explore an area together with an appropriate structure and scaffolding?
- If you are working on an existing play, what is the role and status of the text in the R&D?
- Is it useful to develop community guidelines or agreed values, aims or ways of working as part of your R&D?
- Are there ways to distance R&D from your other work so as to provide a new space for creativity?
- Can your R&D explore form as well as content? What if you start with questions about form? What might these questions reveal about the content (and vice versa)?
- What do you need in the R&D room apart from the people? What furniture, props, pens and so on will help you to explore this idea?
- Record all your ideas in the same place. Keep a sketchbook or notepad, just for this project.
- Think about 'layers' of R&D: the work that goes on in the room and the (often longer and thinner) R&D that continues across the whole timespan of a project.
- Always use R&D to make the thing you really want to make. If you're interested in it, trust that.
- Remind each other (as Alex Kelly did) that you've got to trust the process!

# 13

# Movement direction as research and development

Ayşe Tashkiran

Movement directors are creative collaborators with specialist skills in movement. We work within the parameters of a text, script or score, the spaces in between the text or scenes, and sometimes in the open terrain of newly made or devised work in which spoken language or written text or character is less central. Each theatre project will necessitate a bespoke movement approach and process. The practice of movement direction can be thought of as inherently composed of cycles of research and development (henceforth R&D). Movement directors undertake these cycles alone, with the creative team, and with the acting company. With each iteration of an R&D cycle, co-creative, embodied, dramaturgical propositions, experiments and decisions bring movement directors closer and closer to shaping a physical score that has repeatable aspects for the performer. This repeatable physical score enters the fabric of a production and eventually is performed for an audience who are then part of an embodied experience of the 'development' part of 'research and development'.

For this chapter, I divide my movement direction work into two groups: those with a pre-existing text (plays/opera) and those without, that is, productions that might be known as devised work, dance theatre or new creations. The role of movement direction R&D can be obscured by production methods in mainstream contemporary British theatre, when creative processes are focused on a pre-existing text, or rehearsal room procedures assume the primacy of the text as the terrain of creative exploration. In my experience, R&D is more commonly embedded in the creation of new, physically driven works where text may not be the leading factor, and a phase of movement R&D will be a recognizable, funded part of making that new work.

Two guiding questions structure my exploration: firstly, what constitutes research and development for a movement director in the initial stages of creative processes in the theatre? And secondly, what constitutes movement research and development in the rehearsal room? I will draw on my movement direction of *Doctor Faustus* (Royal Shakespeare Company, the Swan and the Barbican Centre, 2016) and *The Dark* (Peut-Être Theatre, National Tour, 2022) with the creative processes of these productions providing examples of movement research in action. Movement direction, like most theatre arts, is woven into creative relationships and processual possibilities and constraints, and for this chapter I refer to two reflective conversations with two long-term collaborators: director Maria Aberg, and director and artistic director Daphna Attias.

*Doctor Faustus* was directed by Aberg, a Swedish director working in the UK. Being part of Aberg's creative team is characterized by collaborative artistic conversations and the invention of working methods and rehearsal room practice in action, that is, we dialogue through making work and staging productions. Aberg will often redeploy the first weeks of rehearsal as a period of creative experimentation with the actors, movement director and composer. In this way, a type of R&D is imbricated with early rehearsal. All our play-based work at the Royal Shakespeare Company incorporated a period of exploration called 'workshopping', that is, research and development within rehearsal. Over a period of fourteen years working on a variety of productions, Aberg and I have invested in these workshops as a way to explore a research vocabulary within the rehearsal period, and it is here that I have been able to test out movement processes, drawing on our shared critical, feminist perspectives. In the case of *Doctor Faustus*, we pursued world-building research and experimental movement material-making with the whole company in the first weeks of rehearsal and with three of the actors through the whole eight-week rehearsal in an ongoing way. This became key to my ability to use an experimental, embodied process for their movement material. This production was born from a full arc of R&D and a full rehearsal process simultaneously.

The second research and development process that I will examine is with small-scale, independent company Peut-Être Theatre that specializes in deep-rooted explorations of accessibility and inclusivity with a physical, dance-theatre style of work for children. Partnerships with Great Ormond Street Hospital (GOSH) and University of Southampton mean that the artistic team often starts with scientific, medical and specialist conversations, as well as testing out the themes with children themselves. *The Dark* was created with the voices and experiences of visually impaired and blind children at its centre. A blind performer and blind consultants informed the creative processes and performance languages. One motor of this R&D was the experiential nature of the dark for blind, visually impaired and sighted children, and the objective was to create a show that was accessible within the creative making process and audience experience. Director Daphna Attias started the R&D for *The Dark* in 2019 in two week-long studio phases. The development of the show was interrupted by the pandemic, and the production eventually came to fruition in early 2022. This was the third show I had movement directed with the company and the first that had a source text, *The Dark*, a children's book by Lemony Snicket, evocatively illustrated by Jon Klassen (Hachette Children's Group, 2013*)*. In the story a young boy called Laszlo confronts his fear of the Dark, who lives in the cellar of his home. At the time of the R&D, permission to use the actual story had not been finalized, so these early phases were thematically connected to ideas of fear, darkness and home rather than focused on adapting this story.

# Movement direction in the initial stages of research and development

My embodied knowledges and trainings act as sedimentary layers through which movement ideas filter. These layers are in perpetual growth, constantly nourished and influenced by current movement training and lived experiences. Intangible aspects of artistry such as imagination, learning, orientation, aesthetics and creative dialogue start to shape body knowledge into ways of approaching a new project. Skills in movement analysis, translation and communication developed organically over time enable me to move from an intangible movement impulse to a set of creative strategies that are doable for performers.

Part of my early preparation is the discovery of movement possibilities inherent in source material and possible ways into embodiment in the light of mental concepts (of the writer/director/my research). Examples might include fleshing out dynamics, spaces and actions from words and structures in plays or researching abstract concepts to draw myself into an intimate, knowledgeable rapport to the starting point of a devised work. Diving into source material leads to enriching personal research that starts to generate movement initiation points that eventually become organized into embodied experiments and movement tasks for use with actors.

In *Movement Directors in Contemporary Theatre* (Tashkiran 2020), movement directors variously describe this initial examination of source material as 'intuitive' (43), with a view to actualizing (44), 'inventive way of looking at something physically' (81), reading to 'spark movement ideas', 'extrapolating' (83) movement, drawing 'the physicality out' (93) or existing in the realm of the 'non-concrete' (98). Movement directors are unified in describing this period of personal research as multifaceted and bodily. I deliberately engage my felt senses, my body knowledge and informed intuition in dialogue with the source material, often translating it into visual and dynamic forms. In my work, this phase is also structural. I analyse, list, storyboard and unearth the language of the text or source material. I activate and nourish my imagination, while underpinning my informed intuition with firm foundations. Context, politics and the body stories of characters are lenses through which to build familiarity with the source material. My aim is to unify an analytical mode with a more free-ranging approach, in which I intuitively sense the movement within the source material.

With *Doctor Faustus*, my notebook documents two phases of personal research. The first includes the creation of a storyboard of Marlowe's play, which I used to decode the text as written. My storyboard became a tool to understand the sequencing and the internal structure of each scene. This enabled me to identify the weight of each scene, to visualize the spaces/locations and how populated they may be, how the flow of bodies would tell the story. I also created lists to categorize the playwright's language. I listed all verbs spoken by characters (though turned into transitive verbs). I noted repeats of metaphors, animal imagery, references to the body,[1] the weather, time shifts, patterns of relationships, numbers or shapes. This helped me to notice the patterns

---

[1] For a 'humoral reading', see Tashkiran in Flatt, K. (2022), *Movement Direction: Developing Physical Narrative for Performance*, Marlborough: The Crowood Press. Page 98

that existed in the language that eventually became a type of movement map. This is researching the play as authored.

Next in my *Doctor Faustus* notebooks, we find a second phase that captured creative conversations with Aberg and her edit of the play which removed, replaced and added sections to Marlowe's original. This is researching the production text. Three of Aberg's interventions had significant ramifications for movement. Firstly, Aberg introduced a device which meant that the roles of Doctor Faustus and Mephistophilis would be assigned to two actors interchangeably by chance for each show. This meant that for each show we had two possible versions, depending on the striking of a match (this specific game of chance was discovered during a research phase). Aberg's second intervention was the addition of several large movement/song sequences with a chorus of scholars. The third intervention was the incarnation of Helen of Troy as a devil in the shape of an adolescent child. In response, my personal research opened into a new terrain to include the consideration of a performance language for narrative action which included chorus work, chance mechanisms and a physical language for the incarnation of Helen of Troy. Alongside researching our shared texts (Marlowe's play and Aberg's version), I was reading and watching sources that might offer embodied insight and nourish my movement eye with imagery, direct observation and references. For *Doctor Faustus*, I researched a diverse variety of areas, but the history of ritual magic and gender fluid cabaret acts emerged as particularly rich inspirations for movement.

The initial research stage of *The Dark* also involved multiple phases but with a different focus. With *The Dark*, there was no play text, so my personal movement research was mainly in response to Daphna Attias's reasons and mission for this piece, that is, her interest in the audience's sensory experience of darkness and light and this children's story. I went on to develop, detail, add to and translate these starting points. This is the point at which I dive into my physical imagination and engage with my visual and sensorial understanding of movement as it relates to the project. And it is also when I begin to identify and categorize movement principles that I feel, see and imagine. During previous collaborations, Attias and I had developed a working method and shared language, where I would take an abstract concept and identify its dynamics to generate movement material. Our first creative discussions prompted me to explore the personification of darkness and a child's perspective of the architecture of their home, and how fear might grow, animate, dissolve. By the time I entered the rehearsal room, I had synthesized my intuition and research into physical starting points. In the case of *The Dark*, I was also in a learning position with the working methods and politics of working with blind and visually impaired performers and audiences. For this R&D the layers were researching the movement potential of source materials and researching for the production language, which was oriented towards the audiences' sensory experience and age range.

When considering what movement methods to develop for a production, I will often start with a sense of the project's movement dynamic (such as speed, shifts, energy, weight, qualities, patterns) or movement principles (movement foci such as *grounding*) and slowly work backwards to see how that might translate into practice. Working with an informed yet intuitive feel for the movement qualities, I start to locate where the aesthetic centre of the work might be. Whatever the starting point, as movement director, my objective is to get as close as I can to the source material. My aim is to discover its nature with the least amount of interference or judgement, and to circle around it freely, allowing analysis to ignite my imagination. There is much back and forth with the director during this phase. With both Attias and Aberg this is enriching and constructive, forming a shared research terrain. I listen deeply and propose resources and suggestions in relation to movement, which then may become incorporated into our process. There is also a type of dwelling with or immersion in the subjects of the research and allowing for my lived experience to filter through its themes – such as meditations on qualities of darkness in the space that surrounds us and the spaces within us. It is after this phase that I start shaping research discoveries towards what will become movement experimentation: filtering, selecting, designing and anticipating approaches with the company. By this stage, I usually create one thematic movement map with each area populated with potential tasks and improvisations, detailing ways of starting to translate personal preparation and director dialogues into doable movement and methods for working with the actors.

## Movement direction research and development in the rehearsal room

The next phase transforms personal and collaborative research into doable movement and creative movement strategies for specific actors or performers. In my practice, these strategies are *relational and intersubjective groundwork*, improvization for world-building, *generative improvisation* and *task setting*. These areas expand and contract in size depending on the nature of the R&D, and this is the point at which I start turning research into actionable processes: from idea to action, or from mental concept or images into doable things; from words and images to the sensorial. Research becomes active movement experiences, experimentation and embodiment. This involves a sizable shift of focus. After personal research and dialogue with the director, the actor now takes centre stage. In this phase, I enter a complex, shared and live environment.

*Relational, intersubjective groundwork* is fundamental to most theatre processes. This is the creation of the culture of creativity, inclusivity, freedom of movement, actor agency, safe and sustainable use of the body and the parameters of relational exchange between the performers, including shared vocabulary, boundaries, respect and dignity at work. It is the building of an ensemble through movement. For movement direction, the choice of warm-up is key to this groundwork. It informs the kind of creative research and development process I will have with the performers. The warm-up will become a ritual to draw us into physical dialogue with each other and our source material. Here, I take time to construct a bespoke scheme of physical work that will take us from being individual performers into the world of the work. It is often at this time that relevant movement techniques or material might be directly offered to the company. In a technical sense, any warm-up prepares bodies to engage in movement work safely and sustainably. In my process, this leads onto themed movement improvizations. This effectively extends the warm-up, leading the performers into the feel of the world or the physicality of the movement we will explore. These improvisations might be world-building if there is a particular society that we are exploring or more oriented towards a movement dynamic if the theme is abstract.

For *Doctor Faustus*, the warm-up took the form of a guided mobilization of all the major joints from foot to head and then into an improvised rhythmic movement arc from slow to a gradual crescendo made up of free movement. This warm-up increased the heart rate, mobilized the joints, activated the breath and gradually galvanized muscles (activating proprioception and raising certain hormone levels), before building physical connections between the actors as a group. I moved on to guide a full-group physical improvisation that I 'called'[2] as we went along. This kind of improvisation allows actors to invent while in movement connection with each other, while seeing each other moving. Kinaesthetic listening and physical spontaneity arose as we switched partners rapidly and our bodies heated up, perspired, let go, allowing our bodies to lead. After a rhythmic apotheosis, we recalibrated the heart rate and breathing rate (in motion to keep this gradual and safe) – again in communion with each other. Each time I ran this warm-up, I was subtly shifting, adapting, learning the nature of this group of actors and their needs in movement. Group movement became a terrain of embodied research for this show. This choice of warm-up served to lay the foundations for embodied connectivity between the actors and generated movement vocabularies that we harnessed in the production. This ensemble work developed into improvisations and tasks such as competitive choruses led by Faustus and Mephistophilis. It also laid the ground for a series of escalating confrontations between Faustus and his acolyte scholars as he spiralled into chaos. These chorus sections were characterized by loose-limbed, disjointed physical motifs in rave-like movement. At times the chorus could quickly become a pack of snarling, carnal, flesh-eating celebrants. This was seeded and supported by the warm-up and the ensuing group improvisations and tasks.

For *The Dark* the warm-up was very different. Attias and I noted that part of the pleasure of *The Dark* was working with a dancer who had trained in a specific performance vocabulary and two musician/performers who also had their own vocabularies. This warm-up needed to focus on core skills to support performers to increase their stamina, flexibility and connection to movement. With this mix of performers, I was on a learning curve to understand the movement capacities, tendencies and preferences. I was constantly evaluating what techniques and strategies I needed to bring, so we could equitably share a movement terrain for our creative journey. The warm-up started with yoga-based forms combined with elements from other movement systems. The dancer in the company had an extensive dance vocabulary, and the warm-up had to have technical elements to support this wide physical range. This was then followed by variations of contact duet experiments rooted in the weight-bearing of 'push and pull' and 'I am pushed, I am pulled'[3] inspired by Lecoq practices. These generated acute multi-sensory listening (through touch,

---

[2] I am repurposing a term *calling* that is used in folk dance where a caller speaks out the next formation and move in relation to the music (i.e. just ahead of a phrase).

[3] See *The Moving Body: Teaching Creative Theatre* by Jacques Lecoq with Jean-Gabriel Carasso and Jean-Claude Lallias, translated by David Bradby (Methuen Drama 2000: 79–83).

sound, breath) with this group of blind and sighted performers who were discovering their way of moving together. As well as the fundamentals of preparing the body, the warm-up offered the performers a movement vocabulary to use amongst themselves. The guidance for this warm-up laid ground rules of respect, understanding and care for one's own body and for those of fellow performers. Pair work and contact became a terrain of embodied research for this show, weaving through to tasks that resulted in a duet called *The Deep Dark* between the Dark and Laszlo in the cellar. It also laid the ground for playful, sensorial contact between Lazlo and the architecture of his home (staircases, lounge windows in the dead of night, light of the refrigerator).

Prioritizing the intersubjective in the embodied realm of a bespoke warm-up contributes to the context in which movement can happen – a body-positive space that is respectful, care-filled, freeing and stimulating (emotionally and imaginatively). It also needs to be inclusively individualized and harness collective possibility. R&D of movement cannot progress freely if this layer is not carefully planned and well established. In both instances, attention to one's self in the warm-up was followed by the use of gaze/touch, heightened listening, play, improvisation and the occupation of the relational movement space between performers. The warm-ups generated connection within the performers and encouraged freedom to move and experiment. These types of movement director-led warm-ups foreground embodied knowledge as it is the terrain where actors, dancers and movement directors connect. In these kinds of sessions, I am both *inside* the experience, receiving the actor's movement through my body, as well as being a guide who may at any point step *outside*: someone who structures the session, intervenes or signals a new pathway.

*Generative improvisation* and *task setting* are richly creative areas for movement directors in R&D; they feel playful and full of 'what-if' possibilities. Generative improvisation can take many forms. It can be very lightly structured, for example, before the session, I decide upon a movement intention and some key movement principles to use and then I enter the terrain to improvise my way through the guidance with the actors. This type of generative improvisation is when we are all in the activity of moving and, from *inside* and being *in movement*, I am guiding and provoking because I am feeling what is needed and riding the wave towards a certain quality of movement. There is nothing objective about this way of working: it is an intersubjective knowing through the moving body. This is a mix of initiating through offers (both poetic and action based) and through my body in movement: a type of immersive movement research. Another type of generative improvisation is where the parameters are set up in advance with the performers or messages are sent into the 'jam' to add hurdles or problems or ignite specifics. These 'jams' often take the form of long, protracted improvisations that are wholly immersive for the performers but analytical and strategic for me and the director/composer/sound designer/dramaturg and so on. This is movement directing research from a heavily involved, active witness position.

Attias and I have a strong sense memory of some of the *jams* that we undertook in the R&D period for *The Dark,* and for her the analogy is directly musical, that is, we all bring our instruments, we decide on a riff and we all start playing, with an unknown destination. These long-form improvisations were predicated on several factors:

shared languages and parameters; heightened listening; mutuality and extended experiences of time that felt unbound by a need to finish. During these extended, multidisciplinary improvizations, we all worked with a tacit agreement to be inside the jam. Attias saw these jams as having a meditative quality. I recall the strong atmosphere that surrounded us. The nature of these jams is reflective of a group of theatre-makers who improvise in an 'intuitive' way. In the case of this R&D for *The Dark,* our playful jam on the last day of the first week prefigured the final piece. We collated all the movement experiences of the week into one improvization which effectively laid out the tone, the emotional arc and structure for the final show. For Attias in *The Dark* it was imperative to create space and time for experimentation in which immersion was possible. This manifested as extended periods of time of *thematic exploration* where the activities were structured organically, incorporating the voices and participation of all in the room. Having ample time allows space for risk-taking, a deepening of experimentation and a gradual unfolding of the material through testing, adjusting and developing. It is a cumulative process that starts to proliferate with possibilities. In the R&D for *The Dark,* the invitation to play released the potential within the wider creative team, tapping into all our skill sets and extending our artistic input. This set up a multidisciplinary ricochet. We were all invited to play and equally responsible for offering creative starting points. Attias wanted this R&D to be about 'creating textures and emotional connections to material so that you can come back to it more easily'. By not working head-on with narrative material or character, we are afforded greater 'freedom' (Attias 2023).

Key phrases are poetic images designed to generate an open response. I often create a poetic *key phrase* to start a specific movement exploration. Here the research is as much about initiating movement as watching, remembering and responding. The use of key phrases was a rich seam in the process of creating *The Dark*. '*The stairs are full of footsteps*' is an example of a key phrase we used to explore and generate material. Here my intention was to work spatially, knowing that the experience of stairs is widely differing for sighted, blind and visually impaired people, and from a child's point of view. I also knew that we needed to find a physical vocabulary to invoke this architectural element as we were working on a flat floor. This key phrase was a springboard for the performers and all the creatives in the space. Our responses to this phrase produced a playful, acrobatic, energetic movement section in the final production, in which the child character chased stair treads of light that expanded and contracted, disappeared and moved. This is an example of how a movement key phrase can meet an impossible task (creating a staircase on a flat floor) and then be developed into material with the full collaborative force of a creative team. Collectively we generated ludic physical and design solutions, in a multifaceted way for different kinds of audience members, that is, those who were listening and seeing and those who were listening and feeling.

*Task setting* also has many facets. The invention of a movement task already necessitates translating movement intuition into the actionable, communicable and stimulating. As a movement director, I invest in creating dramaturgical propositions while navigating how open or restrictive the parameters for the outcomes might be. In preparation, I first specify the shape of the end point or a desired movement outcome. Next, I reverse engineer, creating stepping stones that might/will get us there – *we start here, we then move onto that, we then bring that and that together and then we select aspects to nourish further.* Once I have a task journey, I step back and ask, 'will I be able to do my task?' Often, I will try out my task myself physically or test it with others. Does it balance the concrete and the possible with the poetic and the impossible? I step away from my task journey to ask in a detailed way what movement skills or experiences the actors need to undertake the task. The slippage between my performer experience and my movement director experience is helpful for this stage. When I have identified what performers may need in terms of physical techniques to be able to flourish within the task, I ensure that we lay those foundations fully. For example, if the actors need to be able to use the floor and the up/down dimension (because I know we need dimensional and topsy-turvy movement) we will prepare physically by making full body contact with the floor, ensuring the safe sequencing of joints and that use of weight is firmly embedded before introducing rolling, spiralling, dropping to and re-emerging from the floor within the task, all of which leads us to the desired topsy-turvy movement. Attias and I circled around my use of verbs[4] as a springboard for exploration, and 'enveloping/escaping' were the ones that resonated strongly during the process of creating *The Dark*. Attias saw this as a key to the final section of what became the show. These two verbs informed movement task journeys. We began by using them to set up a simple progressive structure, for example, working only with the hands to activate the verbs 'envelope' and 'escape'. We changed the timing of the actions and the pathways into and out of the actions. Finally, we incorporated the whole of the body. This is a typical task journey that I might create and one that generated textured movement material that expressed the characters and their relationship to each other. Eventually this became the basis of the dénouement of the final piece: an abstract, tender duet where the Dark repeatedly, softly, enveloped the boy, and from which he slithered away leaving her momentarily with his absent volume imprinted in her arms. The boy's fear progressively dissipated, and he decided to remain in the warm, enveloping embrace of the Dark. We played out this movement task journey in many ways until we all settled on the structure that generated the material for the show. These verbs generated dance-like movement material that was motored by intention rather than abstraction.

Movement task journeys within *Doctor Faustus* contributed to the world surrounding the central characters and, at times, functioned to expand ideas that are only glancingly referenced by Marlowe. At other times, movement tasks allowed for us to connect to the epic gestures contained in the play. In our conversation, Aberg characterized research and development as a 'much freer space where you can explore things that run parallel to, or completely tangentially to the idea or project you are exploring', and that 'it's about what you figure out on the way'. Aberg articulated her desire to start rehearsals in a way that she calls a 'trick of the mind' to reimagine how rehearsal rooms can begin by establishing a shared creative ground for all the company, that is, the actors and the creatives. She problematizes a typical first day of

---

[4] Movement analysis in the Lecoq training is underpinned with forms that are driven by action. See *The Moving Body: Teaching Creative Theatre by* Jacques Lecoq with Jean-Gabriel Carasso and Jean-Claude Lallias, translated by David Bradby (Methuen Drama 2000), for Lecoq's account of the place and scope of verbs.

rehearsal of a play, which feels 'unfree' because 'before you have done anything else here are the limitations and the parameters'. Aberg lays the ground for the company to 'explore and play', and that 'movement is completely integral' to that phase. One example that allowed me to 'explore and play' was to activate my early research into Renaissance sources on magic and incantations. I translated this into a movement task journey for the whole ensemble working individually yet simultaneously. I invited them to '*draw a circle, ensure you are not witnessed, prepare yourself, enter your circle, breathe, become physically ready for your incantation, call the spirits*'. This was an open movement task journey in which each actor offered their unique, individual responses. It enabled the actors to activate their personal research and imaginations within a simple yet comprehensive structure. On reflection, this task served to connect us to the deep-seated impulse of rituals and religious transgressions underpinning the whole play. This contributed to the actors' score and the wider vocabulary of the room. We were all rooted in an embodied way into dark rituals which then filtered into the co-creative, shared realm becoming the frenetic labour of painting circles, burning books, destroying rooms and reifying Doctor Faustus.

As we work through movement tasks, the physical responses, voices and discoveries of the performers are essential – our collective imaginations and artistic insight start to percolate within the task. A theme that emerged in the conversation with Aberg was the nature of *research in action* in the moment. Working with composer Orlando Gough, we took an experimental approach to combining music and song with movement. In the early days of rehearsal, we devised experiments to conduct with the actors. In these experiments, we and the actors bounced suggestions off each other, activating a potent way of creating material. These research sessions prompted ideas and material that translated into sequences in the final production, such as the cabaret number performed by the Seven Deadly Sins for Faustus. The way we worked on this cabaret sequence is typical of a cycle of R&D. After the experimental research sessions with the actors, Aberg, Gough and I would go away to develop the structure, devise and refine moves or write lyrics and music. Then we would roll that into the next rehearsal to further develop the material. Via such means, a rehearsal room is reinvented into a space in which movement, creative agency and embodied sharing manifest from day one. The primacy of the text is challenged: it becomes one of the many elements that builds a production.

Balancing the usable and the indirect through experimentation in periods of research and development is a constant and productive dialogue. The R&D of Doctor Faustus went hand in hand with rehearsal, so undertaking tangential experiments required commitment to their potential. Doing a movement task can also have a diversionary aspect – almost a 'trick of the body'. Conscious activation of a physical task that is enriched by the effort of trying to do it, which then produces a myriad of unconscious physical manifestations. For example, the need to sequence movements speedily means that the actor's whole attention and physical intention is set on doing that. And the fallout of the attempt, such as the tremble caused by effort, the fight to remember or reconstruct a feeling, all become physical manifestations of trying to do the task. It is these that became of interest to me as a movement director for Faustus as these became the springboard for the actual movement material or directly become woven into the fabric of the performer's movement vocabulary. Often by getting into action, the action itself reveals the next development or application, structurally. Movement keeps unfolding. Aberg noted how 'the tentacles of the R&D spread' far into the production. Movement research informed the content and form of *Doctor Faustus*. We were all in training for alternative versions of the whole evening. This reliance on chance then informed how movement was created for the dénouement – a movement-led section of an encounter between Doctor Faustus and a devil incarnation of Helen of Troy, a figment of Faustus's final disintegration. The actor playing Helen of Troy had two different movement versions to be able to partner with either of the actors playing Dr Faustus.

The creation of the Helen of Troy material in *Doctor Faustus* took task-making to a new level as this section always remained a task for the actors playing Helen of Troy and Faustus – all the way through all the performances. Most movement tasks lead to the creation of material that is then composed, edited and learnt/embodied, so it becomes a repeatable, solidified physical score. In this case, doing the task was real for the actors every show, which made elements of the material unpredictable for each performance. The nature of our research and development imprinted the material and the games of chance in the show. During the R&D phases of this duet section, the movement task journey was inspired by partner dance. This acted as an initiation point for generating a duet between Faustus and Helen of Troy. We turned the normally cooperative nature of partnered dancing on its head – playing instead with extremes of weight-giving in partnered contact and unpredictable dynamic shifts (like running, jumping, shaking, abandoning weight unexpectedly). We played with manipulation of Faustus's face and facial expressions by Helen of Troy and constructing/deconstructing each other's physicality. This duet section was researched and developed/structured twice with each of the two male actors with the same underpinning principles of physical manipulation, unpredictable dynamic shifts and secret physical rules (that were withheld from the actor playing Dr Faustus). The game of this section was played for every show – the secret physical rules set by actor Jade Croot playing Helen of Troy meant that she was really in charge of the timing of movement motifs. Withholding the rules of the physical game generated an electric attentiveness between the two actors – the actor playing Doctor Faustus did not know when certain motifs would appear.

For *Doctor Faustus*, I was part of the casting workshop for the actor playing Helen of Troy, enabling the whole process to be inspired and built around the actor's unique presence, emotional landscape and physical gifts. Several considerations informed the process from a very early stage. We sought to explore how this younger female actor might always be the agent of the movement material and in control of everything that played out. We also had to consider how to incorporate safety mechanisms when devising the encounter between Faustus and Helen of Troy. The way Aberg and I dialogued was informed by a deep-seated feminist agenda and our female gaze. This underpinned our working methodology as well as the content of what we staged. We questioned the politics of our research process and the resulting movement material with rigour. These included the creation of a metaphoric language for acts of manipulation and violence; all the structural power was held by Croot as an actor and as a devil playing Helen of Troy and the use of distancing devices for Helen of Troy (cutting in and out of material and interrupting emotional arcs, occupying multiple and contradictory relationships to Faustus). Dramaturgically, the attempt was to trouble the male gaze with a vision of Helen of Troy played by a young female actor who was the motor and witness of the self-destruction of Doctor Faustus.

This duet was followed by a solo movement section for the actors playing Faustus which was generated by a movement task journey that included a mixture of fragments of half-remembered movement re-enacted and poetic key phrases. I called this sequence a 'flicker book' as in my mind's eye it was a shivering, juddering compendium of memories of movement violently running through Faustus's body. For the audience, it appeared to be exhausting because of its apparent absence of logic and the speed with which the actors moved from gesture to gesture and movement motif to movement motif. This whole section was underpinned by movement techniques, as the actors' bodies had to have a sustainable and technical foundation for this material. These safety techniques were foundational and informed the material, which was dependent on the actors' physical capacities. The way we devised this section demanded a spirit of exploration that is key to R&D overall. This is valuable because it means that performers own the movement material, as co-creators rather than interpreters, so the movement material is bespoke to their physicality, strengths and capacities. In R&D, one holds paradoxical positions and is navigating them constantly. That is the desire and need to predict outcomes and yet remain genuinely attentive to possibilities while engaged in dialogue with creative collaborators. The rehearsal process and the R&D processes of Doctor Faustus became unusually and productively intertwined.

By reflecting on these two creative projects, I have identified that cycles of movement R&D have become an underpinning of my creative process as a movement director. Each project enriches the sedimentary layers of embodied experience as I immerse myself and dwell with source material, and in my mind's eye I envisage and invent processes. Early movement-oriented research has an abundant quality. Some of the ideas and movement generated will fall to the wayside. Once in the room I lay down movement techniques to support the performers in the movement language we will explore and may emerge. Directors lead, feed into and shape how those initiation points might develop. The dialogue is opened. After the R&D comes what is recognizable as rehearsal – repetition, attachment processes for performers, integration of all creative elements such as music, light, video and meeting the audiences.

My reflective conversation with Attias about R&D on *The Dark* examined the contribution of movement direction to a physical dance-theatre work made for children. The devised nature of this process and its two stages of R&D were functional and productive, in that the balance between experimentation and open use of time had a very clear correlation to the final work. Attias noted that time between the two R&D phases was equally fertile for her: 'taking time away during periods of R&D there are things that naturally stick [. . .] there are things that you remember *in your body*; these are the things that you know are right' (Attias 2023). This centres the creation of an emotionally resonant movement language with physical images placed in the collective body memory during research. We, too, are developed by the processes we undertake, and R&D is significant in that I was learning about the performer's specific sensorial needs and vocabularies. My work was to harness their capacities productively via movement. Indeed, this is perhaps a key to the way I use R&D. I focus my energy on generating movement material with the specific performers I am working with, at times deliberately distancing myself from the source material and from thinking too much about the audience. In rehearsal, by contrast, I am very focused on construction, legibility and dynamics for the audience's experience.

My reflective conversation with Aberg about *Doctor Faustus* allowed us to revisit a production that was born from a full arc of R&D and a full rehearsal process simultaneously, and one in which I felt sizable artistic growth as a movement director. The play is a conundrum. It is significant that the effortful, deeply investigated starting points translated into shared experiences, that is, rituals and incantations, the ensemble movement of the chorus of scholars, the Helen of Troy duet, Dr Faustus's final descent in the 'flicker book' and the Seven Deadly Sins cabaret number. Productions with long runs highlight the importance of laying down bespoke techniques of movement, that is, safe contact work and sustainability in extreme shifts of dynamics. I had the space and support to invent multiple movement journeys, with a variety of improvisations and tasks that were watched, felt and harnessed by the director. The building of new movement strategies led to experimental material and through collaboration with director, composer and performers became material of the production.

R&D gives me and my collaborators the opportunity to play, to follow tangents and to undertake joint action and make connections. It also temporarily collapses some of the boundaries of roles and responsibilities, replacing them with testing edges and hunches, and avowedly unknowing. My collaborations with Attias and Aberg highlight the importance of synergy, which is a combination of a relational and creative commitment to each other as artists, and to the material of investigation. The material becomes shows for audiences and the synergy becomes ongoing collaboration, prompting the evolution of creative methodologies. I am witness to the way movement research and development can invite actors in explicitly as co-creators.

Fellow movement directors might like to adopt any of the specific approaches I have described above. But I think it is more fundamental that any movement director has their own personal movement journey, following their unique artistic intuition and embodied ways of knowing, that form their distinctive sedimentary layers. Movement director Kate Flatt characterizes the rehearsal process as a 'constant reconfiguring and renegotiating in order to capitalize on the creativity that's emerging' (Tashkiran 2020: 65), and Maria Aberg talked of R&D as a time for 'figuring it out'. R&D is a fulsome way to 'figure it out' in a culture of creativity that invites all to contribute to the process and establishes the rehearsal room as a space for experimentation and co-creation.

## References

Aberg, M. (2023), Unpublished interview with the author, 2 February.
Attias, D. (2023), Unpublished interview with the author, 13 January.
Cope, L. (2023), *Downtime* Podcast, Centre for Applied Dramaturgy (COAD), https://thecoad.org/movement-direction/?utm_source=twitter&utm_medium=organic-social&utm_campaign=s2&utm_id=s2 (accessed 7 January 2023).
Flatt, K. (2022), *Movement Direction: Developing Physical Narrative for Performance*, Marlborough: The Crowood Press.
Fuchs, E. (2015), 'EF's Visit to a Small Planet: Some Questions to Ask a Play', in Magda Romanska (ed.), *The Routledge Companion to Dramaturgy*, 403–7, Oxon: Routledge.
Kemp, R. (2016), 'Lecoq, Emotion and Embodied Cognition', in Mark Evans and Rick Kemp (eds), *The Routledge Companion to Jacques Lecoq*, 199–207, Routledge Companion, Oxon: Routledge.
Lecoq, J., G. Carasso and J-C. Lallias (2000), *The Moving Body: Teaching Creative Theatre*, trans. David Bradby, London: Methuen Drama.
Snicket, L. (2013), *The Dark*, London: Hachette Children's Group.
Tashkiran, A. (2016), 'British Movement Directors', in Mark Evans and Rick Kemp (eds), *The Routledge Companion to Jacques Lecoq*, 227–35, Oxon: Routledge.
Tashkiran, A. (2020), *Movement Directors in Contemporary Theatre: Conversations on Craft*, Bloomsbury: Methuen.

## 14

# Interview with Georgina Lamb

**Georgina Lamb** is a movement director, choreographer, director and actor. She was among the earliest members of Frantic Assembly, and worked with the company for thirteen years as creative associate and performer, performing in six of their shows as well as directing and leading on their workshop and residency programmes. Georgina's work included several R&D periods with Frantic Assembly, including for *Othello* (2008), Bryony Lavery's *Stockholm* (2007) and Abi Morgan's *Lovesong* (2011). Georgina has been a movement director for the RSC, the Royal Court, Royal Exchange Manchester, Chichester Festival Theatre, Regent's Park Open Air Theatre, the Young Vic and over thirteen productions at Shakespeare's Globe. In New York, her work on the immersive Tooting Arts Club production of *Sweeney Todd* was nominated for a Lucille Lortel award for Outstanding Choreography. Her choreography and movement work on screen has also won a BAFTA. As an actor she has worked at The National Theatre, Shakespeare's Globe, The Almeida, The Old Vic, The Royal Court, National Theatre of Scotland as well as on the BBC, ITV and Channel 4.

In this interview, Georgina describes her route into working as a movement director and the different approaches she has taken to R&D projects from a movement perspective. In particular, she reflects on her creative partnership with directors, and how she moves from research (the 'R' of R&D) to practical work with actors within research and development explorations.

*You've worked on a wide range of projects as a movement director. What was your route into this role?*

I didn't consciously set out to become a movement director. When I first started out, 'movement director' wasn't even really a title, it was still very much 'choreographer'. I graduated in 1995 and started working as an actor; I was with Frantic Assembly for thirteen years on and off as a creative associate and a performer. A lot of my work as a movement director developed through the people I had collaborated with through Frantic's work. Colleagues or pals of mine would contact me and ask me to come and work on a developing project from a movement perspective: to get the piece up on its feet. For example, my friend Matthew Dunster, who is now a really prolific British theatre director, at the time had a company called The Work which was a collaboration between different artists. He called and asked me to work with him, and I've continued to do so with him at The Globe. So, my movement directing work came about when people who knew me as a performer from a physical theatre / dance background asked me to come in and work with their actors. Liam Steel, another prolific movement director and choreographer, couldn't do a job and recommended me, which resulted in me working with Rupert Goold on *Paradise Lost* (Headlong 2006). This led to me working with Rupert on many more of his shows. But back then movement directing was not a constant in theatre – not all companies or shows had a movement director. So gradually, over the years, as the role of movement director became better known, I did less performing and more movement directing and choreographic work.

*How did your process differ with these different collaborators?*

It really does depend on the director and what they need. I worked with Rupert Goold and Matthew Dunster for quite a few years. Both are hugely collaborative in that they will hand the room over to you. They would be very specific about what it was they wanted. They might ask me to look at a particular moment in the play and they would give me a roomful of actors to try things out, and then they'd come back and we might tweak what I'd developed together. Some directors will be much more specific in terms of what they want. They might ask me to come in and work specifically on a couple of transitional moments between scenes, for example. You're still creating the world of the play, but at times you may be problem-solving specific moments rather than working on the overall movement vocabulary for the show. So it really varies. With some shows or projects you'll be in the room nearly full-time, three or four days a week. With others it might be one or two sessions. The role very much depends on the director's creative vision, their rehearsal process, and their needs.

*Are budgetary constraints also a factor in the type of work you do on a project?*

Budgeting has a big impact on my work. The number of times that directors have turned around to me and said 'I would have you in the room every day, if the budgets allowed'. There is a bit of a difference here between movement directing and my work as a choreographer. If you're a choreographer on a musical, you're in the room full-time, but with movement directing, it is often the case that they can pay for nine sessions, or can pay for two days a week. With larger companies like the RSC, and other bigger producing houses, there will be more time as they have the budget. A lot of my work is determined by finances.

*Are there examples where your work was part of a delineated R&D process?*

I remember way back in 2008, Raz Shaw and I made a piece called *Gambling*, a verbatim show curated by Tom Holloway and presented at the Royal Court as one of their Rough Cuts, which were very similar to Battersea Arts Centre's Scratch Nights. Raz Shaw had written a book about his own experience of gambling addiction and wanted to make a show, and he asked me if I could collaborate with him on that from a movement perspective. I think we had two weeks of R&D for the Rough Cut and, off the back of that, we made it into a full piece which was staged at Soho Theatre in 2010. Interestingly, people that saw both said that they preferred the Rough Cut version. I think that's partly to do with subject matter, as well as the use of verbatim interview material, but also the edginess and roughness of R&D. When you present work at the end of an R&D process, it's nice that it doesn't have to be all shiny-edged and complete. People are more accepting and forgiving of an R&D process. It can also allow a creative team and actors to develop work in a slightly more relaxed atmosphere. They're all there to discover this story and put it up on its feet and see what happens. An R&D process can allow for a much more playful headspace. It's the luxury of time. Of having the creative palette to just try stuff and not feeling that kind of pressure or judgement, if something's not working. The revelation of realising that something is completely going down the wrong track. The luxury – the privilege – after a couple of days of chucking stuff on its feet, to say 'This doesn't work does it?' and having the time to then come back together as a team, and start again.

*Where does the 'R' bit of R&D come into your work as a movement director?*

On *Gambling*, there was research before the R&D and within the R&D period itself. At the start of the project, I had very little knowledge of gambling addiction, so I read widely about it before we started the process.

On other projects, the director may ask for some choreography or movement based on a particular historical form of dance that I might have to go away and research. My job is to make sure I come into the room with a knowledge of the world I am entering into, to be able to physically explore and work creatively around those themes or styles.

With *Gambling*, for example, in the R&D itself we visited a residential rehabilitation centre for gambling addicts and interviewed people there. This research was completely fascinating from my perspective as a movement director. It was about how addiction manifests itself in the body. With drug addiction and alcohol addiction it is something you're ingesting into your body, whereas gambling is different. I remember one of the recovering addicts telling us that if you've been awake for 24 hours constantly gambling, the pressure that it puts on your heart is the equivalent of running a marathon because of the stress. The whole research process for *Gambling* was not just humbling, but also massively eye-opening. I was looking at gambling from a physical perspective, exploring how that particular form of addiction manifests itself for individuals physically.

I think – and most artists would say this – everyone loves R&D. Looking at the infrastructure of the theatre world in the UK at the moment, it's probably one of the few places where it feels like there's enough time for creative play and exploration. So when you get the time and opportunity for R&D, it's a joy! You are usually there the whole time with the rest of the creative team. It is about discovering what that world is from a starting point where nobody really knows. Creative leadership is shared. The director is still very much the director and will have their vision and you're very much there to serve that purpose, but it feels like a much more collaborative process as you are all there in the room together full-time. Sometimes, when I visit rehearsals for odd days here and there, I have to start with 'can you remember that sequence we looked at last Tuesday?' Whereas with R&D, you hit the ground running every morning, because you're picking up the baton from where you left it at six o'clock the night before. Creativity is much freer and flowing within a research and development process.

*In the absence of a delineated R&D period, have you been able to bring in some of the practices of R&D into rehearsal processes?*

Yes, I remember this particularly on *Frozen* by Bryony Lavery. This was the production that ran in the West End in 2018, directed by Jonathan Munby and with Suranne Jones, Nina Sosanya and Jason Watkins. There wasn't a distinct R&D process, but the first week was all about research. We spent time doing table work, discussing the subject matters of the piece in great detail. The play is about the disappearance of a child and we had some amazing visits by criminologists and psychologists and people from a charity called Missing, supporting the families of children who have gone missing. I've been really lucky that a lot of projects that I've worked on, the research has been utterly fascinating. As a movement director, you then have to join the dots between research and the project itself. What is the physical impact of a particular subject matter on an individual or a group of people? With *Frozen*, it was about how the psychology of those people might manifest physically. What would be the physical habits of that particular person in that particular moment in that play? It was about creating certain exercises that opened the door for them to physically tap into the psychology of those characters. It was good that there was time for this sort of exploration within the rehearsal period.

By contrast, last year, I was choreographer on *The Great British Bake Off Musical*. It was a brand-new musical and it only had a four-week rehearsal process. It was first staged at the Cheltenham Everyman for two weeks, then the following year did a three-month run at the Noël Coward Theatre in the West End. I've worked with the director, Rachel Kavanaugh, quite a lot, so there was that trust and that creative collaboration immediately. It also meant that she was happy to hand the room over to me. In the first week, Rachel would often work in the writing room with the writers Pippa Cleary and Jake Brunger, and she'd ask me to work on ideas for a particular number. It was nice to have that freedom to explore, but it wasn't the freedom of R&D. Time was of the essence so I had to work to a very clear brief. It would be working out how the performers would make a puff pastry steak pie whilst singing a song! I wanted those actors to feel like they were in a secure space with time to try things out, but I was conscious we only had four weeks. Looking back, a lot of the time in my work as a movement director, I haven't been part of R&D processes. The movement perspective on a piece is often much further down the line in terms of priority.

*You mentioned the freedom of R&D, but is there pressure when the moment of sharing comes? When a producer or director might decide whether this is something to commission or to develop further?*

Yes, that's a huge pressure. Everyone involved is invested to some extent. I remember doing two rounds of R&D at the National Theatre Studio. The director had been invited to come and workshop the project and we had two lots of two weeks. At the end of the first block, the creative leadership team of the National watched the sharing and we were given feedback and were invited back again. But at the end of the second fortnight it didn't get taken further. From a movement director's perspective, because you're not necessarily on board as a creative from the off, you won't necessarily be part of discussions about whether something is going to have a further life. In my experience, I would get a call to say that a project is going to the NT Studio for R&D and they'd like me to come in. So actually, from my perspective, you're slightly removed from the pressure of that. You're hired to do your job and create something. Obviously, you become emotionally engaged in the project and, if it's something you really enjoyed doing, you hope it has another life. There's been a few 'thumbs up / thumbs down' moments. I remember a musical that I collaborated on with a composer and a director and it was brilliant. We did that final showing in front of lots of different theatre houses, but it didn't have a life. So we go again! Next project, we go again.

The other thing to negotiate in an R&D process is navigating the director – movement director relationship. Sometimes you go in and do an R&D and you've maybe not worked with that director before. You don't know what that relationship is going to be before you go into an R&D room and so naturally there is a bit of bouncing off each other and discovering a shared working language. Your job as a movement director is to serve the vision of that director, but you don't know to what capacity they want you to be engaged. With most directors, we'll talk before we go into the R&D and discuss ideas, and they might respond positively to an idea and ask me to try it out. Sometimes I might have a whole morning where they'll happily just observe. In my experience, when directors ask you to lead the room and work creatively with the actors, this encourages a greater sense of trust. Actors see you having that ownership in the space: it's clear that the director trusts you and that the work and movement vocabulary is important and needs time and space.

*What would you say are your tools as a movement director in R&D?*

In terms of the working relationship with the actors, I think it's always just to get a sense of play initially. I have an idea, but I'd never go in and force shapes on a group of people. It's about working with actors and allowing them to use their own physicality to create movement. That's the difference between movement directing and choreography. As a choreographer, often you go in and say 'this is what we're doing' – you've created the material before working in the room with the artists. Whereas with movement directing, it can really depend on what it is you're making. It could be just working with one actor on their breath, or it could be going in and creating a whole movement section or working with a song. So, in terms of my relationship with the actors, I always look to create a sense of play, a sense of trust and always give them creative ownership on whatever that is we're making. I set creative tasks and create the environment so they feel comfortable enough to respond playfully. Then out of that, I then start dropping in nuggets of ideas and tasks based on a particular theme or idea. It's about supporting an environment where they feel able to create movement in whatever capacity they can. That's what I particularly love about research and development processes. When you have the time and space to do that, that is when you get the most creative joy.

My experience of R&D is that a lot of what gets made in the room will end up in the final product, or a version of it. The initial ideas that come from an R&D process form the foundation. The end production will be a bigger shinier version of the ideas generated in that room. I don't think I've ever had a bad experience in a research and development process. I've always found that we are all in the room together, wanting to achieve the same thing. Everyone feels that you are in a privileged position of getting a research and development period. It feels like a warm, open and collaborative environment. In the current political and economic landscape for the arts, R&D feels like even more of a privilege. From my perspective as a movement director, it feels like the landscape has changed and support for R&D has been squeezed. Hopefully this will improve.

26 January 2024
Interviewed by Mark Love-Smith

## Questions and Prompts #7

- What is your source material for the R&D? How will you begin your work on the source material? Might lists or storyboards be productive in your preparation?
- What tasks might you set for those involved? What preparation might they do?
- If you don't have a specific R&D period, how might you build R&D into the start of the rehearsal period? Are there ways to explore the project collectively and to find room for experimentation?
- Consider how the R&D might allow you to develop a shared vocabulary for the project.
- Consider starting your R&D from the perspective of 'world-building' – that is, collectively constructing the world in which the story/play/project takes place.
- How will warm-ups, and the starts of each R&D session, be designed to build a sense of collective preparation for this collaborative endeavour? How might warm-ups connect to the experimentation and discovery that will follow?
- Consider the politics of your R&D process: who has structural power (both within the R&D group and within each exercise and each game you play)?
- Incorporate safety mechanisms when experimenting so that everyone feels supported and safe.
- How might you use time at the end of each R&D session to reflect on what you've done? How will you document and record key discoveries as you go? Is it useful to take photos, write in a notebook, make voice notes? You might want to draw, sing or dance your reflections instead (or as well), if this fits with your practice and process.

# Afterword

## Duška Radosavljević

What makes a suitable 'Afterword' on the subject of 'Research and Development'? Aside from wishing to express gratitude for having been included in this conversation that is so close to my academic heart and to unreservedly amplify this book's key points – the demand that artistic R&D be properly included in the British government's policymaking and tax legislation, the call for greater academic and sectoral recognition for this crucial aspect of theatre-making practice, and the appreciation for the necessary and endemic specificities of each and every creative process – the most apposite thing left for me to add at this point would be the conceptual importance of 'open-endedness'.

'Research and Development' entails structured activity that is by its nature never finite and as such should also fit with sustainability-seeking agendas of the twenty-first century. But in response to this particular invitation to think about a UK-based academic 'work in progress' from a base in continental Europe, I find myself in a familiar position of liminality – a perpetual expat/immigrant – a position not dissimilar from my often held professional role of a dramaturg or an 'outside eye' as it has been known in the British context. And this makes me aware of yet another kind of openness habitual to this position: 'open-mindedness'.

In order to move on, in order to reach new places or new insights, in order to honestly ask questions to which we do not yet know answers, it is necessary to expose and shed preconceptions, discern the substance of real value from attractive but obsolete tools and ideas, and perhaps in order to determine where (as co-travellers or not) we are going, it is necessary to chart the way in which we have got here. Specifically for the purpose of this chapter, and with true appreciation for this volume's collaborative undertaking, I'd like to prompt some questions and possible cues for further research, starting with: How and why the placing of the artistic R&D on the agenda of Theatre and Performance Studies has taken so long?

In the context of Theatre and Performance Studies as a subject, the distinctiveness of this endeavour plays out not only in this volume's stated set of questions pertaining to the methods of teaching but also in the production of REF-able research itself, knowledge exchange in action and the inextricable interdependences of these three areas of academic activity which have been cleaved apart in British academia over the past few decades.

I entered British academia as an undergraduate student of Theatre Studies in the 1990s. At the time, the key words in our learning were 'process' and then, depending on personal predilection, 'devising', 'physical theatre' or 'performance art' ('experimental', 'visual', 'avant-garde' and 'total' theatre still had currency though they had just begun to fizzle out as hot terms). We all studied theatre history, aspects of theatre pedagogy or theatre in 'social situations' and dramatic texts as well, of course, but the opportunity to really get creative was sought under the headings above. Even in the 1990s, especially after polytechnics were made into universities in 1992 and drama schools gradually gained degree-awarding powers, there were around a hundred providers of BA degrees involving Drama, Theatre and/or Performance as a subject. The magnitude of this makes it difficult to see from the inside how exceptional the UK provision is in this respect by comparison to the rest of Europe, where the options for studying the subject at undergraduate level are very narrowly specialized from the outset, often exclusive, and comparatively difficult to access. From the continental perspective, the British model might appear lacking in rigour, standards or likelihood of employment upon graduation. From the British perspective many continental contexts might seem slow to change, elitist and overly conventional. The truth is neither extreme is ideal, but I'll get to that later.

My academic career and particularly my monographs *Theatre-Making* (2013) and *Aural/Oral Dramaturgies* (2023) are directly focused on understanding contemporary British theatre and performance by reference to this model of embodied Theatre Studies and the consequent formal, contextual and methodological innovations in theatre-making practice. From a historical perspective, informed by the work of Gerald Graff (1987) and Shannon Jackson (2004) in the United States, and Simon Shepherd (2012) and others in the UK, I have come to understand this change in the ways of working and divisions of labour as part of a paradigm shift from the industrial to the post-industrial era. Unburdened by the strict allocation of roles (actor, director, writer, designer, composer), contemporary theatre ensembles, emerging from universities, work as both research teams and garage bands, generating material in more organic ways, using newfound tools and technologies, improvising and innovating along the way. In my view this represents a perfect meeting of top-down and bottom-up generative processes.

At long last, the book that is before us shines a spotlight on prominent examples of cultural institutions and individuals who helped to grow and nurture – often from the ground up – experimental ways of working and the particularity of creative processes in British theatre. Whatever the terms that have been used in connection with this work over the decades – from 'rehearsal', 'trial', 'sharing', 'work in progress', 'experiment' and 'laboratory' to 'studio', 'scratch', 'devising', 'new work', 'workshopping' or 'DIY' – what many of these processes have in common, I argue, is that they were seeded within the context of British universities and/or the specific ecosystems of their Drama/Theatre/Performance Studies degrees. Having interviewed hundreds of artists over the years as part of my research I have learnt that the specificity of their creative practice can always in some way be traced back to how, where and alongside whom they began their journey.

What I have just incidentally referred to as 'embodied Theatre Studies' denotes a disciplinary innovation that was instigated in the UK, according to one way of looking at it, at the University of Bristol in 1947 as a result of a desire to teach drama to students of language and literature through the material considerations of staging. This broke away from the Oxbridge model of 'reading' a subject by demanding to have a theatre space at the centre of the learning process, and the successful initiation of the Drama Department at Bristol was then followed by similar initiatives in Manchester in 1962, Hull in 1963, Birmingham in 1964 and Glasgow in 1966. Although many of these graduates ended up working in theatre, film and TV, they were not trained specifically for these careers. Rather the point was to gain experiential understanding of theatre-making, and in some ways, perhaps, the cultural imperative of knowledge production characteristic of university contexts per se might have shaped these learning processes too. By 1984 Exeter University grew an iconic theatre company that would go on to be hailed internationally as a highly influential example of a new way of working and performance style: Forced Entertainment. And throughout the 1990s and 2000s many other examples of innovative though unfortunately often short-lived university-grown companies have popped up in other places: Suspect Culture (Bristol University), Frantic Assembly (Swansea University), Unlimited Theatre (Leeds University), Little Bulb (Kent), RashDash (Hull), Middle Child (Hull). Thanks to the growth and illustrious achievements of theatre and performance scholarship over the decades we now know that live performance is notoriously difficult to record, that theatre history has provided a partial or skewed picture of relevant practices due to the predominance of text as key surviving documentation, and that the workings of unconscious bias have continuously eclipsed some valuable historic contributions from the margins. In this spirit I believe it is absolutely crucial to capture, document and study the cumulative effects of the correlations between the practical university study of theatre, the ensemble way of working and artistic innovation.

A comprehensive cultural history of Theatre Studies in the UK is sorely missing – if nothing else in order to save from oblivion the growing number of now historic examples of places such as Dartington College and Bretton Hall whose contributions to the British cultural scene only exist in scattered artist biographies, anecdotal testimonies or unacknowledged transmission of embodied practices – but also and chiefly because governments always need hard evidence for the cultural value of the arts. At the time of writing over sixty British universities are running redundancy programmes where arts subjects are the first earmarked for cuts (https://qmucu.org/qmul-transformation/uk-he-shrinking/). Yet some of those same arts departments were both individually and cumulatively responsible for producing 'world leading' research in Theatre and Performance Studies and for the grassroots development and growth of new theatre-making methodologies and forms, as well as artists and companies.

It is certainly possible to critique the massification of British and anglophone higher education by reference to the advent of neoliberal capitalism and the subsequent marketization of the sector (Trow 2000, 2006; Lynch 2006; Calderon 2018). Similar kinds of critique can be aimed at the dissolution of the 'repertory theatre' model in Margaret Thatcher's Britain in favour of 'freeing' the artists to pursue individual projects and careers and to ultimately sink or swim at the mercy of the market economy. A comparative study of the independent or fringe theatre in the UK and other European contexts on the basis of the criteria, extent and allocation processes of government funding is needed in order to gain a proper overview, but it can be safely asserted that, despite its insidious nature, this neoliberal move has resulted in the fact that the independent theatre sector in the UK has had a longer, more substantial, creatively fruitful and more academically documented history than has so far been the case elsewhere. The necessity for critique does not – and should not – preclude capacity for creativity and care.

So why has it taken so long to place R&D on the scholarly agenda?

I have argued before that the intoxicating authoritativeness of critique as a key research method in cultural studies, from the Frankfurt School onwards, has rendered other possibilities in Theatre and Performance Studies as of lesser epistemic value, effect, reach or significance. In the past ten years, additionally, there has been a refreshing and welcome resurgence of academic writing in the field motivated by activism in favour of specific worthy causes: climate crisis, anti-racism, identity politics and socially just futures. Academic writing about performance process, on the other hand, risks coming across as acritical, hagiographic, journalistic or, in the case of practice as research or autoethnography, as solipsistic or self-serving. My position is that there must certainly be a third way, beyond the given polarization between the critical and acritical, political and apolitical, ideology and art for art's sake. One example is this book, which unequivocally places theatre-making on the political agenda by properly equating creative process with the economic rubric of R&D in government spending.

We must not underestimate the difficulty of doing the academic work that seems as simple as finding the right terms and articulating the familiar in new ways. It takes a lot of cumulative effort within a field over time to break new ground. In academia, like in theatre, even when one is working solo, one is always building on collectively erected foundations. One might think one has made a point, or shown something to be the case, but it takes multiple iterations, and then – hopefully – sufficiently attentive reading by others, interpretation and amplification by means of academic citations, for a particular point to land. Unfortunately in the arts and humanities, where research is often conducted in isolation rather than in teams, the overproduction imperative of the recent years has inevitably led to a certain degree of underappreciation and cursory engagement with each other's work. This volume, on the other hand, represents a particularly efficient model of the best of academic collaboration, constituted through dialogue, exchange, polyphony and synergistic action, with the shared outcome of crystalizing a new perspective.

To be precise: articulation is difficult. And it is an inspired move to denote the creative processes studied under so many different microcosmic and idiosyncratic terms so far – such as experimental theatre, avant-garde, devising, theatre-making – using a more macrocosmic term: R&D, both exact and capacious; legible equally accurately to artists, scholars, industry people as well as, importantly, policymakers and funders.

That said, Research and Development is not exactly a politically neutral term, either. My own dip into the archives for the purpose of this publication has revealed that one of the earliest uses of this particular collocation is to be found in the money pages of the mid-nineteenth-century British newspapers referring to the government-funded research and development of the natural resources of Africa and documenting its subsequent standing in the daily stock exchange reports. A more common association that survives to the present day is of course one linked with technical innovation within industrial settings – most often in the chemical industry, as documented for example by the newspaper reports of the annual general meeting addresses Lord McGowan gave to Imperial Chemical Industries, which he chaired from 1930 to 1950 (Anon. 1939). His speeches often acknowledge the importance of Research and Development for the company, and on 11 May 1939, he makes a direct remark about the inspiration derived in this regard from the American company DuPont. Both companies, it might be worth noting, had lines of military and non-military production throughout their lifetimes; DuPont, now famous for nylon, Teflon and Lycra, had been the main supplier of gunpowder during the American Civil War, and it is no accident that the need for Research and Development is perceived as of special importance on the eve of another world war. In the late twentieth and early twenty-first centuries the term R&D most often crops up in the British Newspaper Archive in the context of Irish economic growth and Ireland's self-styling as a 'knowledge-based' economy. A 2003 business article, informed by an interview with a consultant from the National Institute of Transport and Logistics (NITL), profiles a post-industrial vision of Ireland as a 'virtual hub' and an intellectual and logistical 'centre of excellence', where the actual manufacture of products has been outsourced to lower-cost economies, while it retains the virtual supply chain management and R&D departments. It is a vision arising in line with the pressures of neoliberal capitalism for sure, though it might be said that it is made possible by a considered and opportune harnessing of technological developments as well as a valorization of the local resources and the existing human expertise (Kennedy 2003).

This swift overview of the semantic remit of a term changing, over 150 years, to replace its extractionist connotations with 'enabling' ones is intended, in the spirit of open-endedness, as yet another cue for some further speculation and/or new lines of enquiry stemming from the intersection of the ideas explored in this text and this book so far. Perhaps the last set of questions for me to put on the table would include the following: What would the world be like without R&D? What would it be like if there was no space allowed for trial and error, for open questions, for blue sky thinking, for wild goose chases, for dreaming, intuiting and speculating? And conversely, what exactly does it mean when according to the UNESCO Institute for Statistics (https://data.uis.unesco.org/Index.aspx?DataSetCode=SCN_DS) for five years running, from 2016 to 2021, the same countries – Israel, Republic of Korea and Sweden – have consistently and persuasively topped the charts when it comes to 'Research and Development spending as a proportion of GDP'? How much of that funding has, in each specific case, been apportioned to science and technology and how much exactly to the creative arts? What are the respective areas of similarity and difference among those three chart toppers? Ultimately also, what are the advantages and disadvantages of conducting R&D in the industry as opposed to the university sector? How exactly is each of those processes funded? What are the ethical implications of either way of working? And how different would industry-based R&D processes be if university research did not exist in the first place?

This is only a beginning: Welcome to the R&D department of Theatre and Performance Studies.

## References

Anon. (1939), 'Imperial Chemical Industries, Difficult Trading Conditions: Competition in Overseas Markets, Lord McGowan's Review', *Northern Whig*, 12 May.

Calderon, A. (2018), *Massification of Higher Education Revisited*, Melbourne: ReMIT. https://cdn02.pucp.education/academico/2018/08/23165810/na_mass_revis_230818.pdf.

Graff, G. (1987), *Professing Literature: An Institutional History*, Chicago and London: The University of Chicago Press.

Jackson, S. (2004), *Professing Performance: Theatre in the Academy from Philology to Performativity*, Cambridge: Cambridge University Press.

Kennedy, J. (2003), 'Ireland as a Virtual Hub?'. https://www.siliconrepublic.com/enterprise/ireland-as-a-virtual-hub.

Lynch, K. (2006), 'Neo-liberalism and Marketisation: The Implications for Higher Education', *European Educational Research Journal*, 5 (1): 1–17.

Radosavljević, D. (2013), *Theatre-Making: Interplay Between Text and Performance in the 21st Century*, Basingstoke: Palgrave.

Radosavljević, D. (2023), *Aural/Oral Dramaturgies: Theatre in the Digital Age*, London and New York: Routledge.

Shepherd, S. (2012), *Direction*, Basingstoke: Palgrave.

Trow, M. (2000), *From Mass Higher Education to Universal Access: The American Advantage*, UC Berkley: Research and Occasional Paper Series, Center for Studies in Higher Education.

Trow, M. (2006), 'Reflections on the Transition from Elite to Mass to Universal Access: Forms and Phases of Higher Education in Modern Societies since WWII', in J. J. F. Forest and P. G. Altbach (eds), *International Handbook of Higher Education*, 243–80, Dordrecht: Springer.

# Index

1927
   *The Animals and Children Took to the Streets* 93–5
   *Between the Devil and the Deep Blue Sea* 91–5
   *Golem* 95

Aberg, Maria 171–4, 178–82
   *Doctor Faustus* 170–3, 175, 178–81
accessibility 23–4, 171, *see also* disability, diversity, and inclusivity
Action Hero 101–2, 108, 167
   *Hoke's Bluff* 101–2
actor training 20, 23, 95–6, 175
animation 27, 91–4
Arches, The 57, 65–6, 106
archives 35, 42, 194
Arts Council England (ACE) 9–10, 48, 52, 68, 72, 108–11, 166
   Developing Your Creative Practice (DYCP) 9–10, 97, 109–11
   National Portfolio Organisations (NPOs) 9, 72, 166
Arts Council of Northern Ireland (ACNI) 10, 120
Arts Council of Wales 10
Attias, Daphna 171–82, 173–4, 176, 181–2
   *The Dark* 171, 173, 175–8
audience feedback 43, 47, 49, 51, 53–4, 60–2, 70
audio description 23–4
audition 80, 106
   autobiographical storytelling 104–5, 122, 163–4, *see also* lived experience research

Battersea Arts Centre (BAC) 9, 30, 42–8, 54–5, 57, 93–4, 105–6
Blackman, Paul 45–6
Blythe, Alecky 71–2, 76–87
   *London Road* 71–2, 76–80, 83–4, 88

body, performer's 18, 20, 22–3, 26–7, 114, 133, 136, 172, 174, 176, 181
Bristol, University of 192–3
Bristol Old Vic 80
British Council 51, 102, 112, 127
British Festival of Visual Theatre 46, 48, 125

choreography, *see* movement direction
commissions 12, 39, 78–9, 84–5, 106, 112–13, 164–6, 112, *see also* funding
community guidelines 157–8, 169
Complicité (Théâtre de) 54, 159–60
consent cultures 148–9, 152
Cork, Adam 71–2, 76–88
   *London Road* 71–2, 76–80, 83–4, 88
Covid pandemic 40, 91, 96–7, 131, 171
Creative Scotland 10, 66

dance 35, 126, 130, 175, 178, 180–1, *see also* movement direction
Dark Room residency, the 102–3
devising 3–4, 101–2, 132, 154–5, 158, 163, 168, 170–2, 179, 181, 191–2
DICE Festival 112, 114
directing 85–6, 122, 185, 188
director, historic primacy of 2, 124, *see also* hierarchies in theatre-making
disability 40, 171, 176–7, *see also* accessibility
diversity and inclusivity 12, 153, 171, 174
dramaturgy 51, 79, 97–8, 102, 114, 122, 127, 129–131, 134–6, 149, 153

Edinburgh Fringe 46, 51, 92, 104–5, 107, 128
employment
   freelance 12, 108, 112

precarious and unpaid   12–13, 68–9, 29–31, 96–7, 106, 112, 130–1
ensemble   2–3, 28–9, 41, 154–5, 179, 182
Essex, University of   148–51, 154–60
ethics in performance   40
Exeter, University of   148–51, 160

Field, Eleanor   126, 131–2, 134–5
Forced Entertainment   34, 100, 193
Forest Fringe   101–7
form, experimenting with   163–4, 169
Frantic Assembly   55, 73, 132, 184
*Frascati Manual*   7–8
Fuel (production company)   53
funding, *see also specific funding bodies and commissions by name* …
  arts   5–11, 52, 68, 166
  science and technology   5–6, 195
  self-   31, 111, 193
  theatre   11, 31, 38–9, 46, 52, 68, 96, 108–12, 120, 135, 142, 185

Gardner, Lyn   4, 48
Germany   139–41
Glasgow   57, 63–6, 193

Halberstam, Jack   61, 64
Hall, Ruth   130, 131, 135
Hariu, Shizuka   125–6, 131
hierarchies in theatre-making   124, 132, 134–5, 143, 185, *see also* director, historic primacy of
Hohki, Kazuko   43–4
Hungary   104, 112
Hytner, Nicholas   74–6, 80, 85–6

immersive community research   117–20
installation   104, 107, 143
intimacy coordination   149, 151, 156–7
intuitive work   120, 172–3, 177, 182, 195

Jenkinson, Rosemary
  *The Bonefire*   117–20
Jubb, David   43, 47, 56–7, 62–6, 105

Lecoq, Jacques   54, 157, 159, 175, 178 n.4
Leeds Playhouse   60, 64, 66, 68

Furnace programme   61, 66–7
lighting   127–8, 133–4
Little Bulb Theatre   19, 30
  *Orpheus*   28, 30
lived experience research   117, 172, 174, *see also* autobiographical storytelling
Lobel, Brian   107–8, 114–15

mentoring   9–10, 109, 167–8
Micklem, David   56–7, 105
Mitchell, Katie   21, 73
Morell, Purni   72–6, 81–5, 88
Morris, Tom   42–8, 52–3, 56, 79–80
movement direction   25, 29, 126, 151, 158, 170–4, 177, 180–2, 184–9
music   18, 27–8, 46, 76–9, 91–4, 97–8
musical theatre   76–7, 84, 97–8, 187

National Theatre (England)   9, 21, 47, 66, 71–88, 91, 97, 131, 184
National Theatre of Scotland   65
National Theatre Studio   9, 34, 39, 66, 71–88, 97, 112, 187–8
  Writers and Composers Week   76–88
Norwich and Norfolk Festival   100, 107, 112–13

Paintin, Gemma   102, 110–11
Pastor, Eugénie
  *Pube*   26–7
Pearson, Deborah
  *History History History* (*HHH*)   100–13
performance design, *see also* scenography
  and actors   130, 133
  costume design   22, 124–5, 130
  as dramaturgy   134–6
  R&D   123–9, 135–6, 139–42, 145–7
  sound design   21
performance language   24, 28, 70, 133, 135–6, 145–6, 157, 160, 171, 173–5, 179, 181, 188
performance materiality   123–5, 127, 133–4, 139, 142, 147, *see also* scenography and props
playwriting   40, 101–2, 117–21, 165, *see also* script development
practice research   124, 194

props   36–7, 41, 127, 133, 147, 165, 169, 186, *see also* performance materiality

R&D
  definition   2, 103
  end product   70, 81–4, 87, 99, 107–8, 113–14, 155–5, 160, 188
  failure and risk   60, 64, 68, 70, 82–4, 99, 131–6, 142–3, 147, 158, 195
  ownership   84–7, 99
  tax relief   6–8
race in the arts   35, 39–40, 153, *see also* diversity and inclusivity
rehearsals   1, 4, 17, 23, 25, 78–9, 86, 96, 158, 165, 171, 175–7, 179–82, 186–7, 192
residencies   30, 102, 107, 112, 146
Rough Magic   117–18
Royal Court
  Rough Cuts   185–6
  Young Writers programme   48, 142

Scene Change movement   131
scenography   36–7, 123–4, 127–31, 134–5, 143, *see also* performance design
scratch nights
  and 'ladder of development'   48, 50, 105–6
  and capitalism   49–52, 56
  as ecology and culture   48–9, 56–7
  origin of   43–4
  and stand-up comedy   46–7, 106
script development   3–4, 36, 102, 120–1, 142, 165, 172, *see also* playwriting and devising
Shakespeare   148–51, 156
sharings   4, 42, 47, 54–6, 77, 105–6, 122, 128, 133, 187–8, 192, *see also* scratch nights

She Goat   12, 19, 22–4, 27, 30
  *DoppelDänger*   22–3, 29
  *The Undefinable*   23–4
skill
  acquisition   17–20, 24–5, 27, 31, 41, 157, 175
  performance of   18, 22, 25, 27
  sharing   75–6, 88, 94, 97–8
solo performance   19, 26, 28, 36, 61, 100, 139
Southside Studios (Glasgow)   63–6
space modelling   126, 141–3
spectators, and experience of performance   18, 22
Stringer, Ruth   130, 135
studio practice   52–7, 192

Talawa   9
task setting and generative improvization   174, 176–7
teaching   1, 19–20, 61–2, 152–3, 191
The TEAM   4
text analysis   124, 172
theatre and the real   22, 25
theatre materials, sourcing   134, 153, 165
Theatre Re   125, 127, 132–3
Third Angel   9, 162
  *Presumption*   163–5
Thompson, Selina
  *Race Cards*   35, 107
  *salt*   37, 39–40
  *Twine*   35, 40
Troubles, the   120

undisciplining   61–2, 69–70

warm-ups   174–6, 190
work-in-progress, *see* sharings and scratch nights
workshops, *see* rehearsals
world-building   171, 190